Fodor's

THIRD EDITION

New

Provence &
the Riviera

"When it comes to information on regional history,
what to see and do, and shopping, these guides are
exhaustive."

—USAir Magazine

"Usable, sophisticated restaurant coverage, with an
emphasis on good value."

—Andy Birsh, *Gourmet Magazine* columnist

"Valuable because of their comprehensiveness."

—*Minneapolis Star-Tribune*

"Fodor's always delivers high quality...thoughtfully
presented...thorough."

—*Houston Post*

"An excellent choice for those who want everything
under one cover."

—*Washington Post*

Reprinted from *Fodor's France*

Fodor's Travel Publications, Inc.
New York • Toronto • London • Sydney • Auckland
http://www.fodors.com/

Fodor's Provence & the Riviera

Editor: Natasha Lesser

Editorial Contributors: Steven K. Amsterdam, Rob Andrews, Robert Blake, David Brown, Audra Epstein, Nigel Fisher, Laura M. Kidder, Jennifer Paull, Heidi Sarna, Helayne Schiff, Mary Ellen Schultz, M. T. Schwartzman, George Semler, Dinah Spritzer

Creative Director: Fabrizio La Rocca

Associate Art Director: Guido Caroti

Photo Researcher: Jolie Novak

Cartographers: David Lindroth; Mapping Specialists Ltd.

Cover Photograph: Sonja Bullaty © 1991

Design: Between the Covers

Copyright

Third Edition

ISBN 0–679–03304–1

Special Sales

Fodor's Travel Publications are available at special discounts for bulk purchases for sales promotions or premiums. Special editions, including personalized covers, excerpts of existing guides, and corporate imprints, can be created in large quantities for special needs. For more information, contact your local bookseller or write to Special Markets, Fodor's Travel Publications, 201 East 50th Street, New York, NY 10022. Inquiries from Canada should be directed to your local Canadian bookseller or sent to Random House of Canada, Ltd., Marketing Department, 1265 Aerowood Drive, Mississauga, Ontario L4W 1B9. Inquiries from the United Kingdom should be sent to: Fodor's Travel Publications, 20 Vauxhall Bridge Road, London, England SW1V 2SA.

PRINTED IN THE UNITED STATES OF AMERICA

10 9 8 7 6 5 4 3 2

CONTENTS

ON THE ROAD WITH FODOR'S

WE'RE ALWAYS THRILLED to get letters from readers, especially one like this:

It took us an hour to decide what book to buy and we now know we picked the best one. Your book was wonderful, easy to follow, very accurate, and good on pointing out eating places, informal as well as formal. When we saw other people using your book, we would look at each other and smile.

Our editors and writers are deeply committed to making every Fodor's guide "the best one"—not only accurate but always charming, brimming with sound recommendations and solid ideas, right on the mark in describing restaurants and hotels, and full of fascinating facts that make you view what you've traveled to see in a rich new light.

About Our Writers

Our success in achieving our goals—and in helping to make your trip the best of all possible vacations—is a credit to the hard work of our extraordinary writers and editors.

Much of this book was updated by **Nigel Fisher,** the peripatetic writer and knowledgeable publisher of "Voyager International," a newsletter on world travel. His particular interests are in telling his readers about art, about divine places to stay, and about the most delicious food. Everywhere he goes, he talks to people and makes friends; so he always knows which chefs are striving for the second Michelin star and which are resting on their laurels.

Editor **Natasha Lesser** has lived in Washington, D.C., California, Iowa, Kenya, and France. After exploring every boulevard and back rue in Paris, many a mile of coast in Normandy, and the heights of the French Alps, she has stayed long enough at her desk in New York to pass her knowledge on to you.

George Semler actually lives over the border in Spain, but he's acquainted with each trout in the Pyrénées, of Spanish *and*

French persuasion. He loves every bump in those mountain roads and has contributed a grand tour of the region, cannily feeding and lodging us along the way.

We'd especially like to thank Marion Fourestier at the French Government Tourist Office in New York.

Fodor's Web Site

Be sure to check out Fodor's Web site (http://www.fodors.com/), where you'll find travel information on major destinations around the world and an ever-changing array of interactive features.

How to Use this Book

Organization

Up front is the **Gold Guide.** Its first section, **Important Contacts A to Z,** gives addresses and telephone numbers of organizations and companies that offer destination-related services and detailed information and publications. **Smart Travel Tips A to Z,** the Gold Guide's second section, gives specific information on how to accomplish what you need to in Provence and the Riviera as well as tips on savvy traveling. Both sections are in alphabetical order by topic.

The Provence and Riviera chapters are divided by geographical area; within each area, towns are covered in logical geographical order, and attractive stretches of road and minor points of interest between them are indicated by the designation En Route. Throughout, Off the Beaten Path sights appear after the places from which they are most easily accessible. And within town sections, all restaurants and lodgings are grouped together.

To help you decide what to visit in the time you have, the chapters begin with recommended itineraries. A section called When to Tour points out the optimal time of day, day of the week, and season for your journey. The A to Z section that ends the chapters covers getting there, getting around, and helpful contacts and resources.

At the end of the book you'll find Portraits, a chronology and an evocative essay on the region by Peter Mayle.

Icons and Symbols

★ Our special recommendations
✕ Restaurant
🏠 Lodging establishment
✕🏠 Lodging establishment whose restaurant warrants a detour
🖒 Rubber duckie (good for kids)
☞ Sends you to another section of the guide for more information
✉ Address
☎ Telephone number
FAX Fax number
🕓 Opening and closing times
💷 Admission prices (those we give apply only to adults; substantially reduced fees are almost always available for children, students, and senior citizens)

Numbers in white and black circles—② and ❷, for example—that appear on the maps, in the margins, and within the tours correspond to one another.

Dining and Lodging

The restaurants and lodgings we list are the cream of the crop in each price range. Price charts appear in the Pleasures and Pastimes section that follows each chapter introduction.

Hotel Facilities

We always list the facilities that are available—but we don't specify whether they cost extra: When pricing accommodations, always ask what's included.

Assume that hotels operate on the **European Plan** (EP, with no meals) unless we note that they use the **Full American Plan** (FAP, with all meals), the **Modified American Plan** (MAP, with breakfast and dinner daily), the **Continental Plan** (CP, with a Continental breakfast daily), or are **all-inclusive** (all meals and most activities).

Restaurant Reservations and Dress Codes

Reservations are always a good idea; we note only when they're essential or when they are not accepted. Book as far ahead as you can, and reconfirm when you get to town. Unless otherwise noted, the restaurants listed are open daily for lunch and dinner. We mention dress only when men are required to wear a jacket or a jacket and tie. Look for an overview of local habits under Dining in Smart Travel Tips A to Z and in the Pleasures and Pastimes section that follows each chapter introduction.

Credit Cards

The following abbreviations are used: **AE,** American Express; **D,** Discover; **DC,** Diners Club; **MC,** MasterCard; and **V,** Visa.

Don't Forget to Write

You can use this book in the confidence that all prices and opening times are based on information supplied to us at press time; Fodor's cannot accept responsibility for any errors. Time inevitably brings changes, so always confirm information when it matters—especially if you're making a detour to visit a specific place. In addition, when making reservations be sure to mention if you have a disability or are traveling with children, if you prefer a private bath or a certain type of bed, or if you have specific dietary needs or any other concerns.

Were the restaurants we recommended as described? Did our hotel picks exceed your expectations? Did you find a museum we recommended a waste of time? If you have complaints, we'll look into them and revise our entries when the facts warrant it. If you've discovered a special place that we haven't included, we'll pass the information along to our correspondents and have them check it out. So send your feedback, positive *and* negative, to the Provence & the Riviera Editor at 201 East 50th Street, New York, New York 10022—and have a wonderful trip!

Karen Cure

Karen Cure
Editorial Director

France

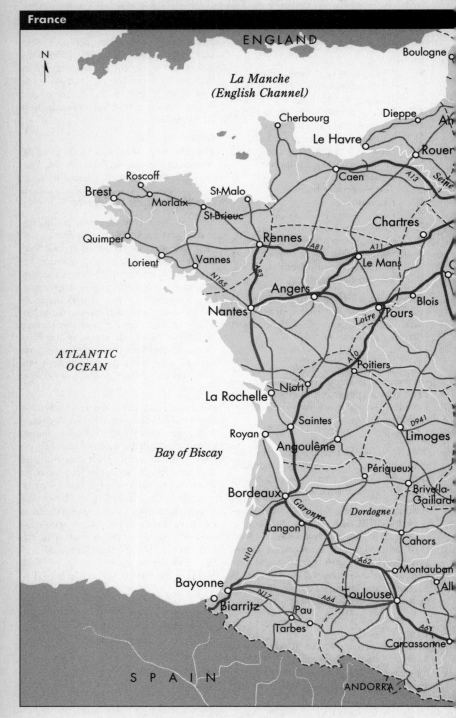

ENGLAND

La Manche
(English Channel)

Boulogne

Cherbourg

Dieppe

Le Havre

Rouen

Caen

Roscoff

St-Malo

Brest

Morlaix

St-Brieuc

Chartres

Quimper

Rennes

Le Mans

Lorient

Vannes

Angers

Blois

Nantes

Tours

Loire

ATLANTIC
OCEAN

Poitiers

Niort

La Rochelle

Saintes

Limoges

Royan

Angoulême

Bay of Biscay

Périgueux

Brive-la-
Gaillard

Bordeaux

Garonne

Dordogne

Langon

Cahors

Montauban

Bayonne

Toulouse

Biarritz

Pau

Tarbes

Carcassonne

SPAIN

ANDORRA

Calais
A26/E15
Lille
Arras
BELGIUM
Cambrai
iiens
St. Quentin
Beauvais
A26
LUXEMBOURG
Reims
A4
Metz
Paris
A26
Châlons-en-
Champagne
Nancy
Sens
Strasbourg
Rhine
A5
Troyes
GERMANY
Orléans
A6
Auxerre
Mulhouse
Bourges
Dijon
Belfort
Nevers
Beaune
Besançon
A36
SWITZERLAND
Montluçon
Mâcon
Saône
Bourg-en-
Bresse
A72
A40
Clermont-
Ferrand
Lyon
Rhône
ITALY
Le Puy
A7
Chambéry
Rhône
Aurillac
Grenoble
Rodez
Montélimar
Millau
THE
RIVIERA
Nîmes
Avignon
Nice
MONACO
Montpellier
PROVENCE
Aix-en-Provence
Monte Carlo
Narbonne
Marseille
A8
Cannes
Perpignan
A9
Toulon
Mediterranean Sea
Corsica

0   50 mi
0   75 km

Corsica
Calvi
Bastia
Corte
Ajaccio
N198
Bonifacio

Europe

Reykjavik
ICELAND

NORWAY
Bergen

NORTHERN IRELAND
SCOTLAND
Edinburgh
North Sea
Skagerrak
DENMARK

IRELAND
Belfast
Irish Sea
UNITED KINGDOM
Dublin
Hamburg

WALES
ENGLAND
NETHERLANDS
Amsterdam
GERM

Cardiff
London
The Hague
Rotterdam

ATLANTIC OCEAN
English Channel
Brussels
Bonn
BELGIUM
Frankfurt

Paris
LUXEMBOURG

FRANCE
Zürich
Munich
Bern
SWITZERLAND
LIECHTENSTEIN

Lyon
Milan
Venic

Monte Carlo
Nice
MONACO
Florence

Marseille

PORTUGAL
Madrid
ANDORRA
Corsica

Lisbon
Barcelona

SPAIN
Sardinia

Seville
Granada
Balearic Islands
Tyrrhenia

Gibraltar
Mediterranean Sea

MOROCCO
ALGERIA
TUNISIA

0   400 miles
0   600 km

World Time Zones

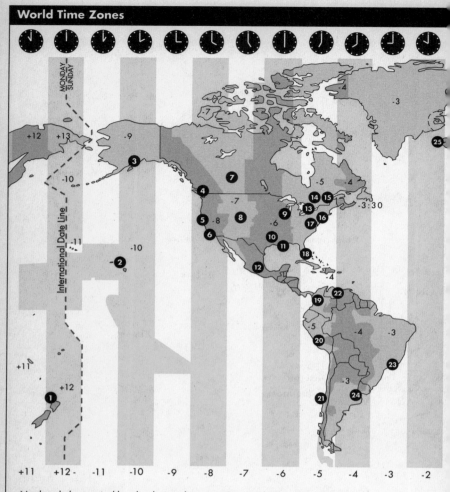

Numbers below vertical bands relate each zone to Greenwich Mean Time (0 hrs.).
Local times frequently differ from these general indications,
as indicated by light-face numbers on map.

Algiers, **29**

Anchorage, **3**

Athens, **41**

Auckland, **1**

Baghdad, **46**

Bangkok, **50**

Beijing, **54**

Berlin, **34**

Bogotá, **19**

Budapest, **37**

Buenos Aires, **24**

Caracas, **22**

Chicago, **9**

Copenhagen, **33**

Dallas, **10**

Delhi, **48**

Denver, **8**

Djakarta, **53**

Dublin, **26**

Edmonton, **7**

Hong Kong, **56**

Honolulu, **2**

Istanbul, **40**

Jerusalem, **42**

Johannesburg, **44**

Lima, **20**

Lisbon, **28**

London
(Greenwich), **27**

Los Angeles, **6**

Madrid, **38**

Manila, **57**

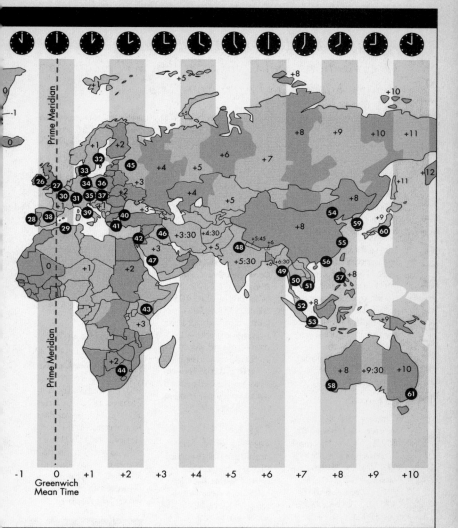

Mecca, **47**
Mexico City, **12**
Miami, **18**
Montréal, **15**
Moscow, **45**
Nairobi, **43**
New Orleans, **11**
New York City, **16**

Ottawa, **14**
Paris, **30**
Perth, **58**
Reykjavík, **25**
Rio de Janeiro, **23**
Rome, **39**
Saigon (Ho Chi Minh City), **51**

San Francisco, **5**
Santiago, **21**
Seoul, **59**
Shanghai, **55**
Singapore, **52**
Stockholm, **32**
Sydney, **61**
Tokyo, **60**

Toronto, **13**
Vancouver, **4**
Vienna, **35**
Warsaw, **36**
Washington, D.C., **17**
Yangon, **49**
Zürich, **31**

XII

THE GOLD GUIDE / IMPORTANT CONTACTS

IMPORTANT CONTACTS A TO Z

An Alphabetical Listing of Publications, Organizations, and Companies that Will Help You Before, During, and After Your Trip

A

AIR TRAVEL

The major gateways to France include Paris's Orly Airport (☎ 01–49–75–52–52) and Charles de Gaulle (Roissy) Airport (☎ 01–48–62–22–80).

Marseille and Montpellier are served by frequent flights from Paris and London, and daily flights from Paris arrive at the smaller airport at Nîmes. In summer, there are direct flights from the United States to the Riviera's international airport in Nice (☎ 04–93–21–30–12).

CARRIERS

Carriers serving France include **Air France** (☎ 800/237–2747), **American Airlines** (☎ 800/433–7300), **British Airways** (☎ 800/247–9297), **Continental** (☎ 800/231–0856), **Delta** (☎ 800/241–4141), **TWA** (☎ 800/892–4141), **United Airlines** (☎ 800/241–6522), and **USAir** (☎ 800/428–4322).

FROM THE U.K.➤ Carriers from the United Kingdom include **Air France** (☎ 0181/742–6600), **British Airways** (☎ 0181/759–2313), and **Caledonian Airways** (☎ 01293/567100). Charter flights often offer the best value; contact **Bluebird Express** (⌧ Vanguard House, 277 London Rd., Burgess Hill, RH5 9QU, ☎ 01444/235–678), which flies from Gatwick, Manchester, and Birmingham.

COMPLAINTS

To register complaints about charter and scheduled airlines, contact the U.S. Department of Transportation's **Aviation Consumer Protection Division** (⌧ C-75, Washington, DC 20590, ☎ 202/366–2220). Complaints about lost baggage or ticketing problems and safety concerns may also be logged with the **Federal Aviation Administration (FAA) Consumer Hotline** (☎ 800/322–7873).

CONSOLIDATORS

For the names of reputable air-ticket consolidators, contact the **United States Air Consolidators Association** (⌧ 925 L St., Suite 220, Sacramento, CA 95814, ☎ 916/441–4166, FAX 916/441–3520). For services that will help you find the lowest airfares, *see* Discounts & Deals, *below.*

PUBLICATIONS

For general information about charter carriers, ask for the Department of Transportation's free brochure **"Plane Talk: Public Charter Flights"** (⌧ Aviation Consumer Protection Division, C-75, Washington, DC 20590, ☎ 202/366–2220). The Department of Transportation also publishes a 58-page booklet, **"Fly Rights,"** available from the Consumer Information Center (⌧ Supt. of Documents, Dept. 136C, Pueblo, CO 81009; $1.75).

For other tips and hints, consult the Consumer Union's monthly **"Consumer Reports Travel Letter"** (⌧ Box 53629, Boulder, CO 80322, ☎ 800/234–1970; $39 1st year).

WITHIN FRANCE

France's domestic airline service, **Air Inter** (☎ 01–45–46–90–00), has flights from Paris to all major cities. For journeys from Paris to Provence and the Riviera, air travel is a time saver, though train travel is always much cheaper. Most domestic flights from Paris leave from **Orly Airport.**

B

BARGE TRAVEL

For information on cruising France's inland waterways, contact **Bourgogne Voies Navigables** (⌧ 1 quai de la République, 89000 Auxerre, ☎ 01–86–52–18–99). For barge tours, *see* Theme Trips *in* Tour Operators, *below.*

BETTER BUSINESS BUREAU

For local contacts in the hometown of a tour

operator you may be considering, consult the **Council of Better Business Bureaus** (⊠ 4200 Wilson Blvd., Suite 800, Arlington, VA 22203, ☎ 703/276–0100, FAX 703/525–8277).

For information on cycling in France, contact the **Fédération Française de Cyclotourisme** (⊠ 8 rue Jean-Marie-Jégo, 75013 Paris, ☎ 01–44–16–88–88). The yellow Michelin maps (1:200,000 scale) are fine for roads, but the best large-scale maps are prepared by the **Institut Géographique National** (⊠ IGN, 107 rue La Boétie, 75008 Paris, ☎ 42–56–06–68). Try their blue series (1:25,000) or orange series (1:50,000). Both indicate elevations and steep grades. Several good bike routes are described in detail in the chapters that follow. Also *see* Theme Trips *in* Tour Operators, *below.*

For service from the United Kingdom, contact **Eurolines** (☎ 0171/730–3499), the international affiliate of **National Express.**

WITHIN FRANCE

Excursions and bus holidays are organized by the **SNCF** (⊠ 88 rue St-Lazare, 75009 Paris, ☎ 01–45–82–50–50) and other tourist organizations, such as **Horizons Européens.** Ask for the brochure at any major travel agent, or contact **France-Tourisme** (⊠ 1 rue d'Auber, 75009 Paris, ☎ 01–47–42–27–40).

The major car-rental companies represented in France are **Avis** (☎ 800/331–1084; in Canada, 800/879–2847), **Budget** (☎ 800/527–0700; in the U.K., 0800/181181), **Dollar** (known as Eurodollar outside North America, ☎ 800/800–4000; in the U.K., 0990/565–656), **Hertz** (☎ 800/654–3001; in Canada, 800/263–0600; in the U.K., 0345/555–888), and **National InterRent** (sometimes known as Europcar InterRent outside North America; ☎ 800/227–3876; in the U.K., 01345/222–525). Rates in France begin at 375 francs a day and 1225 francs a week for an economy car with unlimited mileage. This does not include tax on car rentals, which is 20.6%.

Local car-rental firms in Paris include **Rent-A-Car** (⊠ 79 rue de Bercy, 75012, ☎ 01–43–45–15–15), which offers small Fiat Pandas or larger Rover 214s. Other outfits include **Dergi** (⊠ 60 bd. St-Marcel, 75005, ☎ 01–45–87–27–04); **Locabest** (⊠ 104 bd. Magenta, 75010, ☎ 01–44–72–08–05); and **ACAR** (⊠ 99 bd. Auguste-Blanqui, 75013, ☎ 01–45–88–28–38), with economy cars and Renault Espace minivans.

RENTAL WHOLESALERS

Contact **Auto Europe** (☎ 207/828–2525 or 800/223–5555), **Europe**

by Car (☎ 800/223–1516; in CA, 800/252–9401), or the **Kemwel Group** (☎ 914/835–5555 or 800/678–0678).

For information, contact **Le Shuttle** (in the U.S., ☎ 800/388–3876; in the U.K., 0990/353535), which transports cars, or **Eurostar** (in the U.S., ☎ 800/942–4866; in the U.K., 0345/881–881), the high-speed train service between London (Waterloo) and Paris (Gare du Nord). Eurostar tickets are available in the U.K. through **InterCity Europe,** the international wing of BritRail (⊠ Victoria Station, London, ☎ 0171/834–2345 or 0171/828–0892 for credit-card bookings), and in the United States through **Rail Europe** (☎ 800/942–4866) and **BritRail Travel** (☎ 800/677–8585).

DISCOUNT RAIL PASSES

The **SNCF** allows children under 4 to travel free (provided they don't occupy a seat) and children 4 to 11 to travel at half fare. The Carte Kiwi (285 francs) allows children under 16 and as many as four accompanying adults to make four journeys at half fare.

FLYING

Look into **"Flying with Baby"** (⊠ Third Street Press, Box 261250, Littleton, CO 80163, ☎ 303/595–5959; $4.95

includes shipping), cowritten by a flight attendant. **"Kids and Teens in Flight,"** free from the U.S. Department of Transportation's Aviation Consumer Protection Division (⊠ C-75, Washington, DC 20590, ☎ 202/366–2220), offers tips on children flying alone. Every two years the February issue of *Family Travel Times* (☞ Know-How, *below*) details children's services on three dozen airlines. **"Flying Alone, Handy Advice for Kids Traveling Solo"** is available free from the American Automobile Association (AAA) (⊠ send stamped, self-addressed, legal-size envelope: Flying Alone, Mail Stop 800, 1000 AAA Dr., Heathrow, FL 32746).

KNOW-HOW

Family Travel Times, published quarterly by Travel with Your Children (⊠ TWYCH, 40 5th Ave., New York, NY 10011, ☎ 212/477–5524; $40 per year), covers destinations, types of vacations, and modes of travel.

LODGING

Novotel (☎ 800/221–4542) and **Sofitel** hotels (☎ 800/221–4542) offer discounts for families; some properties have special programs for children. **Club Med** (⊠ 40 W. 57th St., New York, NY 10019, ☎ 800/258–2633) has a "Baby Club" (from age four months) at its resort in Chamonix, "Mini Clubs" (for ages four to six or eight, depending on the resort), and "Kids Clubs" (for ages eight and up during school holidays)

at most of its resort villages. Some clubs are only French-speaking, so check first.

TOUR OPERATORS

Contact **Grandtravel** (⊠ 6900 Wisconsin Ave., Suite 706, Chevy Chase, MD 20815, ☎ 301/986–0790 or 800/247–7651), which has tours for people traveling with grandchildren ages 7–17; **Families Welcome!** (⊠ 4711 Hope Valley Rd., Durham, NC 27707, ☎ 919/489–2555 or 800/326–0724); or **Rascals in Paradise** (⊠ 650 5th St., Suite 505, San Francisco, CA 94107, ☎ 415/978–9800 or 800/872–7225).

If you're outdoorsy, look into family-oriented programs run by the **American Museum of Natural History** (⊠ 79th St. and Central Park West, New York, NY 10024, ☎ 212/769–5700 or 800/462–8687).

CUSTOMS

U.S. CITIZENS

The **U.S. Customs Service** (⊠ Box 7407, Washington, DC 20044, ☎ 202/927–6724) can answer questions on duty-free limits and publishes a helpful brochure, "Know Before You Go." For information on registering foreign-made articles, call 202/927–0540.

COMPLAINTS➤ Note the inspector's badge number and write to the commissioner's office (⊠ 1301 Constitution Ave. NW, Washington, DC 20229).

CANADIANS

Contact **Revenue Canada** (⊠ 2265 St.

Laurent Blvd. S, Ottawa, Ontario K1G 4K3, ☎ 613/993–0534) for a copy of the free brochure **"I Declare/Je Déclare"** and for details on duty-free limits. For recorded information (within Canada only), call 800/461–9999.

U.K. CITIZENS

HM Customs and Excise (⊠ Dorset House, Stamford St., London SE1 9NG, ☎ 0171/202–4227) can answer questions about U.K. customs regulations and publishes a free pamphlet, **"A Guide for Travellers,"** detailing standard procedures and import rules.

D

DISABILITIES & ACCESSIBILITY

COMPLAINTS

To register complaints under the provisions of the Americans with Disabilities Act, contact the U.S. Department of Justice's **Disability Rights Section** (⊠ Box 66738, Washington, DC 20035, ☎ 202/514–0301 or 800/514–0301, FAX 202/307–1198, TTY 202/514–0383 or 800/514–0383). For airline-related problems, contact the U.S. Department of Transportation's **Aviation Consumer Protection Division** (☞ Air Travel, *above*). For complaints about surface transportation, contact the Department of Transportation's **Civil Rights Office** (☎ 202/366–4648).

LOCAL INFORMATION

Contact the **Comité Nationale Français de**

Liaison pour la Réadaptation des Handicapés (✉ 236b rue de Tolbiac, 75013 Paris, ☎ 01–53–80–66–66) or the **Association des Paralysés de France** (✉ 9 bd. Auguste-Blanqui, 75013 Paris, ☎ 01–45–81–30–63).

ORGANIZATIONS

TRAVELERS WITH HEARING IMPAIRMENTS➤ The **American Academy of Otolaryngology** (✉ 1 Prince St., Alexandria, VA 22314, ☎ 703/836–4444, FAX 703/683–5100, TTY 703/519–1585) publishes a brochure, "Travel Tips for Hearing Impaired People."

TRAVELERS WITH MOBILITY PROBLEMS➤ Contact **Mobility International USA** (✉ Box 10767, Eugene, OR 97440, ☎ and TTY 541/343–1284, FAX 541/343–6812), the U.S. branch of a Belgium-based organization (☞ *below*) with affiliates in 30 countries; **MossRehab Hospital Travel Information Service** (☎ 215/456–9600, TTY 215/456–9602), a telephone information resource for travelers with physical disabilities; the **Society for the Advancement of Travel for the Handicapped** (✉ 347 5th Ave., Suite 610, New York, NY 10016, ☎ 212/447–7284, FAX 212/725–8253; membership $45); and **Travelin' Talk** (✉ Box 3534, Clarksville, TN 37043, ☎ 615/552–6670, FAX 615/552–1182) which provides local contacts worldwide for travelers with disabilities.

TRAVELERS WITH VISION IMPAIRMENTS➤ Contact the **American Council of the Blind** (✉ 1155 15th St. NW, Suite 720, Washington, DC 20005, ☎ 202/467–5081, FAX 202/467–5085) for a list of travelers' resources or the **American Foundation for the Blind** (✉ 11 Penn Plaza, Suite 300, New York, NY 10001, ☎ 212/502–7600 or 800/232–5463, TTY 212/502–7662), which provides general advice and publishes "Access to Art" ($19.95), a directory of museums that accommodate travelers with vision impairments.

IN EUROPE

Contact the **Royal Association for Disability and Rehabilitation** (✉ RADAR, 12 City Forum, 250 City Rd., London EC1V 8AF, ☎ 0171/250–3222) or **Mobility International** (✉ rue de Manchester 25, B-1080 Brussels, Belgium, ☎ 00–322–410–6297, FAX 00–322–410–6874), an international travel-information clearinghouse for people with disabilities.

PUBLICATIONS

Several publications for travelers with disabilities are available from the **Consumer Information Center** (✉ Box 100, Pueblo, CO 81009, ☎ 719/948–3334). Call or write for its free catalog of current titles. The Society for the Advancement of Travel for the Handicapped (☞ Organizations, *above*) publishes the quarterly magazine **"Access to Travel"** ($13 for 1-year subscription).

The 500-page ***Travelin' Talk Directory*** (✉ Box 3534, Clarksville, TN 37043, ☎ 615/552–6670, FAX 615/552–1182; $35) lists people and organizations who help travelers with disabilities. For travel agents worldwide, consult the ***Directory of Travel Agencies for the Disabled*** (✉ Twin Peaks Press, Box 129, Vancouver, WA 98666, ☎ 360/694–2462 or 800/637–2256, FAX 360/696–3210; $19.95 plus $3 shipping).

TRAVEL AGENCIES & TOUR OPERATORS

The Americans with Disabilities Act requires that all travel firms serve the needs of all travelers. That said, you should note that some agencies and operators specialize in making travel arrangements for individuals and groups with disabilities, among them **Access Adventures** (✉ 206 Chestnut Ridge Rd., Rochester, NY 14624, ☎ 716/889–9096), run by a former physical-rehab counselor.

TRAVELERS WITH MOBILITY PROBLEMS➤ Contact **Accessible Journeys** (✉ 35 W. Sellers Ave., Ridley Park, PA 19078, ☎ 610/521–0339 or 800/846–4537, FAX 610/521–6959), a registered nursing service that arranges vacations; **Flying Wheels Travel** (✉ 143 W. Bridge St., Box 382, Owatonna, MN 55060, ☎ 507/451–5005 or 800/535–6790), a travel agency specializing in European cruises and tours; **Hinsdale Travel Service** (✉ 201 E. Ogden Ave., Suite 100, Hinsdale, IL 60521, ☎ 708/325–1335), a travel agency that benefits from the advice of wheelchair traveler Janice Perkins; and **Wheelchair Journeys** (✉ 16979 Redmond Way, Redmond, WA 98052, ☎ 206/885–2210 or 800/313–4751), which can handle arrangements worldwide.

TRAVELERS WITH DEVELOPMENTAL DISABILITIES➤ Contact the nonprofit **New Directions** (✉ 5276 Hollister Ave., Suite 207, Santa Barbara, CA 93111, ☎ 805/967–2841) and **Sprout** (✉ 893 Amsterdam Ave., New York, NY 10025, ☎ 212/222–9575), which specializes in custom-designed itineraries for groups but also books vacations for individual travelers.

TRAVEL GEAR

The **Magellan's** catalog (☎ 800/962–4943, FAX 805/568–5406), includes a range of products designed for travelers with disabilities.

DISCOUNTS & DEALS

AIRFARES

For the lowest airfares to France, call 800/FLY-4-LES.

CLUBS

Contact **Entertainment Travel Editions** (✉ Box 1068, Trumbull, CT 06611, ☎ 800/445–4137; $28–$53, depending on destination), **Great American Traveler** (✉ Box 27965, Salt Lake City, UT 84127, ☎ 800/548–2812; $49.95 per year), **Moment's Notice Discount Travel Club** (✉ 7301 New Utrecht Ave., Brooklyn, NY 11204, ☎ 718/234–6295; $25 per year, single or fam-

ily), **Privilege Card** (✉ 3391 Peachtree Rd. NE, Suite 110, Atlanta, GA 30326, ☎ 404/262–0222 or 800/236–9732; $74.95 per year), **Travelers Advantage** (✉ CUC Travel Service, 49 Music Sq. W, Nashville, TN 37203, ☎ 800/548–1116 or 800/648–4037; $49 per year, single or family), or **Worldwide Discount Travel Club** (✉ 1674 Meridian Ave., Miami Beach, FL 33139, ☎ 305/534–2082; $50 per year for family, $40 single).

HOTEL ROOMS

For hotel room rates guaranteed in U.S. dollars, call **Steigenberger Reservation Service** (☎ 800/223–5652).

PASSES

See Air *and* Train Travel *in* Smart Travel Tips A to Z, *below.*

STUDENTS

Members of Hostelling International–American Youth Hostels (☞ Students, *below*) are eligible for discounts on car rentals, admissions to attractions, and other selected travel expenses.

PUBLICATIONS

Consult *The Frugal Globetrotter,* by Bruce Northam (✉ Fulcrum Publishing, 350 Indiana St., Suite 350, Golden, CO 80401, ☎ 800/9 92–2908; $15.95). For publications that tell how to find the lowest prices on plane tickets, *see* Air Travel, *above.*

F

FERRY TRAVEL

DOVER-CALAIS

Contact **P&O European Ferries** (✉ Channel

House, Channel View Rd., Dover, Kent CT17 9TJ, ☎ 0181/575–8555); **Sealink** (✉ Charter House, Park St., Ashford, Kent TN24 8EX, ☎ 01233/646801); or **Hoverspeed** (✉ International Hoverport, Marine Parade, Dover CT17 9TG, ☎ 01304/240241).

OTHER CROSSINGS

Folkestone–Boulogne crossings are available from Hoverspeed. Newhaven–Dieppe crossings are available from Sealink. The Portsmouth–Le Havre crossing is offered by P&O. For Ramsgate–Dunkerque crossings, contact **Sally Line** (✉ Argyle Centre, York St., Ramsgate, Kent CT11 9DS, ☎ 01843/595522).

G

GAY & LESBIAN TRAVEL

ORGANIZATIONS

The **International Gay Travel Association** (✉ Box 4974, Key West, FL 33041, ☎ 800/448–8550, FAX 305/296–6633), a consortium of more than 1,000 travel companies, can supply names of gay-friendly travel agents, tour operators, and accommodations.

PUBLICATIONS

The 16-page monthly newsletter **"Out & About"** (✉ 8 W. 19th St., Suite 401, New York, NY 10011, ☎ 212/645–6922 or 800/929–2268, FAX 800/929–2215; $49 for 10 issues and quarterly calendar) covers gay-friendly resorts, hotels, cruise lines, and airlines.

TOUR OPERATORS

Toto Tours (✉ 1326 W. Albion Ave., Suite 3W, Chicago, IL 60626, ☎ 312/274–8686 or 800/565–1241, FAX 312/274–8695) offers group tours to worldwide destinations.

TRAVEL AGENCIES

The largest agencies serving gay travelers are **Advance Travel** (✉ 10700 Northwest Fwy., Suite 160, Houston, TX 77092, ☎ 713/682–2002 or 800/292–0500), **Club Travel** (✉ 8739 Santa Monica Blvd., W. Hollywood, CA 90069, ☎ 310/358–2200 or 800/429–8747), **Islanders/Kennedy Travel** (✉ 183 W. 10th St., New York, NY 10014, ☎ 212/242–3222 or 800/988–1181), **Now Voyager** (✉ 4406 18th St., San Francisco, CA 94114, ☎ 415/626–1169 or 800/255–6951), and **Yellowbrick Road** (✉ 1500 W. Balmoral Ave., Chicago, IL 60640, ☎ 312/561–1800 or 800/642–2488). **Skylink Women's Travel** (✉ 2460 W. 3rd St., Suite 215, Santa Rosa, CA 95401, ☎ 707/570–0105 or 800/225–5759) serves lesbian travelers.

H
HEALTH ISSUES

FINDING A DOCTOR

The best bet is to contact the **American Hospital** (✉ 63 bd. Victor-Hugo, Neuilly-sur-Seine, just west of Paris, ☎ 01–46–41–25–25, FAX 01–46–24–49–38) and ask them to

recommend an English-speaking doctor. A midnight visit to a local public hospital could be frightening and confusing, as the interns on duty often speak little English.

For its members, the **International Association for Medical Assistance to Travellers** (✉ IAMAT, membership free; 417 Center St., Lewiston, NY 14092, ☎ 716/754–4883; 40 Regal Rd., Guelph, Ontario N1K 1B5, ☎ 519/836–0102; 1287 St. Clair Ave., Toronto, Ontario M6E 1B8, ☎ 416/652–0137; 57 Voirets, 1212 Grand-Lancy, Geneva, Switzerland, no phone) publishes a worldwide directory of English-speaking physicians meeting IAMAT standards.

MEDICAL ASSISTANCE COMPANIES

The following companies are concerned primarily with emergency medical assistance, although they may provide some insurance as part of their coverage. For a list of full-service travel insurance companies, *see* Insurance, *below.*

Contact **International SOS Assistance** (✉ Box 11568, Philadelphia, PA 19116, ☎ 215/244–1500 or 800/523–8930; Box 466, Pl. Bonaventure, Montréal, Québec H5A 1C1, ☎ 514/874–7674 or 800/363–0263; 7 Old Lodge Pl., St. Margarets, Twickenham TW1 1RQ, England, ☎ 0181/744–0033), **Medex Assistance Corporation** (✉ Box

5375, Timonium, MD 21094–5375, ☎ 410/453–6300 or 800/573–2029), **Near Travel Services** (✉ Box 1339, Calumet City, IL 60409, ☎ 708/868–6700 or 800/654–6700), **Traveler's Emergency Network** (✉ 1133 15th St. NW, Suite 400, Washington DC, 20005, ☎ 202/828–5894 or 800/275–4836, FAX 202/828–5896), **TravMed** (✉ Box 5375, Timonium, MD 21094, ☎ 415/453–6380 or 800/732–5309), or **Worldwide Assistance Services** (✉ 1133 15th St. NW, Suite 400, Washington, DC 20005, ☎ 202/331–1609 or 800/821–2828, FAX 202/828–5896).

HIKING

Contact the **Club Alpin Français** (✉ 24 av. Laumière, 75019 Paris, ☎ 01–42–02–68–64) or the **Fédération Française de la Randonnée Pédestre** (✉ 64 rue de Gergovie, 75014 Paris, ☎ 01–45–45–31–02), which publishes good topographical maps and guides. The IGN maps sold in many bookshops are also invaluable (*see* Bicycling, *above*).

I
INSURANCE

IN CANADA

Contact **Mutual of Omaha** (✉ Travel Division, 500 University Ave., Toronto, Ontario M5G 1V8, ☎ 800/465–0267 in Canada or 416/598-4083).

IN THE U.S.

Travel insurance covering baggage, health, and

trip cancellation or interruptions is available from **Access America** (⊠ Box 6600 W. Broad St., Richmond, VA 23230, ☎ 804/285–3300 or 800/334–7525), **Carefree Travel Insurance** (⊠ Box 9366, 100 Garden City Plaza, Garden City, NY 11530, ☎ 516/294–0220 or 800/323–3149), **Tele-Trip** (⊠ Mutual of Omaha Plaza, Box 31716, Omaha, NE 68131, ☎ 800/228–9792), **Travel Guard International** (⊠ 1145 Clark St., Stevens Point, WI 54481, ☎ 715/345–0505 or 800/826–1300), **Travel Insured International** (⊠ Box 280568, East Hartford, CT 06128, ☎ 203/528–7663 or 800/243–3174), and **Wallach & Company** (⊠ 107 W. Federal St., Box 480, Middleburg, VA 22117, ☎ 540/687–3166 or 800/237–6615).

IN THE U.K.

The **Association of British Insurers** (⊠ 51 Gresham St., London EC2V 7HQ, ☎ 0171/600–3333) gives advice by phone and publishes the free pamphlet **"Holiday Insurance,"** which sets out typical policy provisions and costs.

L
LODGING

For information on hotel consolidators, *see* Discounts, *above*.

APARTMENT & VILLA RENTAL

Among the companies to contact are **At Home Abroad** (⊠ 405 E. 56th St., Suite 6H, New York, NY 10022, ☎ 212/421–9165, FAX 212/752–1591), **At Home in France** (⊠ Box 31404, San Francisco, CA 94131, ☎ 415/920–9628, FAX 415/920–9629), **Europa-Let** (⊠ 92 N. Main St., Ashland, OR 97520, ☎ 541/482–5806 or 800/462–4486, FAX 541/482–0660), **Hometours International** (⊠ Box 11503, Knoxville, TN 37939, ☎ 423/588–8722 or 800/367–4668), **Interhome** (⊠ 124 Little Falls Rd., Fairfield, NJ 07004, ☎ 201/882–6864, FAX 201/808–1742), **Property Rentals International** (⊠ 1008 Mansfield Crossing Rd., Richmond, VA 23236, ☎ 804/378–6054 or 800/220–3332, FAX 804/379–2073), **Rental Directories International** (⊠ 2044 Rittenhouse Sq., Philadelphia, PA 19103, ☎ 215/985–4001, FAX 215/985–0323), **Rent-a-Home International** (⊠ 7200 34th Ave. NW, Seattle, WA 98117, ☎ 206/789–9377 or 800/488–7368, FAX 206/789–9379, hmaria@aol.com), **Vacation Home Rentals Worldwide** (⊠ 235 Kensington Ave., Norwood, NJ 07648, ☎ 201/767–9393 or 800/633–3284, FAX 201/767–5510), **Villas and Apartments Abroad** (⊠ 420 Madison Ave., Suite 1003, New York, NY 10017, ☎ 212/759–1025 or 800/433–3020, FAX 212/755–8316), or **Villas International** (⊠ 605 Market St., Suite 510, San Francisco, CA 94105, ☎ 415/281–0910 or 800/221–2260, FAX 415/281–0919). Members of the travel club **Hideaways International** (⊠ 767 Islington St., Portsmouth, NH 03801, ☎ 603/430–4433 or 800/843–4433, FAX 603/430–4444, info@hideaways.com; $99 per year) receive two annual guides plus quarterly newsletters and arrange rentals among themselves.

HOME EXCHANGE

One of the principal clearinghouses is **Home-Link International/Vacation Exchange Club** (⊠ Box 650, Key West, FL 33041, ☎ 305/294–1448 or 800/638–3841, FAX 305/294–1148; $70 per year), which sends members three annual directories, with a listing in one, plus updates.

HOTELS

Directories to small, inexpensive hotels can be obtained from **Logis de France** (⊠ 83 av. d'Italie, 75013 Paris, ☎ 01–45–84–83–84, FAX 01–44–24–08–74; 75 francs) and **France-Accueil** (⊠ 163 av. d'Italie, 75013 Paris, ☎ 01–45–83–04–22, FAX 01–45–86–49–82). Write to **Relais & Châteaux** (⊠ 15 rue Galvani, 75017 Paris, ☎ 01–45–72–90–00, FAX 01–45–72–90–30 or, in the United States, ☎ 212/856–0015 or FAX 212/856–0193) for a guide to the group's network of prestigious inns and hotels.

For reservations and information on the **Gîtes Ruraux,** contact either the **Federation National des Gîtes de France** (⊠ 35 rue Godot-de-Mauroy, 75009 Paris, ☎ 01–49–70–75–75, FAX 01–49–70–75–76), naming which region interests you, or the **French Government Tourist Office** in London

(⌧ 178 Piccadilly, W1V OAL, ☎ 0891/244–123 39p per minute cheap rate and 49p per minute at other times]), which runs a special reservation service.

M
MONEY MATTERS

ATMS

For specific foreign **Cirrus** locations, call 800/424–7787; for foreign **Plus** locations, consult the Plus directory at your local bank.

CURRENCY EXCHANGE

If your bank doesn't exchange currency, contact **Thomas Cook Currency Services** (☎ 800/287–7362 for locations). **Ruesch International** (☎ 800/424–2923 for locations) can also provide you with foreign banknotes before you leave home and publishes a number of useful brochures, including a "Foreign Currency Guide" and "Foreign Exchange Tips."

WIRING FUNDS

Funds can be wired via **MoneyGram**℠ (for locations and information in the U.S. and Canada, ☎ 800/926–9400) or **Western Union** (for agent locations or to send money using MasterCard or Visa, ☎ 800/325–6000; in Canada, 800/321–2923; in the U.K., 0800/833833; or visit the Western Union office at the nearest major post office).

P
PACKING

For strategies on packing light, get a copy of *The Packing Book,* by

Judith Gilford (⌧ Ten Speed Press, Box 7123, Berkeley, CA 94707, ☎ 510/559–1600 or 800/841–2665, ℻ 510/524–4588; $7.95).

PASSPORTS & VISAS

U.S. CITIZENS

For fees, documentation requirements, and other information, call the State Department's **Office of Passport Services** information line (☎ 202/647–0518).

CANADIANS

For fees, documentation requirements, and other information, call the Ministry of Foreign Affairs and International Trade's **Passport Office** (☎ 819/994–3500 or 800/567–6868).

U.K. CITIZENS

For fees, documentation requirements, and to request an emergency passport, call the **London Passport Office** (☎ 0990/210–410).

PHOTO HELP

The **Kodak Information Center** (☎ 800/242–2424) answers consumer questions about film and photography. The *Kodak Guide to Shooting Great Travel Pictures* (available in bookstores; or contact Fodor's Travel Publications, ☎ 800/533–6478; $16.50) explains how to take expert travel photographs.

S
SAFETY

"Trouble-Free Travel," from the AAA, is a booklet of tips for protecting yourself and your belongings when away from home. Send

a stamped, self-addressed, legal-size envelope to Flying Alone (⌧ Mail Stop 75, 1000 AAA Dr., Heathrow, FL 32746).

SENIOR CITIZENS

EDUCATIONAL TRAVEL

The nonprofit **Elderhostel** (⌧ 75 Federal St., 3rd Floor, Boston, MA 02110, ☎ 617/426–7788), for people 60 and older, has offered inexpensive study programs since 1975. Courses cover everything from marine science to Greek mythology and cowboy poetry. Costs for two- to three-week international trips—including room, board, and transportation from the United States—range from $1,800 to $4,500.

For people 50 and over and their children and grandchildren, **Interhostel** (⌧ University of New Hampshire, 6 Garrison Ave., Durham, NH 03824, ☎ 603/862–1147 or 800/733–9753) runs 10-day summer programs that feature lectures, field trips, and sightseeing. Most last two weeks and cost $2,125–$3,100, including airfare.

ORGANIZATIONS

Contact the **American Association of Retired Persons** (⌧ AARP, 601 E St. NW, Washington, DC 20049, ☎ 202/434–2277; annual dues $8 per person or couple). Its Purchase Privilege Program secures discounts for members on lodging, car rentals, and sightseeing.

Sears's **Mature Outlook** (⌧ Box 10448, Des

THE GOLD GUIDE / IMPORTANT CONTACTS

Moines, IA 50306, ☎ 800/336–6330; annual membership $14.95) includes a lifestyle/travel magazine and membership in ITC-50 travel club, which offers discounts of up to 50% at participating hotels and restaurants. (☞ Discounts & Deals *in* Smart Travel Tips A to Z, *below*).

STUDENTS

GROUPS

The major tour operators specializing in student travel are **Contiki Holidays** (⊠ 300 Plaza Alicante, Suite 900, Garden Grove, CA 92640, ☎ 714/740–0808 or 800/266–8454) and **AESU Travel** (⊠ 2 Hamill Rd., Suite 248, Baltimore, MD 21210-1807, ☎ 410/323–4416 or 800/638–7640).

HOSTELING

In the United States, contact **Hostelling International–American Youth Hostels** (⊠ 733 15th St. NW, Suite 840, Washington, DC 20005, ☎ 202/783–6161 or 800/444–6111 for reservations at selected hostels, FAX 202/783–6171); in Canada, **Hostelling International–Canada** (⊠ 205 Catherine St., Suite 400, Ottawa, Ontario K2P 1C3, ☎ 613/237–7884); and in the United Kingdom, the **Youth Hostel Association of England and Wales** (⊠ Trevelyan House, 8 St. Stephen's Hill, St. Albans, Hertfordshire AL1 2DY, ☎ 01727/855215 or 01727/845047). Membership (in the U.S., $25; in Canada, C$26.75; in the U.K., £9.30) gives you access to 5,000 hostels in 77 countries that charge $5–$30 per person per night.

Information is also available from the French headquarters, **Fédération Unie des Auberges de Jeunesse** (⊠ 27 rue Pajol, 75018 Paris, ☎ 44–89–87–28, FAX 44–89–87–10).

ORGANIZATIONS

A major contact is the **Council on International Educational Exchange** (⊠ mail orders only: CIEE, 205 E. 42nd St., 16th Floor, New York, NY 10017, ☎ 212/661–1450, info@ciee.org). The **Educational Travel Centre** (⊠ 438 N. Frances St., Madison, WI 53703, ☎ 608/256–5551 or 800/747–5551, FAX 608/256–2042) offers rail passes and low-cost airline tickets, mostly for flights that depart from Chicago.

In Canada, also contact **Travel Cuts** (⊠ 187 College St., Toronto, Ontario M5T 1P7, ☎ 416/979–2406 or 800/667–2887).

T
TELEPHONE MATTERS

CALLS TO AND WITHIN FRANCE

The country code for France is 33 and for Monaco, 337. Two digits have been added to French telephone numbers, so there is no longer a code when calling the Paris region from the provinces (16–1) or calling the provinces from Paris (16). The new prefixes are as follows: 01 for Paris and Ile-de-France; 02 for the northwest; 03 for the northeast; 04 for the southeast; and 05 for the southwest. Drop the zero if you are calling France from abroad.

To find a number in France, dial 12 for information. For local access numbers abroad, contact **AT&T** USADirect (☎ 800/874–4000), **MCI** Call USA (☎ 800/444–4444), or **Sprint** Express (☎ 800/793–1153).

CALLS FROM FRANCE

To make a direct international call from France, dial 00 and wait for the tone, then dial the country code (1 for the United States and Canada; 44 for the United Kingdom), area code (minus any initial 0), and number.

OPERATORS AND INFORMATION➤ When calling home from France, local access numbers to the English-speaking operators of U.S. long-distance carriers are: **AT&T:** 0–800–99–0011; **MCI:** 0–800–99–0019, and **Sprint:** 0–800–99–0087. For international inquiries, dial 00–33 plus the country code.

TOUR OPERATORS

Among the companies that sell tours and packages to France, the following are nationally known, have a proven reputation, and offer plenty of options.

GROUP TOURS

SUPER-DELUXE➤ **Abercrombie & Kent** (⊠ 1520 Kensington Rd., Oak Brook, IL 60521-2141, ☎ 708/954–2944 or 800/323–7308,

FAX 708/954–3324) and **Travcoa** (✉ Box 2630, 2350 S.E. Bristol St., Newport Beach, CA 92660, ☎ 714/476–2800 or 800/992–2003, FAX 714/476–2538).

DELUXE➤ **Tauck Tours** (✉ Box 5027, 276 Post Rd. W, Westport, CT 06881, ☎ 203/226–6911 or 800/468–2825, FAX 203/221–6828).

PACKAGES

The French Experience (✉ 370 Lexington Ave., New York, NY 10017, ☎ 212/986–1115, FAX 212/986–3808) has a great variety of packages. Just about every airline that flies to France sells packages that include round-trip airfare and hotel accommodations. Among U.S. carriers, contact **American Airlines Fly AAway Vacations** (☎ 800/321–2121), **Delta Dream Vacations** (☎ 800/872–7786), and **USAir Vacations** (☎ 800/455–0123). Other packagers include **Abercrombie & Kent** (☞ Group Tours, *above*), **Alek's Travel** (✉ 519A S. Andrews Ave., Fort Lauderdale, FL 33301, ☎ 954/462–6767, FAX 954/462–8691), **DER Tours** (✉ 11933 Wilshire Blvd., Los Angeles, CA 90025, ☎ 310/479–4140 or 800/782–2424), **Five Star Touring** (✉ 60 E. 42nd St., #612, New York, NY 10165, ☎ 212/818–9140 or 800/792–7827, FAX 212/818–9142), and **Jet Vacations** (✉ 1775 Broadway, New York, NY 10019, ☎ 212/474–8740 or 800/538–2762). **Funjet Vacations** based in Milwaukee, Wisconsin, sells packages only through travel agents.

THEME TRIPS

Travel Contacts (✉ Box 173, Camberley, GU15 1YE, England, ☎ 011/44/1/27667–7217, FAX 011/44/1/2766–3477), which represents 150 tour operators, can satisfy virtually any special interest in France.

ART AND ARCHITECTURE➤ **Endless Beginnings Tours** (✉ 9825 Dowdy Dr., #105, San Diego, CA 92126, ☎ 619/566–4166 or 800/822–7855, FAX 619/549–9655) and **Esplanade Tours** (✉ 581 Boylston St., Boston, MA 02116, ☎ 617/266–7465 or 800/426–5492, FAX 617/262–9829) explore the art, culture, history, and natural beauty of southern France.

BARGE/RIVER CRUISES➤ **Abercrombie & Kent** (☞ Group Tours, *above*) has more than 30 years experience barging in France. **Alden Yacht Charters** (✉ 1909 Alden Landing, Portsmouth, RI 02871, ☎ 401/683–1782 or 800/662–2628, FAX 401/683–3668) represents a variety of barges and boats throughout France. **European Waterways** (✉ 140 E. 56th St., #4C, New York, NY 10022, ☎ 212/688–9489 or 800/217–4447, FAX 212/688–3778 or 800/296–4554, cellular@interport.net) represents barges that carry 6 to 12 passengers; hot-air ballooning and bicycling are available from most barges. **Fenwick & Lang** (✉ 100 W. Harrison, South Tower, #350, Seattle, WA 98119, ☎ 206/216–2903 or 800/243–6244, FAX 206/216–2973) has more than 35 years of experience in booking barge tours of France. For barges with room for up to 50 passengers in the south of France, try **Kemwel's Premier Selections** (✉ 106 Calvert St., Harrison, NY 10528, ☎ 914/835–5555 or 800/234–4000, FAX 914/835–5449). **Le Boat** (☎ 201/342–1838 or 800/922–0291) has one of France's most diverse barge fleets and runs theme tours around food and wine, gardens, and sketching and art. **KD River Cruises of Europe** (✉ 2500 Westchester Ave., Purchase, NY 10577, ☎ 914/696–3600 or 800/346–6525, FAX 914/696–0833) has been cruising the rivers of Europe since 1827 and operates ships accommodating 104 to 184 passengers.

BICYCLING➤ Bike trips through Provence are available for five days to two weeks. Contact **Backroads** (✉ 1516 5th St., Berkeley, CA 94710–1740, ☎ 510/527–1555 or 800/462–2848, FAX 510/527–1444, goactive@Backroads.com), **Bridges Tours** (✉ 2855 Capital Dr., Eugene, OR 97403, ☎ 541/484–1196, FAX 541/687–9085), **Butterfield & Robinson** (✉ 70 Bond St., Toronto, Ontario, Canada M5B 1X3, ☎ 416/864–1354 or 800/678–1147, FAX 416/864–0541, info@butterfield.com), **Chateaux Bike Tours** (✉ Box 5706, Denver, CO 80217, ☎ 303/393–6910 or 800/678–

2453, FAX 303/393–6801), **Classic Adventures** (✉ Box 153, Hamlin, NY 14464-0153, ☎ 716/964–8488 or 800/777–8090, FAX 716/964-7297), **Euro-Bike Tours** (✉ Box 990, De Kalb, IL 60115, ☎ 800/321–6060, FAX 815/758–8851), **Himalayan Travel** (✉ 112 Prospect St., Stamford, CT 06901, ☎ 203/359–3711 or 800/225–2380, FAX 203/359–3669), **Progressive Travels** (✉ 224 W. Galer Ave., #C, Seattle, WA 98119, ☎ 206/285–1987 or 800/245–2229, FAX 206/285–1988), **Rocky Mountain Worldwide Cycle Tours** (✉ Box 1978, Canmore, Alberta, Canada TOL OMO, ☎ 403/678–6770 or 800/661–2453, FAX 403/678–4451, RMCT@CIA.COM, http://www.worldweb.com/rmct), and **Uniquely Europe** (✉ 2819 1st Ave., #280, Seattle, WA 98121-1113, ☎ 206/441–8682 or 800/426–3615, FAX 206/441–8862).

FOOD AND WINE➤ **Annemarie Victory Organization** (✉ 136 E. 64th St., New York, NY 10021, ☎ 212/486–0353) offers a week at a cooking school in Provence. **Cuisine International** (✉ Box 25228, Dallas, TX 75225, ☎ 214/373–1161 or FAX 214/373–1162, CuisineInt@aol.com) has weeklong cooking programs led by expert chefs.

GOLF➤ **Golf International** (✉ 275 Madison Ave., New York, NY 10016, ☎ 212/986–9176 or 800/833–1389, FAX 212/986–3720) has golf packages in several

European countries. **ITC Golf Tours** (✉ 4134 Atlantic Ave., #205, Long Beach, CA 90807, ☎ 310/595–6905 or 800/257–4981) custom designs golf itineraries in France.

HISTORY➤ History buffs should look into **Herodot Travel** (✉ 775 E. Blithedale, Box 234, Mill Valley, CA 94941, ☎ FAX 415/381–4031).

HORSEBACK RIDING➤ For weeklong tours contact **FITS Equestrian** (✉ 685 Lateen Rd., Solvang, CA 93463, ☎ 805/688–9494 or 800/666–3487, FAX 805/688–2943).

LEARNING➤ **Smithsonian Study Tours and Seminars** (✉ 1100 Jefferson Dr., SW, Room 3045, MRC 702, Washington, DC 20560, ☎ 202/357–4700, FAX 202/633–9250) focus on art and culture.

NATURAL HISTORY➤ **Questers** (✉ 381 Park Ave. S, New York, NY 10016, ☎ 212/251–0444 or 800/468–8668, FAX 212/251–0890) explores the wild side of southern France in the company of expert guides.

SPAS➤ **Great Spas of the World** (✉ 211 E. 43rd St., #1404, New York, NY 10017, ☎ 212/599–0382 or 800/826–8062) and Spa-Finders (✉ 91 5th Ave., #301, New York, NY 10003-3039, ☎ 212/924–6800 or 800/255–7727) represents spas in France.

TENNIS➤ **Steve Furgal's International Tennis Tours** (✉ 11828 Rancho Bernardo Rd.,

#123-305, San Diego, CA 92128, ☎ 619/487–7777 or 800/258–3664) can take you to the Monte Carlo Open and arrange for a variety of accommodations and activities.

VILLA RENTALS➤ Contact **Eurovillas** (✉ 1398 55th St., Emeryville, CA 94608, ☎ 707/648–0266), **B&V Associates** (✉ 140 E. 56th St., #4C, New York, NY 10022, ☎ 800/546–4777, FAX 212/688–9467), **Chez Vous** (✉ 1001 Bridgeway, #245, Sausalito, CA 94965 ☎ 415/331–2535, FAX 415/331–5296), and **Villas International** (✉ 605 Market St., San Francisco, CA 94105, ☎ 415/281–0910 or 800/221–2260, FAX 415/281–0919).

WALKING➤ Try **Abercrombie & Kent** (☞ Group Tours, *above*), **Above the Clouds Trekking** (✉ Box 398, Worcester, MA 01602, ☎ 508/799–4499 or 800/233–4499, FAX 508/797–4779), **Adventure Center** (✉ 1311 63rd St., #200, Emeryville, CA 94608, ☎ 510/654–1879 or 800/227–8747), **Mountain Travel-Sobek** (✉ 6420 Fairmount Ave., El Cerrito, CA 94530, ☎ 510/527–8100 or 800/227–2384, FAX 510/525–7710, Info @MT-Sobek.com, http://www.MTSobek.com), and **Wilderness Travel** (✉ 801 Allston Way, Berkeley, CA 94710, ☎ 510/548–0420 or 800/368–2794, FAX 510/548–0347, info@wildernesstravel.com). Also try **Backroads, Butterfield & Robinson, Euro-Bike Tours, Himalayan Travel,**

Progressive Travels, and **Uniquely Europe** (☞ Bicycling, *above*).

YACHT CHARTERS➤ **Huntley Yacht Vacations** (✉ 210 Preston Rd., Wernersville, PA 19565, ☎ 610/678–2628 or 800/322–9224, FAX 610/670–1767, yachts4u@enter.net), **Lynn Jachney Charters** (✉ Box 302, Marblehead, MA 01945, ☎ 617/639–0787 or 800/223–2050, FAX 617/639–0216), **The Moorings** (✉ 19345 U.S. Hwy. 19 N, 4th floor, Clearwater, FL 34624-3193, ☎ 813/530–5424 or 800/535–7289, FAX 813/530–9474), **Ocean Voyages** (✉ 1709 Bridgeway, Sausalito, CA 94965, ☎ 415/332–4681, FAX 415/332–7460).

ORGANIZATIONS

The **National Tour Association** (✉ NTA, 546 E. Main St., Lexington, KY 40508, ☎ 606/226–4444 or 800/755–8687) and the **United States Tour Operators Association** (✉ USTOA, 211 E. 51st St., Suite 12B, New York, NY 10022, ☎ 212/750–7371) can provide lists of members and information on booking tours.

PUBLICATIONS

Contact the USTOA (☞ Organizations, *above*) for its **"Smart Traveler's Planning Kit."** Pamphlets in the kit include the "Worldwide Tour and Vacation Package Finder," "How to Select a Tour or Vacation Package," and information on the organization's consumer protection plan. Also get copy of the Better Business Bureau's **"Tips on Travel Packages"** (✉ Publication 24-195, 4200 Wilson Blvd., Arlington, VA 22203; $2).

TRAIN TRAVEL

Train-ferry travel from the United Kingdom is provided by **Sealink** (☎ 0233/647047) and **British Rail International** (☎ 0171/834–2345).

For information on rail travel within France, contact the **SNCF** (✉ 88 rue St-Lazare, 75009 Paris, ☎ 45–82–50–50).

DISCOUNT PASSES

Eurail and EuroPasses are available through travel agents and **Rail Europe** (✉ 226-230 Westchester Ave., White Plains, NY 10604, ☎ 914/682–5172 or 800/438–7245; ✉ 2087 Dundas E., Suite 105, Mississauga, Ontario L4X 1M2, ☎ 416/602–4195), **DER Tours** (✉ Box 1606, Des Plaines, IL 60017, ☎ 800/782–2424, FAX 800/282–7474), or **CIT Tours Corp.** (✉ 342 Madison Ave., Suite 207, New York, NY 10173, ☎ 212/697–2100 or 800/248–8687 or 800/248–7245 in western U.S.).

TRAVEL GEAR

For travel apparel, appliances, personal-care items, and other travel necessities, get a free catalog from **Magellan's** (☎ 800/962–4943, FAX 805/568–5406), **Orvis Travel** (☎ 800/541–3541, FAX 703/343–7053), or **TravelSmith** (☎ 800/950–1600, FAX 415/455–0554).

ELECTRICAL CONVERTERS

Send a self-addressed, stamped envelope to the **Franzus Company** (✉ Customer Service, Dept. B50, Murtha Industrial Park, Box 142, Beacon Falls, CT 06403, ☎ 203/723–6664) for a copy of the free brochure "Foreign Electricity Is No Deep, Dark Secret."

TRAVEL AGENCIES

For names of reputable agencies in your area, contact the **American Society of Travel Agents** (✉ ASTA, 1101 King St., Suite 200, Alexandria, VA 22314, ☎ 703/739–2782), the **Association of Canadian Travel Agents** (✉ Suite 201, 1729 Bank St., Ottawa, Ontario K1V 7Z5, ☎ 613/521–0474, FAX 613/521–0805) or the **Association of British Travel Agents** (✉ 55-57 Newman St., London W1P 4AH, ☎ 0171/637–2444, FAX 0171/637–0713).

U

U.S.
GOVERNMENT
TRAVEL BRIEFINGS

The U.S. Department of State's American Citizens Services office (✉ Room 4811, Washington, DC 20520; enclose SASE) issues **Consular Information Sheets** on all foreign countries. These cover issues such as crime, security, political climate, and health risks as well as listing embassy locations, entry requirements, currency regulations, and providing other useful information. For the latest information, stop in at any U.S. passport office, consulate, or embassy; call the interactive hot line (☎ 202/647–5225, FAX 202/647–3000); or,

THE GOLD GUIDE / IMPORTANT CONTACTS

with your PC's modem, tap into the department's computer bulletin board (☎ 202/647–9225).

V

VISITOR

INFORMATION

Contact the **French Government Tourist Office.**

IN THE U.S.

Nationwide: ☎ 900/990–0040 (costs 95¢ per minute).

New York: ✉ 610 5th Ave., New York, NY 10020, ☎ 212/315–0888 or 212/757–1125, FAX 212/247–6468.

Chicago: ✉ 676 N. Michigan Ave., Chicago, IL 60611, ☎ 312/751–7800.

Los Angeles: ✉ 9454 Wilshire Blvd., Beverly Hills, CA 90212, ☎ 310/271–2358, FAX 310/276–2835.

IN CANADA

Montreál: ✉ 1981 McGill College Ave., Suite 490, Montréal, Québec H3A 2W9, ☎ 514/288–4264, FAX 514/845–4868.

Toronto: ✉ 30 St. Patrick St., Suite 700, Toronto, Ontario M5T 3A3, ☎ 416/593–4723, FAX 416/979–7587.

IN THE U.K.

French Government Tourist Office: (✉ 178 Piccadilly, London WIV OAL, ☎ 0891/244–123). Calls cost 49p per minute peak rate or 39p per minute cheap rate.

W

WEATHER

For current conditions and forecasts, plus the local time and helpful travel tips, call the **Weather Channel Connection** (☎ 900/932–8437; 95¢ per minute) from a Touch-Tone phone.

The *International Traveler's Weather Guide* (✉ Weather Press, Box 660606, Sacramento, CA 95866, ☎ 916/974–0201 or 800/972–0201; $10.95 includes shipping), written by two meteorologists, provides month-by-month information on temperature, humidity, and precipitation in more than 175 cities worldwide.

SMART TRAVEL TIPS A TO Z

*Basic Information on Traveling in Provence and the
Riviera and Savvy Tips to Make Your Trip a Breeze*

A
AIR TRAVEL

If time is an issue, **always look for nonstop flights,** which require no change of plane. If possible, **avoid connecting flights,** which stop at least once and can involve a change of plane, even though the flight number remains the same; if the first leg is late, the second waits.

For better service, **fly smaller or regional carriers,** which often have higher passenger satisfaction ratings. Sometimes they have such in-flight amenities as leather seats or greater legroom and they often have better food.

CUTTING COSTS

The Sunday travel section of most newspapers is a good place to look for deals. *See also* Travel Passes, *below.*

MAJOR AIRLINES➤ The least-expensive airfares from the major airlines are priced for round-trip travel and are subject to restrictions. Usually, you must **book in advance and buy the ticket within 24 hours** to get cheaper fares, and you may have to **stay over a Saturday night.** The lowest fare is subject to availability, and only a small percentage of the plane's total seats is sold at that price. It's smart to **call a number of airlines,** and when you are quoted a

good price, book it on the spot—the same fare may not be available on the same flight the next day. Airlines generally allow you to change your return date for a $25 to $50 fee. If you don't use your ticket, you can apply the cost toward the purchase of a new ticket, again for a small charge. However, most low-fare tickets are nonrefundable. To get the lowest airfare, **check different routings.** If your destination has more than one gateway, **compare prices to different airports.**

FROM THE U.K.➤ To save money on flights, **look into an APEX or Super-Pex ticket.** APEX tickets must be booked in advance and have certain restrictions. Super-PEX tickets can be purchased right at the airport.

TRAVEL PASSES

You can **save on air travel** within Europe if you plan on traveling to and from Paris aboard Air France. As part of their Euro Flyer program, you then can buy between three and nine flight coupons, valid on these airlines' flights to more than 100 European cities. At $120 each, these coupons are a good deal, and the fine print still allows you plenty of freedom.

ALOFT

AIRLINE FOOD➤ If you hate airline food, **ask for special meals when**

booking. These can be vegetarian, low-cholesterol, or kosher, for example; commonly prepared to order in smaller quantities than standard fare, they can be tastier.

SMOKING➤ Smoking is not allowed on flights of six hours or less within the continental United States. Smoking is also prohibited on flights to Canada. For U.S. flights longer than six hours or international flights, **contact your carrier regarding smoking policy.** Some carriers have prohibited smoking only on certain routes throughout their system; others allow smoking only on certain routes or even certain departures of that route.

Foreign airlines are exempt from these rules but do provide no-smoking sections. British Airways has banned smoking; some countries have banned smoking on all domestic flights, and others may not allow smoking on some flights. Talks continue on the feasibility of broadening no-smoking policies.

B
BARGE TRAVEL

Contact a travel agent; ask for a "Tourisme Fluvial" brochure in any French tourist office; or contact Bourgogne Voies Navigables. Also *see* Theme Trips *in* Tour Operators *in*

Important Contacts A to Z.

BUS TRAVEL

France's excellent train service means that long-distance buses are rare; regional buses are found mainly where the train service is spotty. Excursions and bus holidays are organized by the SNCF and other tourist organizations.

FROM THE U.K.

Eurolines (☞ Bus Travel *in* Important Contacts A to Z, *above*) runs bus trips (via Hovercraft or ferry) out of London. Buses depart from London for Paris and the Riviera.

BUSINESS HOURS

BANKS

Banks are open weekdays, generally from 9:30 to 4:30. Most banks take a one-hour, or even a 90-minute, lunch break. In a pinch, **money can also be exchanged at 24-hour exchange offices** in the larger French cities.

MUSEUMS

Usual opening times are from 9:30 to 5 or 6, but some are only open Sunday afternoons. Many close for lunch (noon–2). Most are closed one day a week (generally Monday or Tuesday) and on national holidays: **check museum hours before you go.**

SHOPS

Large stores in big towns are open from 9 or 9:30 until 7 or 8. Smaller shops often open earlier (8 AM) and close later (8 PM) but take a lengthy lunch break (1–4) in the south of France. Corner groceries, often run by immigrants (*"l'Arabe du coin"*), frequently stay open until around 10 PM.

IN TRANSIT

Always **keep your film tape, or disks out of the sun;** never put them on a car dashboard. Carry an extra supply of batteries, and **be prepared to turn on your camera, camcorder, or laptop computer for security personnel** to prove that it's real.

X-RAYS

Always **ask for hand inspection at security.** Such requests are virtually always honored at U.S. airports, and are usually accommodated abroad. Photographic film becomes clouded after successive exposure to airport X-ray machines. Videotape and computer disks are not harmed by X-rays, but **keep your tapes and disks away from metal detectors.**

CUSTOMS

Before departing, **register your foreign-made camera or laptop with U.S. Customs.** If your equipment is U.S.-made, call the consulate of the country you'll be visiting to find out whether it should be registered with local customs upon arrival.

CAR RENTAL

Renting cars in France is expensive—about twice as much as in the United States. In addition, the price doesn't usually take into account the 20.6% VAT tax. You won't need a car in the capital, so **wait to pick up your rental until the day you leave Paris.**

CUTTING COSTS

To get the best deal, **book through a travel agent who is willing to shop around.** Ask your agent to **look for fly-drive packages,** which also save you money, and **ask if local taxes are included** in the rental or fly-drive price. These can be as high as 20% in some destinations. Don't forget to find out about required deposits, cancellation penalties, drop-off charges, and the cost of any required insurance coverage.

Also **ask your travel agent about a company's customer-service record.** How has it responded to late plane arrivals and vehicle mishaps? Are there often lines at the rental counter, and—if you're traveling during a holiday period—does a confirmed reservation guarantee you a car?

Always **find out what equipment is standard** at your destination before specifying what you want; automatic transmission and air-conditioning are usually optional—and very expensive.

Be sure to **look into wholesalers**—companies that do not own their own fleets but rent in bulk from those that do and often offer better rates than traditional car-rental operations. Prices are best during off-peak periods; rentals booked through wholesalers must be paid for before you leave the United States.

INSURANCE

When driving a rented car, you are generally responsible for any damage to or loss of the rental vehicle. Before you rent, **see what coverage you already have** under the terms of your personal auto insurance policy and credit cards.

If you do not have auto insurance or an umbrella insurance policy that covers damage to third parties, purchasing CDW or LDW is highly recommended.

Collision policies that car-rental companies sell for European rentals typically do not cover stolen vehicles. Before you buy additional coverage for theft, find out if your credit card or personal auto insurance will cover the loss.

LICENSE REQUIREMENTS

In France your own driver's license is acceptable. An International Driver's Permit is a good idea; it's available from the American or Canadian automobile associations, or, in the United Kingdom, from the AA or RAC.

SURCHARGES

Before you pick up a car in one city and leave it in another, **ask about drop-off charges or one-way service fees,** which can be substantial. Note, too, that some rental agencies charge extra if you return the car before the time specified on your contract. To avoid a hefty refueling fee, **fill the tank just before you turn in the car**—but be aware that gas stations near the rental outlet may overcharge.

THE CHANNEL TUNNEL

The "Chunnel" is the fastest way to cross the English Channel short of flying—35 minutes from Folkestone to Calais, 60 minutes from motorway to motorway, or 3 hours from Waterloo, London, to Paris's Gare du Nord. It consists of two large 50-kilometer-long (31-mile-long) long train tunnels, and a smaller service tunnel running between them.

CHILDREN & TRAVEL

When traveling with children, **plan ahead** and **involve your youngsters** as you outline your trip. When packing, **include a supply of things to keep them busy** en route (☞ Children & Travel in Important Contacts A to Z). On sightseeing days, try to **schedule activities of special interest to your children,** like a trip to a zoo or a playground. If you **plan your itinerary around seasonal festivals,** you'll never lack for things to do. In addition, **check local newspapers for special events** mounted by public libraries, museums, and parks.

BABY-SITTING

For recommended local sitters, **check with your hotel desk.**

DRIVING

If you are renting a car, don't forget to **arrange for a car seat when you reserve.** Sometimes they're free.

FLYING

Always **ask about discounted children's fares.** On international flights, infants under 2 not occupying a seat generally travel free or for 10% of the accompanying adult's fare; the fare for children ages 2–11 is usually half to two-thirds of the adult fare. On domestic flights, children under 2 not occupying a seat travel free, and older children are charged at the lowest applicable adult rate.

BAGGAGE➣ In general, the adult baggage allowance applies to children paying half or more of the adult fare. If you are traveling with an infant, **ask about carry-on allowances** before departure. In general, for infants charged 10% of the adult fare you are allowed one carry-on bag and a collapsible stroller; you may be limited to less if the flight is full.

SAFETY SEATS➣ According to the FAA, it's a good idea to **use safety seats aloft** for children weighing less than 40 pounds. Airline policies vary. U.S. carriers allow FAA-approved models but usually require that you buy a ticket, even if your child would otherwise ride free, since the seats must be strapped into regular seats. Foreign carriers may not allow infant seats, may charge a child rather than an infant fare for their use, or may require you to hold your baby during takeoff and

SMART TRAVEL TIPS / THE GOLD GUIDE

landing—defeating the seat's purpose.

FACILITIES> When making your reservation, **request children's meals or freestanding bassinets** if you need them; the latter are available only to those seated at the bulkhead, where there's enough legroom. If you don't need a bassinet, **think twice before requesting bulkhead seats**—the only storage space for in-flight necessities is in inconveniently distant overhead bins.

GAMES

In local toy stores, look for travel versions of popular games such as Trouble, Sorry, and Monopoly ($5–$8).

TRAIN TRAVEL

Changing compartments for infants are available on all TGVs.

LODGING

Most hotels allow children under a certain age to stay in their parents' room at no extra charge; others charge them as extra adults. Be sure to **ask about the cutoff age.**

CLOTHING SIZES

To figure out the French equivalent of U.S. clothing and shoe sizes, **do the following, simple calculations.**

To change U.S. men's suit sizes to French suit sizes, add 10 to the U.S. suit size. To change French suit sizes to U.S. suit sizes, subtract 10 from the French suit size. For example, a U.S. size 42 is a French size 52.

To change U.S. men's collar sizes to French

collar sizes, multiply the U.S. collar size by 2 and add 8. To change French collar sizes to U.S. collar sizes, subtract 8 from the French collar size and divide by 2. For example, a U.S. size 15 is a French size 38. A U.S. size 15½ is a French size 39.

French men's shoe sizes vary in their relation to U.S. shoe sizes. A U.S. men's size 6½ is a French size 39; a size 7 is a 39; an 8 is a 40; a 9 is a 41; a 10 is a 42; a 10½ is a 43; and an 11 is a 45.

To change U.S. dress/coat/blouse sizes to French sizes, add 28 to the U.S. size. To change French dress/coat/blouse sizes to U.S. sizes, subtract 28 from the French size. For example, a U.S. women's size 8 is a French size 36.

To change U.S. women's shoe sizes to French shoe sizes, add 32 to the U.S. shoe size. To change French shoe sizes to U.S. shoe sizes, subtract 32 from the French shoe size. For example, a U.S. size 7 is a French size 39.

CUSTOMS & DUTIES

To speed your clearance through customs, **keep receipts for all your purchases abroad.** If you feel that you've been incorrectly or unfairly charged, you can **appeal assessments in dispute.** First ask to see a supervisor. If you are still unsatisfied, **write to the port director** at your point of entry, sending your customs receipt and any other appropriate documentation. The address will

be listed on your receipt. If you still get results, you can take your case to customs headquarters in Washington, D.C.

IN FRANCE

There are two levels of duty-free allowance for travelers entering France: one for goods obtained (tax paid) within another European Union (EU) country and the other for goods obtained anywhere outside the EU or for goods purchased in a duty-free shop within the EU.

In the first category, you may import duty-free: 300 cigarettes or 150 cigarillos or 75 cigars or 400 grams of tobacco; 5 liters of table wine and (1) 1½ liters of alcohol over 22% volume (most spirits), (2) 3 liters of alcohol under 22% by volume (fortified or sparkling wine), or (3) 3 more liters of table wine; 90 milliliters of perfume; 375 milliliters of toilet water; and other goods to the value of 2,400 francs (620 francs for those under 15).

In the second category, you may import duty-free: 200 cigarettes or 100 cigarillos or 50 cigars or 250 grams of tobacco (these allowances are doubled if you live outside Europe); 2 liters of wine and (1) 1 liter of alcohol over 22% volume (most spirits), (2) two liters of alcohol under 22% volume (fortified or sparkling wine), or (3) 2 more liters of table wine; 60 milliliters of perfume; 250 milliliters of toilet water; and other goods to the value of 300 francs (150 francs for those under 15).

IN THE U.S.

You may bring home $400 worth of foreign goods duty-free if you've been out of the country for at least 48 hours and haven't already used the $400 allowance, or any part of it, in the past 30 days.

Travelers 21 or older may bring back 1 liter of alcohol duty-free, provided the beverage laws of the state through which they reenter the United States allow it. In addition, regardless of their age, they are allowed 100 non-Cuban cigars and 200 cigarettes. Antiques and works of art more than 100 years old are duty-free.

Duty-free, travelers may mail packages valued at up to $200 to themselves and up to $100 to others, with a limit of one parcel per addressee per day (and no alcohol or tobacco products or perfume valued at more than $5); on the outside, the package should be labeled as being either for personal use or an unsolicited gift, and a list of its contents and their retail value should be attached. Mailed items do not affect your duty-free allowance on your return.

IN CANADA

If you've been out of Canada for at least seven days, you may bring in C$500 worth of goods duty-free. If you've been away for fewer than seven days but for more than 48 hours, the duty-free

allowance drops to C$200; if your trip lasts between 24 and 48 hours, the allowance is C$50. You cannot pool allowances with family members. Goods claimed under the C$500 exemption may follow you by mail; those claimed under the lesser exemptions must accompany you.

Alcohol and tobacco products may be included in the seven-day and 48-hour exemptions but not in the 24-hour exemption. If you meet the age requirements of the province or territory through which you reenter Canada, you may bring in, duty-free, 1.14 liters (40 imperial ounces) of wine or liquor or 24 12-ounce cans or bottles of beer or ale. If you are 16 or older, you may bring in, duty-free, 200 cigarettes, 50 cigars or cigarillos, and 400 tobacco sticks or 400 grams of manufactured tobacco. Alcohol and tobacco must accompany you on your return.

An unlimited number of gifts with a value of up to C$60 each may be mailed to Canada duty-free. These do not affect your duty-free allowance on your return. Label the package "Unsolicited Gift—Value Under $60." Alcohol and tobacco are excluded.

IN THE U.K.

If your journey was wholly within European Union (EU) countries, you no longer need to pass through customs when you return to the United Kingdom. If you plan to bring back large

quantities of alcohol or tobacco, check in advance on EU limits.

D

DINING

France is two-big-meals-a-day country, with good restaurants around every corner. If you prefer to eat lighter, you can **try a brasserie for rapid, straightforward fare.** French breakfasts are relatively skimpy: good coffee, fruit juice if you request it, bread, butter, and croissants. Although you can have breakfast in hotels, it's a good idea to **eat breakfast in cafés.** Tap water is safe, though not always appetizing.

DISABILITIES & ACCESSIBILITY

The French government is doing much to ensure that public facilities provide for visitors with disabilities. A number of monuments, hotels, and museums—especially those constructed within the past decade—are equipped with ramps, elevators, and special toilet facilities. Lists of regional hotels include a symbol to indicate which hotels have rooms that are accessible to people using wheelchairs. Similarly, the SNCF has special cars on some trains that have been reserved exclusively for people using wheelchairs and can arrange for those passengers to be escorted on and off trains and assisted in making connections (the latter service must be requested in advance).

When discussing accessibility with an operator

or reservationist, **ask hard questions.** Are there any stairs, inside *or* out? Are there grab bars next to the toilet *and* in the shower/tub? How wide is the doorway to the room? To the bathroom? For the most extensive facilities, meeting the latest legal specifications, **opt for newer accommodations,** which more often have been designed with access in mind. Older properties or ships must usually be retrofitted and may offer more limited facilities as a result. Be sure to **discuss your needs before booking.**

DISCOUNTS & DEALS

You shouldn't have to pay for a discount. In fact, you may already be eligible for all kinds of savings. Here are some time-honored strategies for getting the best deal.

LOOK IN YOUR WALLET

When you **use your credit card to make travel purchases,** you may get free travel-accident insurance, collision damage insurance, medical or legal assistance, depending on the card and bank that issued it. Visa and MasterCard provide one or more of these services, so **get a copy of your card's travel benefits.** If you are a member of the AAA or an oil-company-sponsored road-assistance plan, always **ask hotel or car-rental reservationists for auto-club discounts.** Some clubs offer additional discounts on tours, cruises, or admission to attrac-

tions. And don't forget that auto-club membership entitles you to free maps and trip-planning services.

DIAL FOR DOLLARS

To save money, **look into "1-800" discount reservations services,** which often have lower rates. These services use their buying power to get a better price on hotels, airline tickets, and sometimes even car rentals. When booking a room, always **call the hotel's local toll-free number** (if one is available) rather than the central reservations number—you'll often get a better price. Ask the reservationist about special packages or corporate rates, which are usually available even if you're not traveling on business.

JOIN A CLUB?

Discount clubs can be a legitimate source of savings, but you must use the participating hotels and visit the participating attractions in order to realize any benefits. Remember, too, that you have to pay a fee to join, so **determine if you'll save enough to warrant your membership fee.** Before booking with a club, **make sure the hotel or other supplier isn't offering a better deal.**

GET A GUARANTEE

When shopping for the best deal on hotels and car rentals, **look for guaranteed exchange rates,** which protect you against a falling dollar. With your rate locked in, you won't pay more even if the price goes up in the local currency.

SENIOR CITIZENS & STUDENTS

As a senior-citizen traveler, you may be eligible for special rates, but you should mention your senior-citizen status up front. If you're a student, or under 26, you can also get discounts, especially if you have an official ID card (☞ Senior-Citizen Discounts *and* Students on the Road, *below*).

DRIVING

If you plan to drive through France, **get a Michelin map,** for each region you'll be visiting. The maps are available from most bookshops and newsagents. For the fastest roads between two points, **look for roads marked A** for *autoroutes.* Most are toll roads.

GAS

When possible, **buy gas before you get on the expressway.** Also **don't let your tank get too low in rural areas,** as you can go for many miles in the country without hitting a gas station. Keep an eye on pump prices, which vary enormously: anything between 5.75 and 6.50 francs per liter.

PARKING

Parking is a nightmare in Paris and is often difficult in large towns. Meters and ticket machines (pay and display) are commonplace (be sure to **have a supply of 1-franc coins**). Before you park, **check the signs,** as rules vary.

RULES OF THE ROAD

In France, you **drive on the right.** Also remember that drivers on the right have the right of way. You must **wear your seat belt,** and children under 12 may not travel in the front seat. Speed limits range from 50 kph (31 mph) in towns to 130 kph (81 mph) on expressways. You may use your home driver's license in France.

G
GAY & LESBIAN TRAVEL

The gay and lesbian communities are low-key and reserved in public, although active and easily accessible to visitors. Discos and nightclubs are numerous and popular.

I
INSURANCE

Travel insurance can protect your monetary investment, replace your luggage and its contents, or provide for medical coverage should you fall ill during your trip. Most tour operators, travel agents, and insurance agents sell specialized health-and-accident, flight, trip-cancellation, and luggage insurance as well as comprehensive policies with some or all of these coverages. Comprehensive policies may also reimburse you for delays due to weather—an important consideration if you're traveling during the winter months. Some health-insurance policies do not cover preexisting conditions, but waivers may be available in specific cases. Coverage is sold by the companies listed in Important Contacts A to Z; these companies act as the policy's administrators. The actual insurance is usually underwritten by a well-known name, such as The Travelers or Continental Insurance.

Before you make any purchase, **review your existing health and homeowner's policies** to find out whether they cover expenses incurred while traveling.

BAGGAGE

Airline liability for baggage is limited to $1,250 per person on domestic flights. On international flights, it amounts to $9.07 per pound or $20 per kilogram for checked baggage (roughly $640 per 70-pound bag) and $400 per passenger for unchecked baggage. Insurance for losses exceeding the terms of your airline ticket can be bought directly from the airline at check-in for about $10 per $1,000 of coverage; note that it excludes a rather extensive list of items, shown on your airline ticket.

COMPREHENSIVE

Comprehensive insurance policies include all the coverages described above plus some that may not be available in more specific policies. If you have purchased an expensive vacation, especially one that involves travel abroad, comprehensive insurance is a must; **look for policies that include trip delay insurance,** which will protect you in the event that weather problems cause you to miss your flight, tour, or cruise. A few insurers will also sell you a waiver for preexisting medical conditions. Some of the companies that offer both these features are Access America, Carefree Travel, Travel Insured International, and TravelGuard (☞ Important Contacts A to Z).

FLIGHT

You should **think twice before buying flight insurance.** Often purchased as a last-minute impulse at the airport, it pays a lump sum when a plane crashes, either to a beneficiary if the insured dies or sometimes to a surviving passenger who loses his or her eyesight or a limb. Supplementing the airlines' coverage described in the limits-of-liability paragraphs on your ticket, it's expensive and basically unnecessary. Charging an airline ticket to a major credit card often automatically provides you with coverage that may also extend to travel by bus, train, and ship.

HEALTH

Medicare generally does not cover health care costs outside the United States; nor do many privately issued policies. If your own health insurance policy does not cover you outside the United States, **consider buying supplemental medical coverage.** It can reimburse you for $1,000–$150,000 worth of medical and/or dental expenses incurred as a result of an accident or illness during a trip. These policies also may include a personal-accident, or death-and-dismemberment, provision, which pays a lump sum ranging from $15,000 to $500,000 to your beneficiaries if you die or to you if you lose one or more limbs or your eyesight, and a medical-assistance provision, which may either reimburse you for the cost of referrals, evacuation, or repatriation and other services, or automatically enroll you as a member of a particular medical-assistance company (☞ Health Issues *in* Important Contacts A to Z).

U.K. TRAVELERS

You can buy an annual travel insurance policy valid for most vacations during the year in which it's purchased. If you are pregnant or have a preexisting medical condition make sure you're covered before buying such a policy.

TRIP

Without insurance, you will lose all or most of your money if you cancel your trip regardless of the reason. Especially if your airline ticket, cruise, or package tour is nonrefundable and cannot be changed, it's essential that you **buy trip-cancellation-and-interruption insurance.** When considering how much coverage you need, look for a policy that will cover the cost of your trip plus the nondiscounted price of a one-way airline ticket should you need to return home early. Read the fine print carefully, especially sections that define "family member" and "preexisting medical conditions." Also

consider default or bankruptcy insurance, which protects you against a supplier's failure to deliver. Be aware, however, that if you buy such a policy from a travel agency, tour operator, airline, or cruise line, it may not cover default by the firm in question.

L

LANGUAGE

English is widely understood in major tourist areas, and no matter what the area, at least one person in most hotels can explain things to you. It also helps if you **try to master a few French words.** *See* the French Vocabulary and Menu Guide at the back of the book.

LODGING

Prices must, by law, be posted at the hotel entrance and should include taxes and service. Rates are always by room, not per person, and you should always **check what bathroom facilities the price includes,** if any. Because replumbing drains is often prohibitive, if not impossible, old hotels may have added bathrooms—often with showers, not tubs—to the guest rooms, but not toilets. Breakfast is not always included in the price, but you are usually expected to have it and are sometimes charged for it regardless. In smaller rural hotels you may be expected to have your evening meal at the hotel, too. When making your reservation, **ask for a *grand lit* if you want a double**

bed. Negotiating rates has become acceptable. Although you may not be able to reduce the price, you might get an upgrade to a newly redecorated, larger, or deluxe room.

APARTMENT & VILLA RENTAL

If you want a home base that's roomy enough for a family and comes with cooking facilities, **consider taking a furnished rental.** This can also save you money, but not always—some rentals are luxury properties (economical only when your party is large). Home-exchange directories list rentals—often second homes owned by prospective house swappers—and some services search for a house or apartment for you (even a castle if that's your fancy) and handle the paperwork.

BED-AND-BREAKFAST

B&Bs, known in France as *chambres d'hôte,* are increasingly popular, especially in rural areas. Check local tourist offices for details.

HOME EXCHANGE

If you would like to find a house, an apartment, or some other type of vacation property to exchange for your own while on holiday, **become a member of a home-exchange organization,** which will send you its updated listings of available exchanges for a year, and will include your own listing in at least one of them. Arrangements for the actual exchange are made by the two parties involved, not by the organization.

M
MAIL

Letters and postcards to the United States and Canada cost 4.30 francs (about 75/) for 20 grams. Letters and postcards to the United Kingdom cost 2.80 francs (about £2.70) for up to 20 grams. Letters and postcards within France cost 2.80 francs. Stamps can be bought in post offices (La Poste) and cafés sporting a red TABAC sign outside.

RECEIVING MAIL

If you're uncertain where you'll be staying, **have mail sent to the local post office,** addressed as "poste restante," or to American Express, but remember that during peak seasons, American Express may refuse to accept mail.

MEDICAL ASSISTANCE

No one plans to get sick while traveling, but it happens, so **consider signing up with a medical assistance company.** These outfits provide referrals, emergency evacuation or repatriation, 24-hour telephone hot lines for medical consultation, cash for emergencies, and other personal and legal assistance. They also dispatch medical personnel and arrange for the relay of medical records.

MONEY & EXPENSES

The units of currency in France are the franc (fr) and the centime. Bills are in denominations of 500, 200, 100, 50, and 20 francs. Coins are 20, 10, 5, 2, and 1 francs and 50, 20, 10, and 5 centimes. At press time (1996), the exchange rate was about 4.80 francs to the U.S. dollar, 3.70 to the Canadian dollar, and 7.45 to the pound sterling.

ATMS

CASH ADVANCES➤ Before leaving home, **make sure that your credit cards have been programmed for ATM use.** Note that Discover is accepted mostly in the United States. Local bank cards often do not work overseas either; **ask your bank about a Global Access debit card,** which works like a bank card but can be used at any ATM displaying a Visa logo. Cirrus, Plus, and many other networks that connect automated teller machines operate internationally. Four-digit numbers are commonly used overseas; **ask whether your card's PIN must be reprogrammed** for use in France.

TRANSACTION FEES➤ On credit-card cash advances you are charged interest from the day you receive the money, whether from a teller or an ATM. Although fees charged for ATM transactions may be higher abroad than at home, Cirrus and Plus exchange rates are excellent, because they are based on wholesale rates offered only by major banks.

COSTS

The following prices are for large cities; other areas are often cheaper. Coffee in a bar: 5 francs (standing), 10 francs (seated); beer in a bar: 10 francs (standing), 15 francs (seated); Coca-Cola: 6–10 francs a can; ham sandwich: 15–25 francs; one-mile taxi ride: 35 francs; movie-theater seat: 45 francs (20%–30% cheaper on Monday and Wednesday); foreign newspaper: 10–15 francs.

EXCHANGING CURRENCY

For the most favorable rates, **change money at banks.** You won't do as well at exchange booths in airports or rail and bus stations, in hotels, in restaurants, or in stores, although you may find their hours more convenient. To avoid lines at airport exchange booths, **get a small amount of the local currency before you leave home.**

TAXES

All taxes must be included in posted prices in France. The initials TTC (*toutes taxes comprises*—taxes included) sometimes appear on price lists but, strictly speaking, are superfluous. By law, **restaurant and hotel prices must include 20.6% taxes and a service charge.** If they show up as extra charges on your bill, complain.

VAT➤ A number of shops offer VAT refunds to foreign shoppers. You are entitled to an

Export Discount of 20.6%, depending on the item purchased, but it is often applicable only if your purchases in the same store reach a minimum of 2,800 francs (for U.K. and EU residents) or 1,200 francs (other residents, including U.S. and Canadian residents). Remember to **ask for the refund, as some stores—especially larger ones—offer the service only upon request.**

P

PACKING FOR FRANCE

Baggage carts are scarce in airports and railroad stations, and luggage restrictions on international flights are tight, so **pack light.**

Over the years, **casual dress has become more acceptable.** There is no need to wear a tie and jacket at most restaurants (unless specified), even fancy ones. However, sneakers and shorts are seldom worn in cities—**if you are wearing shorts, you may be denied admission to churches and cathedrals.** For beach resorts, take a cover-up, as wearing bathing suits on the street is frowned upon. Most casinos and nightclubs along the Riviera require jackets and ties.

Provence and the Riviera are hot in the summer, cool in the winter (pack a sweater or a warm jacket for winter stays near the Mediterranean). Since it rains all year round, **bring a raincoat and umbrella.**

If you are staying in budget hotels, **take along soap, many hotels either do not provide it or give you a very limited number.**

Bring an extra pair of eyeglasses or contact lenses in your carry-on luggage, and if you have a health problem, **pack enough medication** to last the trip or have your doctor write you a prescription using the drug's generic name, because brand names vary from country to country. It's important that you **don't put prescription drugs or valuables in luggage to be checked,** for it could go astray. To avoid problems with customs officials, carry medications in the original packaging.

ELECTRICITY

To use your U.S.-purchased electric-powered equipment, **bring a converter and an adapter.** The electrical current in France is 220 volts, 50 cycles alternating current (AC); wall outlets take Continental-type plugs, with two round prongs.

If your appliances are dual-voltage, you'll need only an adapter. Hotels sometimes have 110-volt outlets for low-wattage appliances near the sink, marked FOR SHAVERS ONLY; don't use them for high-wattage appliances like blow-dryers. If your laptop computer is older, carry a converter; new laptops operate equally well on 110 and 220 volts, so you need only an adapter.

LUGGAGE

Airline baggage allowances depend on the airline, the route, and the class of your ticket; ask in advance. In general, on domestic flights and on international flights between the United States and foreign destinations, you are entitled to check two bags. A third piece may be brought on board, but it must fit easily under the seat in front of you or in the overhead compartment. In the United States, the FAA gives airlines broad latitude regarding carry-on allowances, and they tend to tailor them to different aircraft and operational conditions. Charges for excess, oversize, or overweight pieces vary.

If you are flying between two foreign destinations, note that baggage allowances may be determined not by piece but by weight—generally 88 pounds (40 kilograms) in first class, 66 pounds (30 kilograms) in business class, and 44 pounds (20 kilograms) in economy. If your flight between two cities abroad *connects* with your transatlantic or transpacific flight, the piece method still applies.

SAFEGUARDING YOUR LUGGAGE➤ Before leaving home, **itemize your bags' contents** and their worth, and label them with your name, address, and phone number. (If you use your home address, cover it so that potential thieves can't see it readily.) Inside each bag, **pack a copy of your itinerary.** At check-in, **make sure that each bag is correctly tagged** with the destination airport's three-letter code. If your bags arrive damaged—or fail to arrive at all—file a written report with the airline before leaving the airport.

PASSPORTS & VISAS

If you don't already have one, **get a passport.** It is advisable that you **leave one photocopy of your passport's data page** with someone at home and keep another with you, separated from your passport, while traveling. If you lose your passport, promptly call the nearest embassy or consulate and the local police; having the data page information can speed replacement.

U.S. CITIZENS

All U.S. citizens, even infants, need only a valid passport to enter France for stays of up to 90 days (for longer stays, a visa is required). Application forms for both first-time and renewal passports are available at any of the 13 U.S. Passport Agency offices and at some post offices and courthouses. Passports are usually mailed within four weeks; allow five weeks or more in spring and summer.

CANADIANS

You need only a valid passport to enter France for stays of up to 90 days. Passport application forms are available at 28 regional passport offices, as well as post offices and travel agencies. Whether for a first or a renewal passport, you must apply in person. Children under

16 may be included on a parent's passport but must have their own to travel alone. Passports are valid for five years and are usually mailed within two to three weeks of application.

U.K. CITIZENS

Citizens of the United Kingdom need only a valid passport to enter France for stays of up to 90 days. Applications for new and renewal passports are available from main post offices and at the passport offices in Belfast, Glasgow, Liverpool, London, Newport, and Peterborough. You may apply in person at all passport offices, or by mail to all except the London office. Children under 16 may travel on an accompanying parent's passport. All passports are valid for 10 years. Allow a month for processing.

S

SENIOR-CITIZEN DISCOUNTS

Older travelers to France can take advantage of many discounts, such as reduced admissions of 20%–50% to museums and movie theaters. Seniors 60 and older should **buy a Carte Vermeil,** which entitles the bearer to discounts on the French domestic airline (Air Inter), rail and bus travel, and admission prices for films and many cultural events. Cards are available at any rail station (cost: 140 francs).

To qualify for age-related discounts, **mention your senior-**

citizen status up front when booking hotel reservations, not when checking out, and before you're seated in restaurants, not when paying the bill. Note that discounts may be limited to certain menus, days, or hours. When renting a car, **ask about promotional car-rental discounts**—they can net even lower costs than your senior-citizen discount.

SHOPPING

Shop **prices are clearly marked** and bargaining isn't a way of life. Still, at outdoor and flea markets and in antiques stores, you can try your luck. If you're thinking of buying several items, you've nothing to lose by cheerfully suggesting to the proprietor, *"Vous me faites un prix?"* ("How about a discount?").

SPORTS

Many seaside resorts are well equipped for water sports, such as windsurfing and water-skiing, and there are swimming pools in every French town.

Bicycling (☞ Bicycling *in* Important Contacts A to Z) is popular and, like *équitation* (horseback riding), possible in many rural areas. The many rivers of France offer excellent fishing (check locally for authorization rights) and canoeing. Tennis is phenomenally popular in France, and courts are everywhere: Try for a typical *terre battue* (clay court) if you can. Golf and squash have caught on; you may be able to find a course or a court not too far away. The French are not so keen on jogging, but you'll have no difficulty locating a suitable local park or avenue.

STUDENTS ON THE ROAD

Cheap food and lodging are easy to find throughout France, so there's little need to scrounge. In addition, there are student bargains almost everywhere, on train and plane fares, and for movie and museum tickets. All you need is an International Student Identity Card (*see* Students *in* Important Contacts A to Z).

To save money, **look into deals available through student-oriented travel agencies.** To qualify, you'll need to have a bona fide student ID card. Members of international student groups are also eligible (☞ Students *in* Important Contacts A to Z).

T

TELEPHONES

For details on making calls within and to France as well as from France, *see* Telephone Matters *in* Important contacts A to Z, *above.*

LONG-DISTANCE

The long-distance services of AT&T, MCI, and Sprint make calling home relatively convenient, but in many hotels you may find it impossible to dial the access number. The hotel operator may also refuse to make the connection. Instead, the hotel will charge

you a premium rate—as much as 400% more than a calling card—for calls placed from your hotel room. To avoid such price gouging, **travel with more than one company's long-distance calling card**—a hotel may block Sprint but not MCI. If the hotel operator claims that you cannot use any phone card, ask to be connected to an international operator, who will help you to access your phone card. You can also **dial the international operator yourself.** If none of this works, try calling your phone company collect in the United States. If collect calls are also blocked, call from a pay phone in the hotel lobby. Before you go, **find out the local access codes** for your destinations.

PAY PHONES

Telephone booths **can almost always be found at post offices and often in cafés.** A local call costs 75 centimes for every three minutes; half-price rates apply weekdays between 9:30 PM and 8 AM, from 1:30 PM Saturday, and all day Sunday.

Most **French pay phones are operated by *télécartes* (phone cards),** which you can buy from post offices and some tabacs (tobacco shops) for a cost of 40 francs for 50 units and 96 francs for 120. Some pay phones accept 1-, 2- and 5-franc coins (1-franc minimum), but the phone card is the most convenient way to make a call.

TIPPING

The French have a clear idea of when they should be tipped. Bills in bars and restaurants include service, but **it is customary to leave some small change** unless you're dissatisfied. The amount of this varies: 30 centimes if you've merely bought a beer, or a few francs after a meal. Tip taxi drivers and hairdressers about 10%. Give ushers in theaters and movie theaters 1 or 2 francs. In some theaters and hotels, coat check attendants may expect nothing (if there is a sign saying POURBOIRE INTERDIT—tips forbidden); otherwise give them 5 francs. Washroom attendants usually get 5 francs, though the sum is often posted.

If you stay in a hotel for more than two or three days, it is customary to leave something for the chambermaid—about 10 francs per day. In expensive hotels you may well call on the services of a baggage porter (bell boy) and hotel porter and possibly the telephone receptionist. All expect a tip: Plan on about 10 francs per item for the baggage boy, but the other tips will depend on how much you've used their services—common sense must guide you here. In hotels that provide room service, give 5 francs to the waiter (this does not apply to breakfast served in your room). If the chambermaid does some pressing or laundering for you, give her 5 francs on top of the charge made.

Gas-station attendants get nothing for gas or oil, and 5 or 10 francs for checking tires. Train and airport porters get a fixed 6–10 francs per bag, but you're better off getting your own baggage cart if you can (a 10-franc coin—refundable—is sometimes necessary). Museum guides should get 5–10 francs after a guided tour, and it is standard practice to tip tour guides (and bus drivers) 10 francs or more after an excursion, depending on its length.

TOUR OPERATORS

A package or tour to France can make your vacation less expensive and more hassle-free. Firms that sell tours and packages reserve airline seats, hotel rooms, and rental cars in bulk and pass some of the savings on to you. In addition, the best operators have local representatives available to help you at your destination.

A GOOD DEAL?

The more your package or tour includes, the better you can predict the ultimate cost of your vacation. Make sure you know exactly what is covered, and **beware of hidden costs.** Are taxes, tips, and service charges included? Transfers and baggage handling? Entertainment and excursions? These can add up.

Most packages and tours are rated deluxe, first-class superior, first class, tourist, or budget. The key difference is usually accommodations. If the package or tour you are considering is priced lower than

in your wildest dreams, **be skeptical.** Also, **make sure your travel agent knows the accommodations** and other services. Ask about the hotel's location, room size, beds, and whether it has a pool, room service, or programs for children, if you care about these. Has your agent been there in person or sent others you can contact?

BUYER BEWARE

Each year a number of consumers are stranded or lose their money when operators—even very large ones with excellent reputations—go out of business. To avoid becoming one of them, take the time to **check out the operator**—find out how long the company has been in business and ask several agents about its reputation. Next, **don't book unless the firm has a consumer-protection program.** Members of the USTOA and the NTA are required to set aside funds for the sole purpose of covering your payments and travel arrangements in case of default. Non-member operators may instead carry insurance; look for the details in the operator's brochure—and for the name of an underwriter with a solid reputation. Note: When it comes to tour operators, **don't trust escrow accounts.** Although there are laws governing those of charter-flight operators, no governmental body prevents tour operators from raiding the till.

Next, **contact your local Better Business Bureau and the attorney gen-**

eral's offices in both your own state and the operator's; have any complaints been filed? Finally, **pay with a major credit card.** Then you can cancel payment, provided that you can document your complaint. Always **consider trip-cancellation insurance** (☞ Insurance, *above*).

BIG VS. SMALL➤ Operators that handle several hundred thousand travelers per year can use their purchasing power to give you a good price. Their high volume may also indicate financial stability. But some small companies provide more personalized service; because they tend to specialize, they may also be more knowledgeable about a given area.

USING AN AGENT

Travel agents are excellent resources. In fact, large operators accept bookings made only through travel agents. But it's good to **collect brochures from several agencies** because some agents' suggestions may be skewed by promotional relationships with tour and package firms that reward them for volume sales. If you have a special interest, **find an agent with expertise in that area**; ASTA can provide leads in the United States. (Don't rely solely on your agent, though; agents may be unaware of small-niche operators, and some special-interest travel companies only sell direct.)

SINGLE TRAVELERS

Prices are usually quoted per person,

based on two sharing a room. If traveling solo, you may be required to pay the full double-occupancy rate. Some operators eliminate this surcharge if you agree to be matched up with a roommate of the same sex, even if one is not found by departure time.

TRAIN TRAVEL

The SNCF is generally recognized as Europe's best national rail service: It's fast, punctual, comfortable, and comprehensive. The high-speed TGVs, or *Trains à Grande Vitesse* (average 255 kph/160 mph on the Lyon/southeast line, 300 kph/190 mph on the Lille and Bordeaux/southwest lines), are the best domestic trains. They operate between Paris and Lille/Calais, Paris and Brussels, Paris and Lyon/Switzerland/the Riviera, and Angers/Nantes, and Tours/Poitiers/Bordeaux. As with other main-line trains, a small supplement may be assessed at peak hours. You must **always make a seat reservation for the TGV**—easily obtained at the ticket window or from an automatic machine. Seat reservations are reassuring but seldom necessary on other main-line French trains, except at certain busy holiday times.

If you know what station you'll depart from, you can get a free schedule there (while supplies last), or you can access the new multilingual computerized schedule information network at many stations. You can also make reservations and buy your ticket while at the computer.

Get to the station half an hour before departure to ensure that you'll have a good seat. The majority of inter-city trains in France consist of open-plan cars and are known as *Corail* trains. They are clean and extremely comfortable, even in second class. Trains on regional branch lines are currently being spruced up but lag behind in style and quality. The food in French trains can be good, but it's poor value for the money.

Before boarding, you must punch your ticket (but not EurailPass) in one of the orange machines at the entrance to the platforms, or else the ticket collector will fine you 100 francs on the spot.

It is possible to get from one end of France to the other without traveling overnight. Otherwise you have the choice between high-priced *wagons-lits* (sleeping cars) and affordable *couchettes* (bunks, six to a compartment in second class, four to a compartment in first, with sheets and pillow provided, priced at around 90 francs). Special summer night trains from Paris to Spain and the Riviera, geared to young people, are equipped with disco and bar.

DISCOUNT PASSES

If France is your only destination in Europe, **consider purchasing a France Rail Pass,** which allows three days of unlimited train travel in a one-month period. Prices begin at $120 for two adults traveling together in second-class and $160 second-class for a solo traveler. First-class rates are $198 for two adults and $160 for a solo traveler. Additional days may be added for $30 a day in either class. Other options include the France Rail 'n Drive Pass (combining rail and rental car), France Rail 'n Fly Pass (rail travel and one air travel journey within France), and the France Fly Rail 'n Drive Pass (a rail, air, and rental car program all in one).

France is one of 17 countries in which you can **use EurailPasses,** which provide unlimited first-class rail travel, in all of the participating countries, for the duration of the pass. If you plan to rack up the miles, get a standard pass. These are available for 15 days ($522), 21 days ($678), one month ($838), two months ($1,148), and 3 months ($1,468). If your plans call for only limited train travel, **look into a Europass,** which costs less money than a EurailPass. Unlike Eurail-Passes, however, you get a limited number of travel days, in a limited number of countries, during a specified time period. For example, a two month pass ($316) allows between five and fifteen days of rail travel, but costs $200 less than the least expensive EurailPass. Keep in mind, however, that the

Europass is good only in France, Germany, Italy, Spain, and Switzerland, and the number of countries you can visit is further limited by the type of pass you buy. For example, the basic two-month pass allows you to visit only three of the five participating countries.

In addition to standard EurailPasses, **ask about special rail-pass plans.** Among these are the Eurail Youthpass (for those under age 26), the Eurail Saverpass (which gives a discount for two or more people traveling together), a Eurail Flexipass (which allows a certain number of travel days within a set period), the Euraildrive Pass and the Europass Drive (which combines travel by train and rental car).

Whichever pass you choose, remember that you must **purchase your pass before you leave** for Europe.

Many travelers assume that rail passes guaran-

tee them seats on the trains they wish to ride. Not so. You need to **book seats ahead even if you are using a rail pass;** seat reservations are required on some European trains, particularly high-speed trains, and are a good idea on trains that may be crowded—particularly in summer on popular routes. You will also need a reservation if you purchase overnight sleeping accommodations.

TRAVEL GEAR

Travel catalogs specialize in useful items that can **save space when packing** and make life on the road more convenient. Compact alarm clocks, travel irons, travel wallets, and personal-care kits are among the most common items you'll find. They also carry dual-voltage appliances, currency converters and foreign-language phrase books. Some catalogs even carry miniature coffeemakers and water purifiers.

W
WHEN TO GO

June and September are the best months to be in France, as both are free of the midsummer crowds. June offers the advantage of long daylight hours, while cheaper prices and frequent Indian summers, often lasting well into October, make September attractive. Try to avoid the second half of July and all of August, when almost all of France goes on vacation. Huge crowds jam the roads and beaches, and prices are jacked up in resorts. Don't travel on or around July 14 and August 1, 15, and 31. Further, July and August in southern France can be stifling. Anytime between March and November will offer you a good chance to soak up the sun on the Riviera.

CLIMATE

What follows are average daily maximum and minimum temperatures for Nice.

Climate

NICE

Jan.	55F	13C	May	68F	20C	Sept.	77F	25C
	39	4		55	13		61	16
Feb.	55F	13C	June	75F	24C	Oct.	70F	21C
	41	5		61	16		54	12
Mar.	59F	15C	July	81F	27C	Nov.	63F	17C
	45	7		64	18		46	8
Apr.	64F	18C	Aug.	81F	27C	Dec.	55F	13C
	46	8		64	18		41	5

1 Destination: Provence & the Riviera

INTRODUCTION

SUN-BLEACHED, THE ROASTED red clay roofs of the stone cottages skew downhill at Cubist angles, each Romanesque tile, in its snaking row, as alike and as varied as the reeds in a Pan pipe; together, their broad horizontal flow forms a foil for the dark, thrusting verticals of the funeral cypress, the ephemeral, feminine puff of the silvery olive. In the fields behind, white-hot at midday, chill and spare at night, you can stoop down along the pathside and pick wild thyme, rosemary, lavender dried in the arid breeze; their acrid-sweet scent cuts through the crystal air like smelling salts. Goat- and sheep-bells tinkle behind rock walls, and churchbells sound across valleys as easily as over the village wall. Nowhere in France, perhaps nowhere in the Western World, can you touch antiquity with this intimacy—its exoticism, its purity, eternal and alive. Provence and the Côte d'Azur: *Le sud de France* is, as the French say, *primordial*.

Basking luxuriously along the sunny southern flank of France, bordered to the east by Italy, sheltered to the northeast by the Alps, and leaning west and southwest toward its Spanish-influenced neighbors in Languedoc and the Basque country, Provence and its nearby coast, the Riviera, are to the Mediterranean as Eve was to Adam's rib, begotten, as it were, by the Fertile Crescent. The Greeks and Phoenicians first brought classical culture to the Celtic natives of Gaul in 600 BC when they founded Massilia (Marseille), which thrived as a colony until the Ligurians began to impose on them. By the 2nd century BC, Romans were called in for military reinforcement, and turned their weapons on the Greeks instead.

Thus came to be *Provincia Romana*, the first Roman stronghold in Gaul, where the best of Latin culture flourished until the fall of the Empire. Under Roman rule, the Gauls were transformed (as one period writer had it) from "mustachioed, abundantly hairy, exuberant, audacious, thoughtless, boastful, passionate warriors" into disciplined hard workers—at least temporarily. In its wake, Rome left its physical mark as well: The theater and triumphal arch at Orange; more arches at Cavaillon and Carpentras; the amphitheater at Nîmes, the aqueduct at Pont-du-Gard; the mausoleum at St-Remy-de-Provence; the temple of Augustus and Livia (of *I, Claudius* fame) at Vienne—these monuments, still standing today, are considered among the best of their kind in existence, easily rivaling the Colosseum in Rome; the Maison carrée at Nîmes, built by Agrippa in 16 BC, remains as pure an homage to their Greek forebears as the Romans ever produced. Vivid details in Roman artifacts bring the stories to life: The creamy marble bust of Octavian found at Arles shows a peach-fuzz beard on his all-too-young face—a Roman sign of mourning for the assassination of Julius Caesar.

Yet the noble remains of Rome have taken on a patina and given way to the culture of modern Provence, where the hustling, burly streetlife of Marseille still punches out at *sieste* time for a milky *pastis* (the local, anise-based aperitif), a bowl of nutty black olives, or a game of *boules*. Today, the south of France implies a lazy, laissez-faire lifestyle, a barefoot idyll, three-hour lunches, sultry terrace nights, and a splash in the Mediterranean. In fact, most of the hordes of both French and foreign tourists that descend on Provence and the Riviera today think Caesar is a salad, though they might be able to name the last five film directors to place at Cannes. Far from searching for the classical perfection of a 2nd-century column, they seek out the glamor that drew Grace Kelly and other Hollywood stars of the '50s—who were in turn drawn by the gentry and the international literary jet-set, the Nicks and Noras of the Lost Generation. On these slim rocky beaches, if anywhere in the world, were nurtured the first Perfect Tans, cultivated with tantalizing exhibitionism on every flauntable inch of skin. And still today, oblivious to the Ozone Hole, rank on rank of nearly bare bodies crowd flank to flank on the Mediterranean shore.

Yet caveat emptor—the glamour of the Riviera has, for the most part, been crowded down to the shoreline and swept out to sea: honky-tonk tourist traps and project-like high rises dominate much of the region, while the wealthy hoard their seaside serenity in private, isolated villas. At greasy brasseries along the waterfront, sunburned visitors and leathery locals fight for the waiter's attention just to gulp down a *'ot dog* and a lukewarm Coke, or to strain through the canned crab in a mass-produced *bourride*.

To find the grace and antiquity of the region, and the sun if not the beach, visitors would do well to hunt out the smaller towns, both nestled along the waterfront and rising like ziggurats on stony hilltops behind the coast. Here, you'll discover the crystalline light and elemental forms that inspired Cezanne, Pissarro, Bonnard, Van Gogh, Matisse, Braque, Léger, Miró, Chagall, and Picasso. The *volupté* of the Mediterranean saturates their work—sensual fruit, lush flowers, fundamental forms, light and color analyzed, interpreted, transformed, revealed. They, like the literati who retreat here today, found in this primeval setting the peace and stimulation to create.

That's the sort of epiphany you may face in *le Sud,* whether standing humbled inside the 5th-century baptistry in Saint-Sauveur at Aix; breakfasting on a wrought-iron balcony overlooking turquoise Mediterranean tides; contemplating the orbs and linear perspective of a melon field outside Cavaillon; or sipping the sea-perfumed elixir of a great bouillabaisse (surely the Phoenicians sipped something similar 2,600 years ago) along the piers of Marseille. Provocative, tranquil, earthy, primordial: Like a woven rope of garlic, it's the essence of Latin France.

—Nancy Coons

Author of *Fodor's Switzerland* and a regular contributor to Fodor's publications, Nancy Coons has written on European topics for the *Wall Street Journal, National Geographic Traveler, Opera News,* and *European Travel and Life.*

WHAT'S WHERE

Provence

Hot, fragrant Provence, full of well-preserved Roman ruins, feels like summer, with dozens of produce and flower and fish markets, and outdoor sports (even bullfighting). Come to Nîmes (in Languedoc) to see the Pont du Gard aqueduct, the amphitheater, the museums, and the beautiful Maison Carré temple. You'll pass through the marshy Camargue en route to Arles, with its Roman arena and theater. Visit Daudet's Moulin in charming Fontvieille, inspect the tiny medieval streets and ancient houses in Les Baux, and stop in Avignon to see the Papal Palace and the famous bridge. Orange has a Roman theater and triumphal arch, and elegant Aix-en-Provence has museums, fountains, and the beautiful Cours Mirabeau boulevard.

The Riviera

Invisible celebrities, pebbly beaches, backed-up traffic, hordes of sunburned bathers—why do people come? Medieval hilltop villages (St-Paul-de-Vence, Mougins, Gassin, Vence, Peillon, even touristy Eze), fields of fragrant flowers that supply the Grasse perfume factories, wonderful museums, and the lovely, limpid light are still as magnetic as ever. Stylish boutiques, great art, splendid food, exciting nightlife, and spectacular views of crystal bays and cliff-side villas don't hurt either. Wander the cobble streets of Nice's old town, visit its Shell Museum, and have a flutter at Monte Carlo's casino.

PLEASURES AND PASTIMES

Beaches

If you like your beaches sandy, stick to those between St-Tropez and Antibes; most of the others are pebbly, though Menton and Monaco have imported vast tons of sand to spread around their shores. Private beaches are everywhere. You'll have to pay to use them (between 80 and 140 francs a day), but they usually have a café or restaurant, cabanas and showers, mat-

4   Destination: Provence & the Riviera

tresses and umbrellas, and a parade of people in stylish swimwear.

Bicycling

There is no shortage of wide, empty roads and flat or rolling countryside in France suitable for biking. The French themselves are great bicycling enthusiasts. Bikes can be hired from many train stations for around 50–90 francs a day (ask for a list at any station); you need to show your passport and leave a deposit of 500–1,000 francs (unless you have Visa or Master-Card). In general, you must return the bike to a station within the same *département* (county or region). Bikes may be sent as accompanied luggage from any station in France; some trains in rural areas transport them without any extra charge.

Boules

The sport that is closest to French hearts is *boules* or *pétanque*—an easy-to-grasp version of bowling, traditionally played beneath plane trees with a glass of *pastis* (similar to anisette) at hand. The local *boulodrome* is a social focal point in southern France.

Bullfighting

Provence's most popular summer spectator sport is bullfighting, both Spanish-style or the kinder *courses libres,* where the bulls have star billing and are often regarded as local heroes (they always live to fight another day). Spectacles are held in the Roman arenas in Arles and Nîmes and in surrounding villages.

NEW AND NOTEWORTHY

There's good transportation news in France. **Eurostar** reduced the price of train travel through the Channel Tunnel in 1996 to £49 ($74) from £69, for the least-expensive round-trip ticket. A new fleet of **super-rapid boats** traveling between Corsica and Marseille, Toulon, Nice, and Genoa was introduced in 1996. Although these vessels are not hydrofoils, they have special hulls that allow for high speeds. **Air Inter** has increased the number of domestic flights in France and the result is greater convenience and cheaper fares.

Finally, because of a need for more telephone lines, **two digits have been added to all French phone numbers and Monaco has been give its own country code.** *See* the Gold Guide for details.

FESTIVALS AND SEASONAL EVENTS

France is a festival all year round, with special events taking place throughout the country. The most complete listing of festivals comes in a small pamphlet published by **Maison de la France** (✉ 8 av. de l'Opéra, Paris 75001, ☎ 01–42–96–10–23). The *International Herald Tribune* also lists special events in its weekend edition, but not in great detail.

Annual highlights include the Monte Carlo Motor Rally in January, Nice's Carnival in February, the Monte Carlo Open in April, and the Cannes Film Festival in May.

WINTER

DEC.➤ On the 24th, a Christmas celebration known as the **Shepherd's Festival,** featuring midnight Mass and picturesque "living crèches," is held in Les Baux, Provence.

JAN.➤ The **International Circus Festival,** featuring top acts from around the world, and the **Monte Carlo Motor Rally,** one of the motoring world's most venerable races, are held in Monaco.

FEB.➤ The **Carnival de Nice** provides an exotic blend of parades and revelry during the weeks leading up to Lent. Other cities and villages also have their own smaller versions.

SPRING

APRIL➤ The **Monte Carlo Open Tennis Championships** get under way at the ultraswank Monte Carlo Country Club.

MAY➤ The **Cannes Film Festival** sees two weeks of star-studded events. Classical concert festivals get underway throughout the country.

SUMMER

JULY➤ **Summer arts festival season** gets into full swing, particularly in Provence. Avignon offers a month of top-notch

theater, Aix-en-Provence specializes in opera, Carpentras in religious music, Châteauvallon in dance, and Nice holds a big Jazz Festival, starting with a Grand Parade. Arles mounts a big photography festival. Most important, the **Tour de France,** the world's most famous bicycle race, dominates national attention for over three weeks before crossing the finish line on the Champs-Elysées.

On **July 14** all of France celebrates Bastille Day, commemorating the Storming of the Bastille in 1789—the start of the French Revolution. Look out for fireworks, free concerts, and street festivities beginning the evening of the 13th, with the **Bals des Pompiers** (Firemen's Ball) organized by local firemen.

AUTUMN

NOV.➤ On the third Thursday of the month, France celebrates the arrival of the Beaujolais Nouveau.

2 Provence

Nîmes, Arles, Avignon, and Marseille

Provence means dazzling light and rugged, rocky countryside interspersed with vineyards, fields of lavender, and olive groves. The Romans staked their first claim here and left riches behind; Van Gogh and Cézanne taught us to see it through their eyes; then Peter Mayle bought a house and the world was not far behind. From Montpellier to Toulon, from Orange to the sea, this ancient, alluring land is still seducing visitors.

AS YOU APPROACH PROVENCE, there is a magical moment when the north is finally left behind: Cypresses and red-tile roofs appear; you hear the screech of the cicadas and catch the scent of wild thyme and lavender. Even on the modern highway, oleanders flower on the central strip against a backdrop of harsh, brightly lit landscapes that inspired the paintings of Paul Cézanne and Vincent van Gogh.

Updated by
Nigel Fisher

Provence lies in the south of France, bordered by Italy to the east and the blue waters of the Mediterranean. The Romans called it Provincia—the Province—for it was the first part of Gaul they occupied. Roman remains litter the ground in well-preserved profusion. The theater and triumphal arch at Orange, the amphitheater at Nîmes, and the aqueduct at Pont-du-Gard are considered the best of their kind.

Provençal life continues at an old-fashioned pace. Hot afternoons tend to mean siestas, with signs of life discernible only as the shadows under the *platanes* (plane trees) start to lengthen and lethargic locals saunter out to play *boules* (the French version of bocce) and drink long, cooling *pastis,* an anise-based aperitif. The famous mistral—a fierce, cold wind that races through the Rhône Valley—is another feature of Provence. Thankfully, clear blue skies usually follow in its wake.

The Rhône, the great river of southern France, splits in two at Arles, 24 kilometers (15 miles) before reaching the Mediterranean: The Petit Rhône crosses the marshy region known as the Camargue on its way to Stes-Maries-de-la-Mer, while the Grand Rhône heads off to Fos, an industrial port just along the coast from Marseille. North of Marseille lies Aix-en-Provence, whose old-time elegance reflects its former role as regional capital. Provence's traditional boundaries have been extended westward slightly into Languedoc, to include historic Nîmes and the dynamic university town of Montpellier. The Riviera, too, is part of Provence—but with so much to do there, it has its own chapter.

Pleasures and Pastimes

Dining

In the old days, Provençal cooking was based on olive oil, fruit, and vegetables; garlic and wild herbs improved the scant meat dishes. The current gastronomic scene is a far cry from this frugality: Parisian chefs have created internationally renowned restaurants to satisfy demanding palates. Still, there's a lot to be said for simple Provençal food—pastis, that pale green, anise-based aperitif; *tapenade,* a delicious paste of capers, anchovies, olives, oil; *aïoli,* a garlicky mayonnaise; and grilled lamb and beef with a chilled bottle of rosé. Locals like to end their meal with a round of goat cheese and fruit.

Steer clear of the cheap Marseille fish restaurants, many with brisk ladies out front who deliver throaty sales pitches; fish from the Mediterranean is expensive, so any inexpensive fish menu probably uses frozen imports. The Marseille specialty of bouillabaisse is a case in point: Once a fisherman's cheap stew, it is now a celebration dish, with such heretical additions as lobster. The high-priced versions use fresh fish and can be delicious, but cheaper ones are often of dubious origins.

CATEGORY	COST*
$$$$	over 400 frs
$$$	250–400 frs
$$	125–250 frs
$	under 125 frs

per person for a three-course meal, including tax (20.6%) and tip but not wine.

Lodging

Accommodations are varied in this much-visited part of France and range from luxurious *mas* (converted farmhouses) to modest downtown hotels. Service is often less than prompt, a casualty of the sweltering summer heat. Reservations are essential for much of the year, and many hotels are closed during winter.

CATEGORY	COST*
$$$$	over 800 frs
$$$	550–800 frs
$$	300–550 frs
$	under 300 frs

All prices are for a standard double room for two, including tax (20.6%) and service charge.

Outdoor Activities and Sports

In Provence, you can windsurf and sail at La Grande Motte, Stes-Maries-de-la-Mer, Carry-le-Rouet, Martigues (near Marseille), Cassis, Hyères-Plage, and the island of Porquerolles; ride on a horse rented from a local stable; tool around bikes from the train station; or hike along blazed trails.

Exploring Provence

Provence falls easily into three areas. The marshy Camargue is at the heart of the first, though you might venture briefly into Languedoc to see the fine old towns of Nîmes and Montpellier before wheeling back to visit the Roman remains at Arles and St-Rémy. In the second area, which falls within the boundaries of the Vaucluse, begin at Avignon and head north to Orange and Vaison-la-Romaine; the main natural feature here is Mont Ventoux, towering above the surrounding plains. The third area encompasses Aix, the historic capital of Provence, then stretches south to Marseille and east along the coast to Toulon.

Great Itineraries

The popular book entitled *A Year in Provence* dictates just that, but even a year might not be long enough to soak up all the charm of this captivating region. Provence may be small, but its history and topography are diverse; around each bend there is something of interest. In three days you can see most of the major Roman towns: Nîmes, Arles, and Avignon; with seven days you can easily add Montpellier, Orange, and Aix-en-Provence; with ten days you can cover all the important towns, add Marseilles and the hill towns in the Luberon mountains, and relax on a Mediterranean beach.

IF YOU HAVE 3 DAYS

Numbers in the text correspond to numbers in the margin and on the Provence, Nîmes, Avignon, and Marseille maps.

Begin in **Pont du Gard** ①, the 2,000-year-old Roman aqueduct, then head for ☒ **Nîmes** ②–⑪ to visit the Roman Arènes and spend the night. The next day go to **Arles** ⑯ to see its Arènes. After lunch explore medieval **Les Baux-de-Provence** ⑱ and the castle in **Tarascon** ⑳; enjoy the

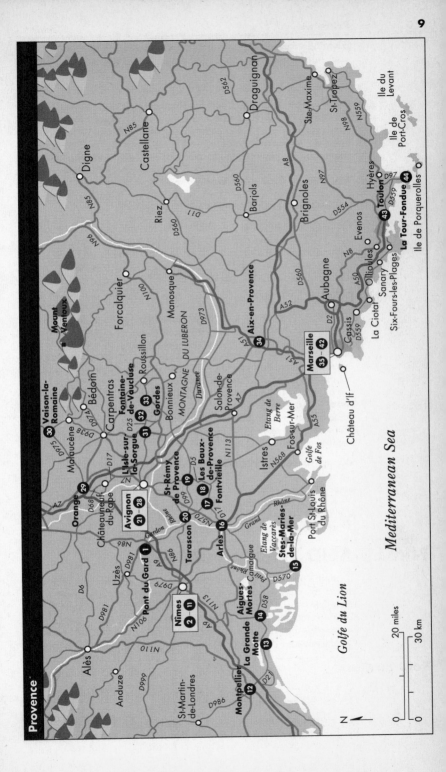

Provence

Mediterranean Sea

Golfe du Lion

N

0 20 miles
0 30 km

countryside en route to ▣ **St-Rémy de Provence** ⑲ for the night. On your last day drive to the walled city of **Avignon** ㉑–㉘.

Visit **Orange** ㉙ on your first day before stopping to see the **Pont du Gard** ①. Spend the night and the next morning in ▣ **Nîmes** ②–⑪. In the afternoon, drive to the fortified town of **Aigues-Mortes** ⑭ and through the marshy Carmargue to ▣ **Arles** ⑯. The next day get to **Les Baux-de-Provence** ⑱ by lunchtime, then continue to ▣ **St-Rémy-de-Provence** ⑲ to explore the Roman ruins of Glanum. On the fourth day, wend your way, via **Tarascon** ⑳ to ▣ **Avignon** ㉑–㉘. The following day, head through **L'Isle-sur-la-Sorgue** ㉛ and the other towns in the Luberon Mountains on your way south to spend two nights and a day in ▣ **Aix-en-Provence** ㉞.

Stay in ▣ **Avignon** ㉑–㉘ your first two nights, with a side trip to the Roman theater in **Orange** ㉙, the ruins in **Vaison-la-Romaine** ㉚, and **Mont Ventoux.** On your third day stop at the **Pont du Gard** ① aqueduct on your way to ▣ **Nîmes** ②–⑪ for the afternoon and night. The next day head to the university city of **Montpellier** ⑫, then east past the resort town of **La Grande Motte** ⑬ to medieval **Aigues-Mortes** ⑭. Plan on several hours to explore the marshy Carmargue and visit the fortresslike church at **Stes-Maries-de-la-Mer** ⑮. By nightfall, be in the Roman city of ▣ **Arles** ⑯. Spend the next night only a few miles away at ▣ **St-Rémy-de-Provence** ⑲ and the day visiting **Les Baux-de-Provence** ⑱ and **Tarascon** ⑳. On the sixth day, head to the Luberon Mountains to visit **L'Isle-sur-la-Sorgue** ㉛ and its other picturesque towns. Spend the night in either ▣ **Gordes** ㉝ or ▣ **Fontaine de Vaucluse** ㉜. Stop for two nights in ▣ **Aix-en-Provence** ㉞ to see its marvelous 18th-century mansions and museums and explore the area. Aim for ▣ **Marseille** ㉟–㊷ the next day—it may seem a bit drab at first, but it has its own vitality.

When to Tour Provence

Spring and fall are the best months to experience the dazzling light, rugged rocky countryside, fields of lavender, and fruitful vineyards of Provence. In summer, it gets very hot and very crowded on the beaches. Still, if you are interested in seeing the bullfights, this is the time to come. Winter has nice days, but it often rains.

NÎMES AND THE CAMARGUE

Though Roman remains are found throughout Provence, their presence is strongest where the rivers meander their way to the sea on the region's western flank: the beautiful aqueduct at Pont du Gard, the arenas at Nîmes and Arles, and the excavations at St-Rémy de Provence. Within this area are strange landscapes: the marshy wilderness of the Carmargue and the rocky, arid outcrops around Les Baux.

Pont du Gard

★ ❶ *22 km (13 mi) southwest of Avignon, 37 km (23 mi) southwest of Orange, 48 km (30 mi)north of Arles.*

No other sight in Provence can rival this bridge that symbolically links the 20th century to the Roman grandeur that haunts Provence: the Pont du Gard, midway between Avignon and Nîmes off the N86 highway.

The Pont du Gard is a huge, three-tiered aqueduct, erected 2,000 years ago as part of a 30-mile canal supplying water to Roman Nîmes. It is astonishingly well preserved. Its setting, spanning a rocky gorge 150 feet above the River Gardon, is nothing less than spectacular. There is no entry fee or guide, and at certain times you can have it all to yourself: Early morning is best. Gauge the full majesty of the Pont du Gard by walking along the top.

Nîmes

❷   *20 km (13 mi) southwest of the Pont du Gard, 43 km (26 mi) south of Avignon.*

Few towns have preserved such visible links with their Roman past: Nemausus, as Nîmes was then known, grew to prominence during the reign of Caesar Augustus (27 BC–AD 14) and still boasts a Roman amphitheater (Arènes), temple (Maison Carrée), and watchtower (Tour Magne). Luckily, these monuments emerged relatively unscathed from the flash flood that devastated Nîmes in 1988. A 60-franc "passport," available from the tourist office, admits you to all the town's museums and monuments and is valid three days.

★ ❸   Start out at the **Arènes,** which is more than 140 yards long and 110 yards wide, with a seating capacity of 21,000. After a checkered history—it was transformed into a fortress by the Visigoths and used for housing in medieval times—the amphitheater has been restored almost to its original look. An inflatable roof covers it in winter, when various exhibits and shows occupy the space, and bullfights and tennis tournaments are held here in summer. A smaller version of the Colosseum in Rome, this is considered the world's best-preserved Roman amphitheater. ⊠ *bd. Victor-Hugo,* ☎ *04–66–67–45–76.* 🎟 *22 frs; joint ticket to Arènes and Tour Magne 30 frs. Guided visits only Oct.–April, with approx. 8-frs supplement.* ⊙ *May–Oct. daily 9–6:30; Nov.–Mar. daily 9–noon and 2–5.*

❹   At the **Musée des Beaux-Arts,** a few blocks south of the Arènes, you can admire a vast Roman mosaic; the marriage ceremony depicted provides intriguing insights into the Roman aristocratic lifestyle. Old Master paintings (Nicolas Poussin, Pieter Brueghel, Peter Paul Rubens) and sculpture (Auguste Rodin) form the mainstay of the collection. ⊠ *rue de la Cité-Foulc,* ☎ *04–66–67–38–21.* 🎟 *22 frs.* ⊙ *Tues.–Sat. 11–6.*

❺   The **Musée Archéologique et d'Histoire Naturelle,** a few blocks northeast of the Arènes, is rich in local archaeological finds, mainly statues, busts, friezes, tools, glass, coins, and pottery. ⊠ *bd. de l'Amiral-Courbet,* ☎ *04–66–67–25–57.* 🎟 *22 frs.* ⊙ *Tues.–Sun. 11–6.*

❻   The uninspired 19th-century reconstruction of the **cathedral** is of less interest than either the surrounding streets or the Museum of Old Nîmes.

❼   The **Musée du Vieux Nîmes,** opposite the cathedral in the 17th-century Bishop's Palace, has embroidered garments in exotic and vibrant displays. Nîmes used to be a cloth-manufacturing center and lent its name to what has become one of the world's most popular fabrics—denim (*de Nîmes*—from Nîmes). ⊠ *pl. aux Herbes,* ☎ *04–66–36–00–64.* 🎟 *22 frs.* ⊙ *Tues.–Sun. 11–6.*

★ ❽   Despite its name, which means "square house," the **Maison Carrée** is an oblong Roman temple, dating from the 1st century AD. Today the building is a museum containing an imposing statue of Apollo. The exquisite carvings along the cornice and on the Corinthian capitals rank as some of the finest in Roman architecture. Thomas Jefferson admired the Maison Carrée's chaste lines of columns so much that he had them

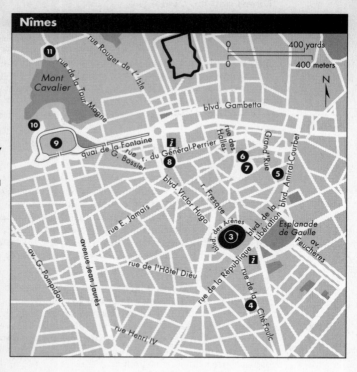

copied for the Virginia state capitol in Richmond. ⊠ *bd. Victor-Hugo.* 🎫 *Free.* 🕑 *May–Oct. daily 9-7; Nov.–Apr. daily 9–6.*

The swanky, glass-fronted Musée d'Art Contemporain, often called the **Carrée d'Art** (it's directly opposite the Maison Carrée), opened in May 1993. It showcases international pictures and sculpture from 1960 onward. ⊠ *pl. de la Maison Carrée,* ☎ *04–66–76–35–35.* 🎫 *22 frs.* 🕑 *Tues.–Sun. 11–6.*

⑨ The **Jardin de la Fontaine,** an elaborate, formal garden, was landscaped on the site of the Roman baths in the 18th century, when the Source de Nemausus, a once sacred spring, was channeled into pools and a canal. Just northwest of the Jardin de la Fontaine you'll see the shat-

⑩ tered Roman ruin known as the **Temple of Diana.**

⑪ At the far end of the Jardin de la Fontaine stands the **Tour Magne**—a stumpy pre-Roman tower that was probably used as a lookout post, which, despite having lost 30 feet during the course of time, still provides fine views of Nîmes for anyone who is energetic enough to climb the 140 steps to the top. ⊠ *quai de la Fontaine,* ☎ *04–66–67–65–56.* 🎫 *Tour Magne: 12 frs; joint ticket as described above,* ☞ *Arènes.* 🕑 *May.–Oct. daily 9–7; Nov.–Apr. daily 9–12:30 and 1:30–6.*

Wave machines, slides, water cannons, and bubble baths make up the fun at **Aquatropic** in Nîmes—an indoor swimming pool with a difference. ⊠ *39 rue de la Hostellerie,* ☎ *04–66–38–31–00.* 🎫 *35 frs.* 🕑 *Weekdays 10–8, weekends 10–7.*

Dining and Lodging

$ ✕ **Nicolas.** You'll hear the noise of this homey place before you open
★ the door. A friendly, frazzled staff serves up delicious *bourride* (fish soup) and other local specialties—all at unbelievably low prices. ⊠ *1 rue Poise,*

☎ 04–66–67–50–47. *MC, V. Closed Mon., first 2 wks in July, and mid-Dec.–first wk in Jan.*

\$\$–\$\$\$ ✕⊞ **Impérator.** This little palace-hotel, just a few minutes' walk from
★ the Jardin de la Fontaine, has been totally modernized in excellent taste. Most rooms retain a Provençal feel. The restaurant, L'Enclos de la Fontaine, is Nîmes's most fashionable eating place, where chef Jean-Michel Nigon provides such inventive dishes as iced, dill-perfumed langoustine soup. The prix-fixe menus are bargains. ⊠ *15 rue Gaston-Boissier, 30900,* ☎ *04–66–21–90–30,* 𝔽𝔸𝕏 *04–66–67–70–25. 59 rooms with bath. Restaurant (closed Sat. lunch). AE, DC, MC, V.*

\$\$ ✕⊞ **Lisita.** This cozy hotel just a stone's throw from the Arènes is a favored haunt of Spanish matadors whenever they're in town for a bull-fight. Rooms are on the small side, but some have a charming view of the plane trees that line the street, and most are tastefully decorated with regional furniture. The restaurant specializes in classic French fish and meat dishes; it is closed Saturday and the first half of August. ⊠ *2 bis bd. des Arènes, 30000,* ☎ *04–66–67–66–20,* 𝔽𝔸𝕏 *04–66–76–22–30. 30 rooms with bath or shower. Restaurant. AE, DC, MC, V.*

Shopping

A **flower market** (⊠ boulevard Jean-Jaurès) takes place Monday mornings.

Montpellier

⑫ *50 km (30 mi) southwest Nîmes, 94 km (58 mi) southwest of Avignon, 152 km (91 mi) north of Perpignan.*

Montpellier is a comparatively young town, a mere 1,000 years old; no Romans settled here. Ever since medieval times, its reputation has been linked to its university, which was founded in the 14th century. Its medical school in particular was so highly esteemed in the 16th century that the great writer François Rabelais left his native Loire Valley to take his doctorate here. Nowadays, the student population of 20,000 helps keep Montpellier young.

The 17th-century town center has been improved by an imaginative urban planning program, and several streets and squares are banned to cars. The heart of Montpellier is **place de la Comédie,** a wide square now free of traffic jams, much to the benefit of the cafés and terraces laid out before the handsome 19th-century facade of the civic theater.

Boulevard Sarrail leads north from place de la Comédie, past the leafy Esplanade with its rows of plane trees, to the **Musée Fabre.** The museum's collection of art highlights important works by Gustave Courbet (notably *Bonjour Monsieur Courbet*) and Eugène Delacroix (*Femmes d'Alger*), as well as paintings by Frédéric Bazille—whose death during the Franco-Prussian War deprived Impressionism of one of its earliest exponents. ⊠ *37 bd. Sarrail,* ☎ *04–67–14–83–00.* 🎟 *20 frs.* ☉ *Tues.–Fri. 9–5:30, weekends 9:30–5.*

In the heart of old Montpellier—a maze of crooked, bustling streets ideal for shopping and strolling—Rue Foch strikes a more disciplined note, slicing straight east to west, to the pride of Montpellier, the **Promenade du Peyrou.** With its majestic steps, this long, broad, tree-shaded terrace has great style. An equestrian statue of Louis XIV rides triumphant, and at the far end carved friezes and columns mask a water tower. Water used to arrive along the **St-Clément aqueduct,** an imposing two-tiered structure and locals still cluster beneath the aqueduct's arches to drink pastis and play boules.

Boulevard Henri IV runs north from the Promenade du Peyrou to France's oldest **botanical garden,** planted by order of Henri IV in 1593. Horticulture buffs and even nongardeners will admire the exceptional range of plants, flowers, and trees that grow here. ✉ *Free.* ⊙ *Gardens Mon.–Sat. 9–noon and 2–5. Greenhouses weekdays 9– noon and 2–5, Sat. 9–noon.*

Dining and Lodging

$$–$$$ ✕ **Le Chandelier.** The only complaints here concern the prices à la carte; ★ the service is impeccable, the trendy pink decor is more than acceptable, and Gilbert Furlan's inventive cuisine is delicious. Try his chilled artichoke and rabbit soup or sea bass with crushed olives. Cinnamon-honey ice cream makes a fine end to your meal. ✉ *3 rue Albert-Leenhardt,* ☎ *04–67–92–61–62. Reservations essential. AE, DC, MC, V. Closed part of Feb., first 2 wks in Aug., Sun., and Mon. lunch.*

$$ ✕ **Petit Jardin.** As the name implies, you can dine here in a charming leafy garden or in the flower-bedecked dining room. Owner Roland Heilmann has made a rapid name for himself with such regional dishes as bourride and the *piperade* omelet with king-size prawns. ✉ *20 rue Jean-Jacques-Rousseau,* ☎ *04–67–60–78–78. Reservations essential. AE, DC, MC, V. Closed Sun. evening, Mon., and Jan.–Mar.*

$$$ ✕🏠 **Métropole.** This venerable 19th-century hotel, halfway between the train station and city center has sumptuous 18th century–style furnishings, marble bathrooms, and a courtyard garden. In La Closerie restaurant, young chef Jean-Luc Rabanel serves regional dishes like mullet with olives or lamb with thyme, accompanied by a good selection of local, fruity wines. The staff tries hard—sometimes too hard—to please. ✉ *3 rue du Clos-René, 34000,* ☎ *04–67–58–11–22,* 🅵🅰🆇 *04–67–92–13– 02. 92 rooms with bath. Restaurant, bar. AE, DC, MC, V.*

Nightlife and the Arts

Montpellier puts on concerts at the 19th-century **Théâtre des Treize Vents** (✉ allée Jules-Milhau, ☎ 04–67–58–08–13). For a lively disco, we suggest **Le Rimmel** (✉ 4 bis rue de Boussairolles).

En Route Between Montpellier and Marseille, from Arles to the Mediterranean lies the haunting, desolate, marshy wilderness of endless horizons, vast pools, low flat plains, and, overhead, innumerable species of migrating birds. This is the **Camargue,** formed by the sprawling Rhône delta and extending over 300 square miles. In October 1993 and January 1994, the swollen river burst its banks, flooding large parts of the area. Much of it is untouched by man; this is a land of black bulls and sturdy, free-roaming gray horses. There are just two towns worthy of the name: Aigues-Mortes and Saintes-Maries-de-la-Mer.

La Grande Motte

⑬ *20 km (12 mi) east of Montpellier, 87 km (54 mi) north of Beziers, 45 km (28 mi) south of Nîmes.*

The arid, rocky Midi landscape begins to change as you head southeast from Montpellier along D21, past pools and lagoons, to La Grande Motte, the most lavish—and, some would say, ugliest—of a string of new resorts built along the Languedoc coast. The mosquitoes that once infested this watery area have finally been vanquished, and tourists have taken their place. La Grande Motte was only a glint in an architect's eye back in the late 1960s; since then, its arresting pyramidal apartment blocks have influenced several French resorts.

Tons of oysters are cultivated in the nearby *Etang* (lagoon) de Thau; you can sample them at the elegant **Alexandre-Amirauté** (✉ 345 esplanade Maurice-Justin, ☎ 04–67–56–63–63).

Outdoor Activities and Sports
La Grande Motte has an excellent 18-hole **golf** course (☎ 04–67–56–05–00).

Aigues-Mortes
🔟4 *13 km (8 mi) east of La Grande Motte, 41 km (25 mi) east of Nîmes, 48 km (30 mi) southwest of Arles.*

Created at the behest of Louis IX (Saint-Louis) in the 13th century Aigues-Mortes is an astonishing relic of early town planning. Medieval streets are usually crooked; at Aigues-Mortes, however, a grid plan was adopted, hemmed in by sturdy walls sprouting towers at regular intervals. The town was originally a port, and Louis used it as a base for his Crusades to the Holy Land. The sea has long since receded, though, and Aigues-Mortes's size and importance have gone away with it.

Unlike most of the medieval buildings, the **fortifications** remain intact. Walk along the top of the city walls and admire some remarkable views across the town and salt marshes. You can also explore the powerful **Tour de Constance**, originally designed as a fortress-keep and used in the 18th century as a prison for Protestants who refused to convert to official state Catholicism. One such unfortunate, Marie Durand, languished here for 38 years. Abraham Mazel was luckier. He spent 10 months chiseling a hole in the wall, while his companions sang psalms to distract the jailers. The ruse worked: Mazel and 16 others escaped. ☎ 04–66–53–73–00. ✉ 27 frs. ☉ *Tower and ramparts open Apr.–Oct., daily 9–7; Nov.–Mar. 9:30–noon and 2–5:30.*

Stes-Maries-de-la-Mer
🔟5 *32 km (20 mi) southeast of Aigues-Mortes, 129 km (80 mi) west of Marseille, 39 km (24 mi) south of Arles.*

Stes-Maries-de-la-Mer is a commercialized resort, frequented mainly by British tourists in search of the Camargue's principal sandy beach. Its tiny, dark fortress-church houses caskets containing relics of the "Holy Maries" after whom the town is named. Legend has it that Mary Jacobi (the sister of the Virgin), Mary Magdalene, Mary Salome (mother of the apostles James and John), and their black servant Sarah were washed up here around AD 40 after being abandoned at sea. Their adopted town rapidly became a site of pilgrimage, the most important site for Gypsies. Sarah was adopted as their patron saint, and to this day, Gypsies from all over the world make pilgrimages to Stes-Maries in late May and late October, while guitar-strumming pseudo-gypsies serenade rich-looking tourists throughout the summer.

In the center of the Carmarque lies the 30-acre **Parc Ornithologique,** itself part of the vast Réserve Nationale centered on the Etang (lagoon) de Vaccarès. It offers a protected environment to vegetation and wildlife: Birds from northern Europe and Siberia spend the winter here, while flamingos flock here in summer. ☎ 04–90–97–82–62. ✉ 35 frs. ☉ *Mar.–Oct., daily 8–dusk; Nov.–Feb., daily 9–dusk.*

Arles
🔟6 *38 km (24 mi) north of Stes-Maries-de-la-Mer, 92 km (57 mi) northwest from Marseille, 36 km (22 mi) south of Avignon.*

The first inhabitants of Arles were probably the Greeks, who arrived from Marseille in the 6th century BC. The Romans, however, left a stronger mark, constructing the theater and amphitheater (Arènes) that remain the biggest tourist attractions. Arles used to be a thriving port before the Mediterranean receded over what is now the Camargue. It was also the site of the southernmost bridge over the Rhône, and became a commercial crossroads; merchants from as far afield as Arabia, Assyria, and Africa would linger here to do business on their way from Rome to Spain or northern Europe.

The Dutch painter Vincent van Gogh produced much of his best work—and chopped off his ear—in Arles during a frenzied 15-month spell (1888–90) just before his suicide at 37. Unfortunately, the houses he lived in are no longer standing—they were destroyed during World War II—but part of one of his most famous subjects remains: the **Pont de Trinquetaille** across the Rhône. Van Gogh's rendering of the bridge, painted in 1888, was auctioned a century later for $20 million. Local art museums can't compete with that type of bidding—which is one reason none of Van Gogh's works are displayed there. Another is that Arles failed to appreciate him; he was jeered at and eventually packed off to the nearest lunatic asylum.

Rather than name the local museum after Van Gogh, Arles chose Jacques Réattu, a local painter of dazzling mediocrity. His works fill three rooms at the **Musée Réattu.** Fortunately, while there is none of Van Gogh's work, there is a collection of modern drawings and paintings by Pablo Picasso, Fernand Léger, and Maurice de Vlaminck and a notable photography section. ⊠ *rue du Grand-Prieuré,* ☎ *04–90–49–37–58.* 🎟 *15 frs; passport to all monuments and museums in Arles: 55 frs.* ⊘ *June–Sept., daily 9:30–7; Nov.–Mar., daily 10–12:30 and 2–5; Apr.–May and Oct., daily 9:30–12:30 and 2–6.*

★ Reminders of Roman society are found at the ruins of the **Palais Constantin,** on the site of the **Thermes de la Trouille,** Provence's largest Roman baths. ⊠ *rue Dominique-Maisto.* 🎟 *12 francs; joint ticket as above.* ⊘ *June–Sept., daily 9:30–7; Nov.–Mar., daily 10–12:30 and 2–5; Apr.–May and Oct., daily 9:30–12:30 and 2–6.*

The most notable Roman sight is the 26,000-capacity **Arènes,** built in the 1st century AD for circuses and gladiator combats. The amphitheater is 150 yards long and as wide as a football field, with each of its two stories composed of 60 arches; the original top tier has long since crumbled, and the three square towers were added in the Middle Ages. Climb to the upper story for some satisfying views. Despite its age, the amphitheater still sees a lot of action, mainly Sunday afternoon bullfights. ⊠ *Rond-Point des Arènes,* ☎ *04–90–96–03–70.* 🎟 *15 frs; joint ticket as above.* ⊘ *June–Sept., daily 8:30–7; Nov.–Mar., daily 9–noon and 2–4:30; Apr.–May and Oct., daily 9–12:30 and 2–6:30.*

★ The bits of marble column scattered around the grassy enclosure of the diminished remains of the **Théâtre Antique** (Roman theater), just 100 yards from the Arènes, hint poignantly at the theater's onetime grandeur. The capacity may have shrunk from 7,000 to a few hundred, but the orchestra pit and a few tiers of seats are still used for the city's Music and Drama Festival each July. ⊠ *rue du Cloître,* ☎ *04–90–96–93–30 for ticket information.* 🎟 *15 frs; joint ticket as above.* ⊘ *June–Sept., daily 8:30–7; Nov.–Mar., daily 9–noon and 2–4:30; Apr.–May and Oct., daily 9–12:30 and 2–6:30.*

The church of **St-Trophime,** on place de la Republique in the center of Arles, dates mainly from the 11th and 12th centuries; subsequent additions have not spoiled its architectural harmony. Take time to admire the accomplished 12th-century sculptures flanking the main portal, featuring the *Last Judgment*, the apostles, the Nativity, and various saints. There are other well-crafted sculptures in the cloisters. ⊠ *rue de l'Hôtel-de-Ville*, ☎ *04–90–49–36–36.* ✉ *Cloisters: 15 frs; joint ticket as above.* ☉ *June–Sept., daily 8:30–7; Nov.–Mar., daily 9–noon and 2–4:30; Apr.–May and Oct., daily 9–12:30 and 2–6:30.*

Housed in a former church next to the 17th-century Hôtel de Ville, opposite the church of St-Trophime, the **Musée d'Art Païen** (Museum of Pagan Art) contains Roman statues, busts, mosaics, and a white marble sarcophagus. You'll also see a copy of the famous statue the *Venus of Arles*; Sun King Louis XIV waltzed off to the Louvre with the original. ⊠ *pl. de la République.* ✉ *12 frs; joint ticket as above.* ☉ *June–Sept., daily 8:30–7; Nov.–Mar., daily 9–noon and 2–4:30; Apr.–May and Oct., 9–12:30 and 2–6:30.*

The **Musée d'Art Chrétien** (Museum of Christian Art) has a magnificent collection of sculpted marble sarcophagi, second only to the Vatican's, that date from the 4th century. Though the building is a former 17th-century Jesuit chapel, it was built on a Roman foundations. Downstairs, you can explore a vast Roman double gallery built in the 1st century BC as a grain store and see part of the great Roman sewer built two centuries later. ⊠ *rue Balze.* ✉ *12 frs; joint ticket as above.* ☉ *June–Sept., daily 8:30–7; Nov.–Mar., daily 9–noon and 2–4:30; Apr.–May and Oct., daily 9–12:30 and 2–6:30.*

The **Muséon Arlaten,** an old-fashioned folklore museum, is housed in a 16th-century mansion next door to the Musée d'Art Chrétien. The charming displays of costumes and headdresses, puppets, and waxworks were lovingly assembled by that great 19th-century Provençal poet Frédéric Mistral. ⊠ *29 rue de la République,* ☎ *04–90–96–08–23.* ✉ *15 frs; joint ticket as above.* ☉ *June–Sept., daily 8:30–7; Nov.–Mar., Tues.–Sun. 9–noon and 2–4:30; Apr.–May and Oct., Tues.–Sun. 9–12:30 and 2–6:30.*

NEED A BREAK? | Join the locals for aperitifs on any one of the sidewalk cafés on leafy **boulevard des Luces.**

The fountains in the **Jardin d'Hiver,** the public garden at the east end of the boulevard des Luces, figure in several of Van Gogh's paintings.

The **Alyscamps** starts at the allée des Sarcophages. This was a prestigious burial site from Roman times through the Middle Ages. A host of important finds have been excavated here, many of which are exhibited in the town's museums. Empty tombs and sarcophagi line the allée des Sarcophages, creating a gloomy atmosphere in dull weather. ☎ *04–90–49–36–87.* ✉ *12 frs.* ☉ *Daily 9–5.*

Dining and Lodging

$$ | ✗ **Le Vaccarès.** In the footsteps of his father and grandfather, chef Bernard Dumas serves classic Provençal dishes. Try his mussels dressed in herbs and garlic. The dining-room decor is as elegant as the cuisine. ⊠ *11 rue Favorin,* ☎ *04–90–96–06–17. Reservations essential. MC, V. Closed mid-Jan.–mid-Feb., Sun. dinner, and Mon.*

$ | ✗ **Le Constantin.** For 89 francs the prix-fixe menu at this tiny, inexpensive restaurant offers three substantial courses: homemade terrines or goat cheese salads for starters to grilled tuna or steaks with pommes frites for the main course, and dessert to fill any corners remaining. Atmosphere is set by exposed brick walls, a cheerful waitress, and red-checkered tablecloths. ⊠ *rue Dominque Maiso,* ☎ *04–90–96–59–33. MC, V. Closed Wed.*

$$$ ✕⊡ **Jules César.** This elegant hotel was originally a Carmelite convent, and many guest rooms overlook the attractive 17th-century cloisters. The rooms are tastefully decorated with antiques. New chef Pascal Renaud pleases his international clientele with nouvelle cuisine and traditional Provençal dishes; the restaurant, Lou Marquès, is the most fashionable place to eat. Try his cod with lentils and fresh cream. ⊠ *bd. des Lices, 13200,* ☎ *04–90–93–43–20,* 𝔽𝔸𝕏 *04–90–93–33–47. 55 rooms with bath. Restaurant, pool. AE, DC, MC, V. Closed Nov.–Dec. 23.*

$$$ ⊡ **Arlatan.** Follow the signposts from place du Forum to the pic-
★   turesque street where you'll find this 15th-century house, former home of the counts of Arlatan, built on the site of a 4th-century basilica (tiled flooring dating from this period is visible below glass casing). Antiques, pretty fabrics, and tapestries lend it a gracious atmosphere. There is an attractive garden and a private bar. ⊠ *26 rue du Sauvage, 13200,* ☎ *04–90–93–56–66,* 𝔽𝔸𝕏 *04–90–49–68–45. 51 rooms with bath. Bar, parking. AE, DC, MC, V.*

$$$ ⊡ **Château de Vergières.** Down an avenue of trees on a 100-acre estate is this small 18th-century château filled with family portraits and bric-a-brac. It's not so much a hotel as a guest house where you can, with reservations, dine with the family and stay overnight. Dinner is excellently prepared by the owners, Marie-Andrée and Jean Pincedé. Rooms are large with high ceilings and wood plank floors. The large bathrooms have deep tubs and rich red bath towels. ⊠ *La Dynamite, 13310 Saint Martin de Crau (15km/9 mi southeast of Arles),* ☎ *04–90–47–17–16,* 𝔽𝔸𝕏 *04–90–47–38–30. 6 rooms all with bath. No credit cards.*

$ ⊡ **Hôtel Gauguin.** The rooms, painted in fresh yellows and blues, are small, but so is the price. Full bathrooms are a little more. Ask for a room in front, looking onto the square. The owner, Mme Dugand, enthusiastically welcomes guests and is happy to try her English. ⊠ *5 pl. Voltaire, 13200 Arles,* ☎ *04–90–96–14–35. 18 rooms. MC, V.*

Nightlife and the Arts

An **International Photography Festival** takes place in July at the Théâtre Antique (⊠ rue de la Calade/rue du Cloître).

Shopping

Delicately patterned Provençal print fabrics and dresses and scarves can be bought at **Souleïado** (⊠ 18 bd. des Lices). Fruit, vegetables, and household goods are sold at Wednesday- and Saturday-morning **markets** (⊠ boulevard des Lices).

Fontvieille

⑰ *10 km (6 mi) east of Arles (take N570 toward Avignon, and almost immediately turn right on D17.)*

The striking village of Fontvieille is best known as the home of writer Alphonse Daudet. In the well-preserved, charming **Moulin de Daudet** (windmill), just up D33 on the outskirts of the village, nineteenth-century writer Alphonse Daudent dreamed up his short stores, *Lettres de Mon Moulin.* Inside there's a small museum devoted to Daudet, and you can walk upstairs to see the original milling system. ☎ *04–90–54–60–78.* 🔳 *10 frs.* ☉ *Apr.–Oct., daily 9–noon and 2–7; Nov.–Dec. and Feb.–Mar., daily 10–noon and 2–5; Jan., Sun. only, 10–noon and 2–5.*

Les Baux-de-Provence

★ ⑱ *18 km (11 mi) northeast of Arles, 29 km (18 mi) south of Avignon.*

Perched on a mighty spur of rock high above the surrounding countryside with its vines, olive trees, and quarries, Les Baux-de-Provence is an amazing place. The mineral bauxite was discovered here in 1821. Half of Les Baux is composed of tiny climbing streets and ancient stone houses inhabited, for the most part, by local craftsmen. The other half, the Ville Morte (Dead Town), is a mass of medieval ruins, vestiges of Les Baux's glorious past, when the town boasted 6,000 inhabitants and the defensive impregnability of its rocky site far outweighed its isolation and poor access. Cars must be left in the parking lot (18 francs) at the entrance to the village.

The 16th-century **Hôtel des Porcelets,** close to the 12th-century church of **St-Vincent** (where local shepherds continue an age-old tradition of herding their lambs to midnight mass at Christmas), features some 18th-century frescoes and a small but choice collection of contemporary art. ⊠ *pl. Hervain,* ☎ *04–90–54–36–99.* ☞ *34 frs; joint ticket with Musée Lapidaire and Ville Morte.* ◷ *Easter–Oct., daily 9–noon and 2–6.*

Enter the **Ville Morte** through the 14th-century Tour-de-Brau on rue Neuve. The tower houses the **Musée Lapidaire,** displaying locally excavated sculptures and ceramics. You can wander at will amid the rocks and ruins of the Dead Town. A 13th-century castle stands at one end of the clifftop and, at the other, the **Tour Paravelle** and the **Monument Charloun Rieu.** From here, you can enjoy a magnificent view of Arles and the Camargue as far as Stes-Maries-de-la-Mer. ⊠ *la Citadelle,* ☎ *04–90–54–37–37.* ☞ *34 frs; joint ticket with museums.* ◷ *Daily 9:15–6:15.*

Half a mile north of Les Baux, off D27, is the **Cathédrale d'Images,** where the majestic setting of the old bauxite quarries, with their towering rock faces and stone pillars, is used as a colossal screen for nature-based films (Jacques Cousteau gets frequent billing). ⊠ *rte. de Maillane,* ☎ *04–90–54–38–65.* ☞ *40 frs.* ◷ *Mid-Feb.–mid-Nov., daily 10–6. Some special exhibitions are held mid-Dec.–mid-Jan.*

Dining and Lodging

$$$$ ✕▥ **L'Oustau de la Baumanière.** The site of this famed hotel is marvelous: Sheltered on three sides by the rocky cliffs with the village of Les Baux perched high above, the hotel looks down the valley toward the Carmargue. The main compound, with a formal terraces and a large swimming pool has the air of a Roman palazzo. Jean-André Charial, grandson of the late Raymond Thuilier, has inherited the kitchen. His signature, sublime dish is ravioli *de truffes aux poireaux* (stuffed with truffles and leeks). Reservations are essential at the restaurant, which is closed Wednesday. All is not perfect, however—the staff can be reserved and repairs are sometimes delayed. On the other hand, rooms are beautifully furnished with a mix of antiques; the nine in the main house have a sense of grandeur—enormous chimneys, sumptuous fabrics, and solid armoires. Most have a superb view of the valley. Two miles away are 15 less-formal rooms and tucked away in a third, small vine-covered building are three more simple but charming rooms. ⊠ *Val d'Enfer, 13520,* ☎ *04–90–54–33–07,* ℻ *04–90–54–40–46. 25 rooms with bath. Restaurant, pool, 2 tennis courts, horseback riding. AE, DC, MC, V. Closed late Jan.–early Mar.*

St-Rémy de Provence

★ ⑲ *8 km (5 mi) north of Les Baux, 24 km (15 mi) east of Arles, 19 km (12 mi) south of Avignon.*

The small town of St-Rémy de Provence was founded in the 6th century BC and known as Glanum to the Romans. St-Rémy is renowned for its outstanding Roman remains: Temples, baths, forum, and houses have been excavated, while the Mausoleum and Arc Municipal (Triumphal Arch) welcome visitors as they enter the town.

The **Roman Mausoleum** was erected around AD 100; the four bas-reliefs around its base, depicting ancient battle scenes, are stunningly preserved. The Mausoleum is composed of four archways topped by a circular colonnade. The nearby **Arc Municipal** is a few decades older and has suffered heavily; the upper half has crumbled away, although you can still make out some of the stone carvings.

Excavations of **Glanum** began in 1921, and a tenth of the original Roman town has now been unearthed. The remains, spread over 300 yards along what was once the Aurelian Way between Arles and Milan, are less spectacular than the arch and mausoleum, but you can still see that they were once temples, fountains, gateways, baths, houses, and a forum. ☎ 04–90–92–23–79. ⊠ 32 frs. ⊙ Apr.–Sept., daily 9–noon and 2–6; Oct.–Mar., daily 9:30–noon and 2–5.

Many of the finds—statues, pottery, and jewelry—can also be examined at the town museum, **Le Musée Archéologique,** in the center of St-Rémy. ⊠ Hôtel de Sade, rue Parage, ☎ 04–90–92–64–04. ⊠ 15 frs. ⊙ June–Oct., daily 9–noon and 2–6; Apr.–May and Oct., weekends 10–noon, weekdays 3–6; closed Nov.–Mar.

Dining and Lodging

$$$–$$$$ ✕🏠 **Vallon de Valrugues.** This luxurious villa is fast making a name for itself. Rooms have a view of the rocky Alpilles hills or across the olive groves. Chef Joël Guillet, who learned his trade at the famous Négresco in Nice, specializes in imaginative regional dishes like sea bass with calamari, pigeon roasted in lavender honey, and fruit desserts that are a refreshing change from chocolate. ⊠ Chemin Canto-Cigalo, 13210, ☎ 04–90–92–04–40, FAX 04–90–92–44–01. 34 rooms and 17 suites with bath. Restaurant, pool, hot tub, sauna. AE, MC, V.

$$$ 🏠 **Château des Alpilles.** This lavishly appointed 19th-century château lords over a fine park off D31. Statesmen and aristocrats stayed here; today the crowd is as sophisticated. Rooms offer the best in classic luxury, with plush carpeting and polished wood furniture. Many rooms are equipped with kitchenettes. ⊠ Ancienne rte. du Grès, 13210, ☎ 04–90–92–03–33, FAX 04–90–92–45–17. 15 rooms and 4 suites with bath. Pool, sauna, 2 tennis courts. AE, DC, MC, V. Closed mid-Nov.–mid-Dec. and Jan.–mid-Mar.

$$$ 🏠 **Château de Roussan.** A manicured 15-acre park makes a lush setting for this well-preserved 18th-century mansion. The quiet and gracious interior appears virtually unaltered, save for the newly renovated bathrooms. Rooms are large and comfortable, and many have pleasant parkland views. ⊠ rte. de Tarascon, 13210 (2 km/1 mi outside town on N99 toward Tarascon), ☎ 04–90–92–11–63, FAX 04–90–92–50–59. 20 rooms with bath. Restaurant. AE, MC, V. Closed mid-Nov.–Dec. 25 and Jan.–mid-Mar.

Tarascon

⓴ 16 km (10 mi) west of St-Rémy. 17 km (11 mi) north of Arles, 25 km (15 mi) east of Nîmes.

The mythical Tarasque, a monster that would emerge from the Rhône to gobble up children and cattle, came from Tarascon. Luckily, Saint Martha, who washed up at Stes-Maries-de-la-Mer, allegedly tamed the

beast with a sprinkle of
it to pieces. This dra
with a parade. Ta
(☞ Fontvielle
known to al

One of the n
tury **château,** n
might be tempted
tle's massive stone w
the Rhône, are among t.
that the castle was used as
the chapels, vaulted royal ap
rior have been restored to less-
93. ✉ 26 frs. ☉ July–Aug., daily
2–6 (Oct.–Mar. 2–5).

Dining and Lodging

$$ ✕▦ **Saint-Jean.** A dozen cozy, spacious, r.
hind the austere facade. The wood-beam dinn.
dishes, including steak with shallot butter and sa.
Victor-Hugo, 13150, ☎ 04–90–91–13–87, FAX 0·
12 rooms with shower or bath. Restaurant. AE, DC,
mid-Dec.–mid-Jan.

THE VAUCLUSE

Though the Roman presence is still evident in this region, especia.
in Orange and at Vaison-la-Romaine, Avignon's more recent history
revolves around its being the seat of the papacy in the 14th century.
The outstanding geographic feature of this hilly landscape stubbly
trees is Mont Ventoux, but it's the small villages in the Luberon moun-
tains that will win your heart.

Avignon

㉑ 24 km (15 mi) northeast of Tarascon, 82 km (51 mi) northwest of Aix-
en-Provence, 95 km (59 mi) northwest of Marseille.

A warren of medieval alleys nestling behind a protective ring of stocky
towers, Avignon is possibly best known for its Pont d'Avignon, the St-
Bénezet bridge, which many will remember singing about during their
nursery-rhyme days. No one dances across the bridge these days, how-
ever; it was amputated in midstream in the 17th century, when a storm
washed half of it away. Still, Avignon has lots to offer, starting with
the Palais des Papes (Papal Palace), where seven exiled popes camped
between 1309 and 1377 after fleeing from the corruption of Rome.
Avignon remained papal property until 1791, and elegant mansions
bear witness to the town's 18th-century prosperity.

From the **tourist office** (41 cours Jean-Jaurès), Avignon's main street,
rue de la République, leads past shops and cafés to place de l'Horloge
and place du Palais.

★ **㉒** The colossal **Palais des Papes** creates a disconcertingly fortresslike im-
pression, underlined by the austerity of its interior decor; most of the
furnishings were dispersed during the French Revolution. Some imag-
ination is required to picture it in medieval splendor, awash with color
and with worldly clerics enjoying what the 14th-century Italian poet

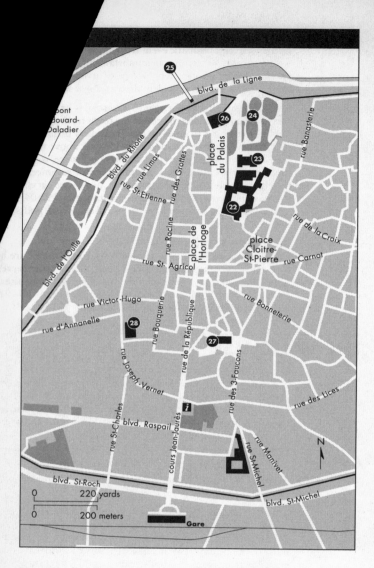

Petrarch called "licentious banquets." On close inspection, two different styles of building emerge at the palace: the severe **Palais Vieux** (Old Palace), built between 1334 and 1342 by Pope Benedict XII, a member of the Cistercian order, which frowned on frivolity, and the more decorative **Palais Nouveau** (New Palace), built in the following decade by the arty, lavish-living Pope Clement VI. The Great Court, where visitors arrive, links the two.

The main rooms of the Palais Vieux are the **consistory** (council hall), decorated with some excellent 14th-century frescoes by Simone Martini; the **Chapelle St-Jean** (original frescoes by Matteo Giovanetti); the **Grand Tinel**, or Salle des Festins, with a majestic vaulted roof and a series of 18th-century Gobelin tapestries; the **Chapelle St-Martial** (more Matteo frescoes); the **Chambre du Cerf**, with a richly decorated ceiling, murals featuring a stag hunt, and a delightful view of Avignon; the **Chambre de Parement** (papal ante-chamber); and the **Chambre à Coucher** (papal bedchamber). The principal attractions of the Palais

Nouveau are the **Grande Audience,** a magnificent two-nave hall on the ground floor, and, upstairs, the **Chapelle Clémentine,** where the college of cardinals gathered to elect the new pope. ⊠ *pl. du Palais,* ☎ *04–90–27–50–73.* ▣ *35 frs. Mar.–Oct., daily 9–7; Nov.–Mar. daily 9–12:45 and 2–6.*

㉓ Avignon's 12th-century **cathedral,** not far from the Palais des Papes,
㉔ contains the Gothic tomb of Pope John XII. The **Rocher des Doms,** a large, attractive garden just east of the cathedral, offers fine views of Avignon and the Rhône.

㉕ The celebrated **Pont St-Bénezet**—built, according to legend, by a local shepherd named Bénezet in the 12th century, was the first bridge to span the Rhône at Avignon. Though only half of the original 900 yards remains, it's worth strolling along, for the views and to visit the tiny **Chapelle St-Nicolas** that juts out over the river. ☎ *04–90–85–60–16.* ▣ *10 frs.* ☉ *Apr.–Sept., daily 9–6:30; Oct.–Mar., Tues.–Sun. 9–1 and 2–5.*

㉖ The medieval **Petit Palais,** situated between Pont St-Bénezet and the Rocher des Doms garden, was once home to cardinals and archbishops. Nowadays it contains an outstanding collection of Old Masters, led by the Italian schools of Venice, Siena, and Florence (note Sandro Botticelli's *Virgin and Child*). ⊠ *21 pl. du Palais,* ☎ *04–90–86–44–58.* ▣ *20 frs.* ☉ *Wed.–Mon. 9:30–noon and 2–6.*

Venture into the narrow, winding, shop-lined streets of old Avignon, south of the Papal Palace. You'll come to a sturdy 17th-century Baroque
㉗ chapel fronted by an imposing facade: the **Musée Lapidaire,** which displays a variety of archaeological finds—including the remains of Avignon's Arc de Triomphe. ⊠ *27 rue de la République,* ☎ *04–90–85–75–38.* ▣ *5 frs.* ☉ *Wed.–Mon. 10–noon and 2–6.*

㉘ An 18th-century town house is home to the **Musée Calvet,** only a few minutes' from the Musée Lapidaire. It features an extensive collection of mainly French paintings from the 16th century on; highlights include works by Théodore Géricault, Camille Corot, Édouard Manet, Raoul Dufy, Maurice de Vlaminck, and the Italian artist Amedeo Modigliani. Greek, Roman, and Etruscan statuettes are also displayed. ⊠ *65 rue Joseph-Vernet,* ☎ *04–90–86–33–84.* ▣ *20 frs.* ☉ *Wed.–Mon. 10–6.*

Dining and Lodging

$$$ ✕ **Hiély-Lucullus.** According to most authorities, this establishment num-
★ bers among the top 50 restaurants in France, although André Chaussy has now taken over as chef for the legendary Pierre Hiély. The upstairs dining room has a quiet, dignified charm and is run with aplomb by Mme. Hiély. Traditional delicacies include crayfish tails in scrambled eggs hidden inside a puff-pastry case. ⊠ *5 rue de la République,* ☎ *04–90–86–17–07. Reservations essential. AE, V. Closed most of Jan., last 2 wks in June, Mon. and Tues. lunch.*

$$$$ ✕▣ **Hôtel de la Mirande.** The most refined and beautifully furnished
★ hotel in Avignon, the Hotel Mirande, is in a former papal palace on a quiet cobbled square at the foot of the Palais des Papes. What was once the central courtyard is now an enclosed, skylit lounge. Tapestries warm the walls of the large airy dining room, where chef Eric Coisel presents his deceptively simple dishes that have complex and exciting flavors. Try the *terrine de gibier* (wild boar) *au fois gras* and the *crepinette de faisan* (pheasant sausage). During the winter, Chef Coisel teams up with other Avignon chefs to give cooking lessons. Rooms are harmoniously decorated with antiques and bathrooms have separate shower stalls and double-ended bathtubs. ⊠ *pl. de la Mirande, 84000,*

☎ 04–90–85–93–93, FAX 04–90–86–26–85. *19 rooms and 1 suite, all with bath. Restaurant, bar, garage. AE, DC, MC, V.*

$$$ ✕🏠 **Cloître Saint-Louis.** Although close to Avignon's train station, sights, and shops, this stately hotel stands calm within its sturdy 17th-century walls. The early Baroque building, erected by the Jesuits in 1611, was a theological school and later a hospital before it became a hotel at the beginning of the decade. Some rooms have exposed beams and most on the top floor have sloping ceilings. There are family suites—unusual in France—for up to four people. ⌨ *20 rue du Portail-Boquier, 84000,* ☎ *04–90–27–55–55,* FAX *04–90–82–24–01. 80 rooms with bath. Restaurant, bar, pool. AE, DC, MC, V.*

$$$ ✕🏠 **Europe.** This 16th-century town house became a hotel in Napoléonic times. In fact, the great man himself was one of the very first customers; since then, everyone from crowned heads of state to Robert and Elizabeth Browning has stayed here. The spacious guest rooms, filled with period furniture, have lavishly appointed modern bathrooms. Make reservations well in advance. The restaurant, La Vieille Fontaine, serves respectable regional cuisine, and you can eat outside in the stone courtyard. Try the chicken with wild mushrooms or the duck liver. It's closed Saturday lunch and Sunday. ⌨ *12 pl. Crillon, 84000,* ☎ *04–90–82–66–92,* FAX *04–90–85–43–66. 47 rooms with bath. Restaurant. AE, DC, MC, V.*

$$$ ✕🏠 **Les Frênes.** This luxurious hotel in a country house has gardens to ramble in, splashing fountains, and individually decorated rooms in styles ranging from subtle modern to art deco. The excellent restaurant specializes in stylish country cuisine; the pigeon with black truffles in a puff-pastry case is always a good bet. ⌨ *645 av. des Vertes-Rives, 84140 Montfavet (5 km/3 mi outside Avignon),* ☎ *04–90–31–17–93,* FAX *04–90–23–95–03. 15 rooms with bath. Restaurant, pool, sauna, 18-hole golf course and 10 tennis courts nearby. AE, DC, MC, V. Closed Nov.–early Mar.*

Nightlife and the Arts

The prestigious **International Music and Drama Festival,** held the last three weeks of July, is centered in the Grand Courtyard of the Palais des Papes (⌨ pl. du Palais, ☎ 04–90–82–67–08). Cabaret fans should try **Les Ambassadeurs** (⌨ 27 rue Bancasse).

Outdoor Activities and Sports

Barthelasse (⌨ Chemin du Mont Blanc, ☎ 04–90–85–83–48) offers lessons for children at Le Poney Club, a children's riding school, and rents horses to more experienced equestrians.

Châteauneuf-du-Pape

18 km (11 mi) north of Avignon, 23 km (14 mi) west of Carpentras.

The hillside village of Châteauneuf-du-Pape was founded in the 14th century. The popes knew their wine: The vineyard here is still regarded as the best of the southern Rhône, even though the vines are embedded less in soil than in stones and pebbles. Several producers stage tastings in the village and sell distinctive wine bottles emblazoned with the crossed-key papal crest.

NEED A   Inexpensive local wines, filling fare, and a cheerful welcome make **La**
BREAK?   **Mule du Pape** (⌨ 2 rue de la République, ☎ 04–90–83–79–22) a good
            choice for lunch; its closed Tuesday.

Orange

29 *10 km (6 mi) north of Châteauneuf, 31 km (19 mi) north of Avignon.*

Orange is a small, pleasant town that sinks into total siesta somnolence during hot afternoons but at other times buzzes with visitors keen on admiring its Roman remains.

★ The magnificent, semicircular **Théâtre Antique,** in the center of town, is the best-preserved remains of a theater from the the ancient world. It was built just before the birth of Christ, to the same dimensions as that of Arles. Orange's theater, however, has a mighty screen wall and steeply climbing terraces carved into the hillside. Seven thousand spectators can crowd in; the acoustics are superb. This is the only Roman theater that still possesses its original Imperial statue, of Caesar Augustus—one of the tallest in existence—which stands, 12 feet tall, in the middle of the screen. ⊠ *pl. des Frères-Mounet,* ☎ *04−90−34−70− 88.* 🖺 *30 frs; joint ticket with Musée Municipal.* ☉ *Apr.−Oct., daily 9−6:30; Nov.−Mar., daily 9−noon and 1:30−5.*

The **Parc de la Colline St-Eutrope,** the banked garden behind the Théâtre Antique, yields a fine view of the theater and of the 6,000-foot Mont Ventoux to the east.

The venerable **Arc de Triomphe**—a 70-foot central arch flanked by two smaller ones, the whole topped by a massive entablature—towered over the old Via Agrippa between Arles and Lyon and was probably built around AD 25 in honor of the Gallic Wars. The carvings on the north side depict the legionnaires' battles with the Gauls and Caesar's naval showdown with the ships of Marseille. Today the arch presides over a busy traffic circle.

Dining and Lodging

$$−$$$ ★ ✕ **Le Pigraillet.** One of Orange's best lunch spots is Le Pigraillet, on the Chemin Colline St-Eutrope at the far end of the gardens. You may want to eat in the garden, but most diners seek shelter from the mistral in the glassed-in terrace. The modern cuisine includes crab ravioli and duck breast in the muscat wine of nearby Beaumes-de-Venise. ⊠ *Chemin de la Colline St-Eutrope,* ☎ *04−90−34−44−25. Reservations essential. MC, V. Closed Jan.−Feb. and Mon.*

$$ 🏨 **Arène.** This stylish old hotel, on a shady square lined with plane trees, prides itself on attentive service and large, air-conditioned rooms. ⊠ *pl. de Langes, 84100,* ☎ *04−90−34−10−95,* 🖷 *04−90−34−91−62. 30 rooms with bath or shower. AE, DC, MC, V. Closed Nov.−mid-Dec.*

Nightlife and the Arts

The **International Opera Festival** takes place the last two weeks of July in the Théâtre Antique (⊠ pl. des Frerès-Mounet).

Shopping

Souleïado's (⊠ 5 rue Joseph-Vernet) beautifully patterned Provençal print fabrics can be bought in lengths or already fashioned into clothes. Fruit, herbs, honey, and truffles can be purchased at the thursday-morning **market** (⊠ cours Aristide-Briand).

Vaison-la-Romaine

30 *27 km (17 mi) northeast of Orange.*

Vaison-la-Romaine, as its name suggests, was a Roman town, now littered with ruins. The **ruins** here are more extensive, though less spectacular than those at Orange; they can be explored on either side of the avenue du Général-de-Gaulle. Parts of houses, villas, a basilica, and a theater have been unearthed; interesting finds are housed in the small museum near the theater. With its lush lawns and colorful flower beds, the entire site suggests a historical garden. ☎ 04–90–36–02–11. ✉ *Ruins and museum 35 frs.* ⊙ *Daily June–Sept. 10–12:30 and 2:30– 5:45 (6:45 June–Aug.); in winter 10–noon and 2–4:30.*

Before leaving Vaison, pause to admire the 2,000-year-old **Roman bridge** over the River Ouvèze and venture briefly into the medieval town across the river.

Dining and Lodging

$$ ✕▥ **Le Beffroi.** This 16th-century mansion, with a nearby 17th-century annex is on a hill in the old town. The spacious, comfortable rooms with old furniture range in price from 300 to 600 francs; the best have attractive views of the gardens. The restaurant offers saddle of hare and gizzard and goose-fillet salad; it is closed for lunch during the week and from late December to early March. ✉ *rue de l'Evêché, 84110,* ☎ *04–90–36–04–71,* ℻ *04–90–36–24–78. 20 rooms, some with bath or shower. Restaurant, free parking. AE, DC, MC, V. Closed mid-Feb–mid-March and mid-Nov.–mid-Dec.*

$$ ▥ **Evêché.** Jean and Aude Verdier offer four rooms in their turreted, 17th-century former bishop's palace in the medieval, hilltop part of town. The warm welcome and the rustic charm of the exposed beams and wooden bedsteads has garnered a loyal following among travelers who prefer character to modern luxury. Breakfast is served on a terrace overlooking the Ouvèze Valley—a good time to try out your French, as the Verdiers' English is rudimentary! ✉ *rue de l'Evêché, 84110,* ☎ *04–90–36–13–46,* ℻ *04–90–36–32–43. 2 rooms with bath, 2 rooms with shower. Reservations essential. No credit cards.*

Mont Ventoux

16 km (10 mi) southeast of Vaison-la-Romaine.

A huge mountain that looms above the surrounding plains, Mont Ventoux is known reverentially as "Le" Ventoux. Weather conditions on this whalelike bulk can vary dramatically: In summer, few places in France experience such scorching heat; in winter, the Ventoux's snow-topped peak recalls the Alps. Its arid heights sometimes provide a grueling setting for the Tour de France cycling race; British bicyclist Tommy Simpson collapsed and died under the Ventoux's pitiless sun in 1967. D974 winds its way from Malaucène up to the summit, 6,250 feet above sea level. Stay on D974 as it doubles back around the southern slopes, then runs from Bédoin toward Carpentras.

L'Isle-sur-la-Sorgue

③① *18 km (11 mi) south of Malaucène, 41 km (25 mi) southeast of Orange, 26 km (16 mi) east of Avignon.*

L'Isle-sur-la-Sorgue is where the River Sorgue, which once turned the waterwheels of the town's silk factories, splits into a number of channels. Silkworms were cultivated locally, one reason for the profusion of mulberry trees in Provence. Some of the waterwheels are still in place, and you can admire them as you stroll along the banks of the river. The richly decorated 17th-century church is also of interest.

Dining

$ ✕ **Le Pescador.** This inexpensive restaurant whose shaded terrace overlooks the arms of the Sorgue is a good place for lunch en route. There

is a wide choice and an excellent-value menu d~~u~~
Partage des Eaux, ☎ *04–90–38–09–69. Closed*

Fontaine-de-Vaucluse

㉜ *8 km (5 mi) east of L'Isle-sur-la-Sorgue, 33 km (20 mi) ea*

The "fountain" in Fontaine-de-Vaucluse is the site of the River ~~S~~
emergence from underground imprisonment: Water shoots up fro~~m~~
cavern as the emerald-green river cascades at the foot of steep cliffs.
This is the picture in springtime or after heavy rains; with summer's
drought and crowds, the scene may be less spectacular.

Dining and Lodging

$$ ✕🏠 **Le Parc.** In the heart of the village, with a terrace overlooking the
River Sorgue, this comfortable hotel has a good choice of prix-fixe menus
and specialties ranging from pasta with foie gras to salmon with mush-
rooms and duckling with berries. ✉ *rue de Bourgades, 84800,* ☎ *04–
90–20–31–57,* ℻ *04–90–20–27–03. 12 rooms with bath or shower.
Restaurant. AE, DC, M, V. Closed Wed. and Jan.–mid-Feb.*

Gordes

㉝ *16 km (10 mi) from Fontaine-de-Vaucluse, 35 km (22 mi) east of
Avignon.*

Gordes is only four miles from Fontaine-de-Vaucluse, but drivers have
to wind their way south, east, and then north on D100-A, D100, D2,
and D15 to skirt the impassable hillside. The golden-stone village of
Gordes with its castle–museum is perched dramatically on its own hill.

On the summit sits the Renaissance **château,** with its collection of mind-
stretching, geometric-pattern paintings by 20th-century Hungarian-
French artist Victor Vasarely. ☎ *04–90–72–02–89.* 🎟 *25 frs.* ⏰
Wed.–Mon. 10–noon and 2–6.

In a wild valley some 4 kilometers (2 miles) north of Gordes (via
D177) stands the beautiful 12th-century **Abbey of Sénanque.** In 1969,
its Cistercian monks moved to the island of St-Honorat, off the shore
of Cannes, and the admirably preserved buildings here are now a cul-
tural center that presents concerts and exhibitions. The dormitory, re-
fectory, church, and chapter house can be visited, along with an odd
museum devoted to the Sahara's Tuareg nomads. ☎ *04–90–72–05–
72.* 🎟 *20 frs.* ⏰ *Mar.–Oct., Mon.–Sat. 10–12 and 2–6, Sun. 2–6;
Nov.–Feb., Mon.–Fri. 2–5, Sat., Sun. 2–6.*

Dining and Lodging

$$$ ✕ **Comptoir du Victuailler.** You'll find only 10 tables at this tiny restau-
rant in the village center, which serves elegantly simple meals using only
the freshest local capon, guinea fowl, asparagus, artichokes, and truffles. The fruit sorbets are a revelation. ✉ *pl. du Château,* ☎ *04–90–
72–01–31. Reservations essential. MC, V. Closed mid-Nov.–mid-Dec.,
mid-Jan.–mid-Mar., Tues. dinner, and Wed. Sept.–May.*

$$$ ✕🏠 **Domaine de l'Enclos.** Small, private stone cottages make up this
charming hotel just outside Gordes; they have deceptively simple ex-
teriors, but inside they have quaint, countrified luxury. The restaurant's
menu of good nouvelle dishes varies with the seasons; if it's offered,
try the excellent aromatic duck. ✉ *rte. de Sénanque, 84220 Gordes,*
☎ *04–90–72–08–22,* ℻ *04–90–72–03–03. 14 rooms with bath.
Restaurant, pool, 1 tennis court. AE, DC, MC, V.*

llon

10 km (6 mi) east of Gordes, 45 km (28 mi) east of Avignon.

Roussillon is a picturesque hilltop village whose houses are built with a distinctive orange and pink stone. This is ocher country, and local quarrying has slashed the cliffs into bizarre shapes.

Bonnieux

11 km (7 mi) south of Roussillon, 45 km (28 mi) north of Aix-en-Provence.

Bonnieux is one of several wondrous villages in the Vaucluse. After exploring, climb to the terrace of the old church (not to be confused with the big 19th-century one below) for a sweeping view north that takes in Gordes, Roussillon, and the ruined château of Lacoste, once home to the notorious marquis de Sade.

AIX-EN-PROVENCE AND THE MEDITERRANEAN COAST

The southeastern part of this area of Provence, on the edge of the Cote d'Azur, is dominated by two major towns: Aix-en-Provence, which is often considered the capital of Provence and is certainly considered the smartest and most cultural town in the region; and Marseilles, a vibrant port that combines seediness and fashion, decrepit buildings, and modern architecture. For a breathtaking experience of the dramatic contrast between the azure Meditteranean sea and the rocky, olive tree-filled hills, a trip along the coast from Marseilles to Toulon and a trip to the Iles d'Hyères is not to be forgotten.

Aix-en-Provence

★ ❸❹ *48 km (29 mi) southeast of Bonnieux, 82 km (51 mi) southeast of Avignon, 176 km (109 mi) west of Nice.*

Many villages, but few towns, are as well preserved as the traditional capital of Provence: elegant Aix-en-Provence. The Romans were drawn here by the presence of thermal springs; the name Aix originates from *Aquae Sextiae* (the waters of Sextius) in honor of the consul who reputedly founded the town in 122 BC. Twenty years later, a vast army of Germanic invaders were defeated by General Marius at a neighboring mountain, known ever since as the Montagne Sainte-Victoire. Marius remains a popular local first name to this day.

Aix-en-Provence numbers two of France's most creative geniuses among its sons: the Impressionist Paul Cézanne (1839–1906), many of whose paintings feature the nearby countryside, especially Montagne Sainte-Victoire (though Cézanne would not recognize it now, after the forest fire that ravaged its slopes in 1990), and the novelist Émile Zola (1840–1902), who, in several of his works, described Aix ("Plassans") and his boyhood friendship with Cézanne.

The celebrated **cours Mirabeau,** flanked with intertwining plane trees, is the town's nerve center, a graceful, lively avenue with the feel of a toned-down, intimate Champs-Elysées. It divides Old Aix into two, with narrow medieval streets to the north and sophisticated, haughty 18th-century mansions to the south. Begin your visit at the west end of cours

Mirabeau (the tourist office is close by at 2 place du Général-de-Gaulle). Halfway down is the Fontaine des Neuf Canons (Fountain of the Nine Cannons), dating from 1691, and farther along is the Fontaine d'Eau Thermale (Thermal Water), built in 1734.

South of cours Mirabeau the streets are straight and rationally planned, flanked with symmetrical mansions imbued with classical elegance. Rue du Quatre-Septembre, three-quarters of the way down cours Mirabeau, leads to the splendid Fontaine des Quatre Dauphins, where sculpted dolphins play in a fountain erected in 1667.

The sumptuous **Hôtel Boyer d'Eguilles,** erected in 1675, is worth a visit for its fine woodwork, sculpture, and murals but is best known as the **Muséum d'Histoire Naturelle.** The highlight is its rare collection of dinosaur eggs, accompanied by life-size models of the dinosaurs that roamed locally 65 million years ago. To get here from Cours Mirabeau, turn left down rue Clemenceau to place St-Honoré, with another small fountain, then make a left again onto rue Espariat. Also notice on rue Espariat the sculpted facade of the **Hôtel d'Albertas** (built in 1707) at No. 10. ⊠ *6 rue Espariat,* ☎ *04–42–26–23–67.* ▣ *15 frs.* ☉ *Mon.–Sat. 10–noon and 2–6, Sun. 2–6.*

Wend your way down rue Aude, lined with ancient town houses, to get to the **Hôtel de Ville** (⊠ pl Hôtel-de-Ville). Pause to admire its 17th-century iron gates and balcony, and the 16th-century **Tour de l'Horloge** (former town belfry) alongside.

It's a mishmash of styles that lack harmony, and the interior feels gloomy and dilapidated, but the **Cathédrale St-Sauveur** (⊠ rue De-la-Roque), just north of the Hôtel de Ville, contains a remarkable 15th-century triptych by Nicolas Froment. Entitled *Tryptique du Buisson Ardent (Burning Bush),* it depicts King René (duke of Anjou, count of Provence, and titular king of Sicily) and Queen Joan kneeling beside the Virgin. Ask the sacristan to spotlight it for you (he'll expect a tip) and to remove the protective shutters from the ornate 16th-century carvings on the cathedral portals. Afterward, wander into the tranquil Romanesque cloisters next door to admire the carved pillars and slender colonnades.

The **Archbishop's Palace,** adjacent to the cathedral, is home to the **Musée des Tapisseries** (Tapestry Museum). Its highlight is a magnificent suite of 17 tapestries made in Beauvais that date, like the palace itself, from the 17th and 18th centuries. Nine woven panels illustrate the adventures of Don Quixote. ⊠ *28 pl. des Martyrs de la Résistance,* ☎ *04–42–23–09–91.* ▣ *14 frs.* ☉ *Wed.–Mon. 10–noon and 2–5:45.*

Cézanne's pioneering work, with its interest in angular forms, paved the way for the Cubist style of the early 20th century. Though no major pictures are on display at the **Musée-Atelier de Paul Cézanne,** the great man's studio remains as he left it at the time of his death in 1906, scattered with his pipe, clothing, and other personal possessions, many of which he painted in his still lifes. Take rue de la Roque up to the broad, leafy boulevard that encircles Old Aix. Head up avenue Pasteur, opposite, then turn right onto avenue Paul-Cézanne. ⊠ *9 áv. Paul-Cézanne,* ☎ *04–42–21–06–53.* ▣ *15 frs.* ☉ *Wed.–Mon. 10–noon and 2–5.*

NEED A BREAK? | Picnic provisions can be had from **Olivier** (⊠ 26 rue Jacques-de-Laroque, near the cathedral) and **Béchard** (⊠ 12 cours Mirabeau).

The **Musée Granet,** south of the cours Mirabeau, is named after another of Aix's artistic sons: François Granet (1775–1849), whose works are good examples of the formal, at times sentimental, style of art popular during the first half of the 19th century. Cézanne is also represented here with several oils and watercolors; there are European paintings from the 16th to the 19th century, plus archaeological finds from Egypt, Greece, and the Roman Empire. ✉ *13 rue Cardinale,· pl. St-Jean de Malte,* ☎ *04–42–38–14–70.* 🎫 *18 frs.* 🕐 *Wed.–Mon. 10–noon and 2–6.*

Dining and Lodging

$$$ ✕ **Le Clos de la Violette.** Aix's best restaurant lies in a residential dis-
★   trict north of the old town. You can eat under the chestnut trees or in the airy pink-and-blue dining room. Chef Jean-Marc Banzo uses fresh, local ingredients in his nouvelle and traditional recipes. Try the *saumon vapeur,* an aromatic steamed salmon, or the oyster and calamari salad. The weekday lunch menu is moderately priced and well worth the trek uptown. ✉ *10 av. de la Violette,* ☎ *04–42–23–30–71. Jacket required. AE, MC, V. Closed Sun., Mon. lunch, early Nov., and most of Mar.*

$$ ✕ **Les Bacchanales.** In the old quarter of Aix, this small, intimate establishment is worth tracking down. From the 130-franc menu, you may want to try the *marbré de lapereau* (stuffed baby rabbit) and the *osso bucco de saumon* (salmon with a light tomato-based sauce). Desserts are particularly good, especially the *tarte aux pommes souf-flés* (apple tart soufflé). ✉ *10 rue de la Couronne,* ☎ *04–42–27–21–06. MC, V. Closed Wed. and Thurs. lunch.*

$ ✕ **Brasserie Royale.** This noisy, bustling eatery on cours Mirabeau serves up hearty Provençal dishes amid a background din of banging pots, vociferous waiters, and tumultuous cries for more wine. The best place to eat is in the glassed-in patio out front. ✉ *17 cours Mirabeau,* ☎ *04–42–26–01–63. MC, V.*

$ ✕ **Domaine de Chasse des Puits de Rians.** In a rural area not far from Aix, this joint venture of two Provençal farmers is characterized by food straight from the land, wine flowing from the flagon, the camaraderie of shared tables, and joyful repartee. Hearty country lunches from a seasonal menu are served. After checking the blackboard you might start with warm goat cheese salad and follow with *jambon de sanglier* (boar haunch) roasted on a spit outside. The room is like a huge work-ing-man's bar, the bare stone floor covered by plain wood tables with well-used checkered tablecloths. A truly baronial hall with a high, vaulted wood ceiling, leading off the main room, is used for big groups. On Sunday local hunters crowd in for a meal, leaving their dogs out-side. ✉ *83560 Rians,* ☎ *04–74–80–58–77. No credit cards.*

$$$$ ✕🏠 **Villa Gallici.** On a slight rise just outside town, this hotel breathes
★   country fragrance. The terrace and the garden with swimming pool are shaded by hundred-year-old cypress trees. In rooms, fabric printed with green and rust chinoiserie scenes covers the walls and the floor-to-ceil-ing windows and there are separate sitting areas. The dining room in the hotel (closed Friday, October to May) is comfortable, but more elab-orate meals are served at Le Clos de la Violette, 100 yards away (closed Sunday). ✉ *av. de la Violette, 13100 Aix-en-Provence,* ☎ *04–42–23–29–23,* 🅵🅰🆇 *04–42–96–30–45. 15 rooms and 4 suites, all with bath. Restaurant, pool. AE, DC, MC, V.*

$$$ ✕🏠 **Relais Ste-Victoire.** At this country inn, the main reason for stay-ing is to dine on Chef Jugy-Berges's modern provençal cooking. Try the *oeufs pochés aux truffes* (eggs poached with truffles) followed by the delicately flavored roast partridge. The most interesting dessert is three different chestnut preparations with thin pastry. The wine list has an extensive selection of Côtes de Provence. The restaurant is closed Sunday dinner and Monday. Rooms are more than adequate: Tile floors shine, fabrics covers the walls, and glass doors lead onto pri-vate balconies. But the single beds joined by one bedspread can slip apart and romantics can finish up on the floor. ✉ *13100 Beaurecueil*

(15 km/9 mi east of Aix), ☎ 04–42–66–94–98, FAX 04–42–66–85–96.10 *rooms all with bath. Restaurant, pool, gardens. AE, DC, MC, V. Closed 1st week Jan., 1 week Feb., and 1 week Nov. (call in advance).*

$$$ 🏨 **Mercure-Paul Cézanne.** Jean-Claude Trésy runs this sophisticated hotel in a stately town house with antiques and ornate furnishings. Rooms are individually decorated with marble, gilt, and period furniture. ⊠ *40 av. Victor-Hugo, 13100,* ☎ *04–42–26–34–73,* FAX *04–42–27–20–95. 56 rooms with bath. AE, DC, MC, V.*

$$–$$$ 🏨 **Nègre-Coste.** A cours Mirabeau location makes this hotel both a convenient and an atmospheric choice. The elegant 18th-century town house has been completely modernized but features a luxurious old-world decor that extends to the guest rooms as well as the public areas. The views and the light make the front rooms worth the extra bit of noise. It's very popular, so make reservations long in advance. ⊠ *33 cours Mirabeau, 13100,* ☎ *04–42–27–74–22,* FAX *04–42–26–80–93. 37 rooms with bath. AE, DC, MC, V.*

Nightlife and the Arts

NIGHTLIFE

Aix has a noteworthy jazz club, **Scat Club** (⊠ 11 rue de la Verrerie). Those who thrive on roulette and blackjack can go to the **Casino Municipal d'Aix Thermal,** which is open from 3 PM to 2 AM (⊠ 2 bis av. Napoléon-Bonaparte, ☎ 04–42–26–30–33).

THE ARTS

The **International Arts and Music Festival,** with first-class opera, symphonic concerts, and chamber music, flourishes from mid-July to mid-August; its principal venue is the Théâtre de l'Archevêché (⊠ pl. des Martyrs-de-la-Résistance). Opera and concerts are performed throughout the year in the 18th-century **Théâtre Municipal** (⊠ 17 rue de l'Opéra, ☎ 04–42–38–44–71).

Outdoor Activities and Sports

Hit the 18-hole course at **Golf International du Château de l'Arc** (⊠ Fuveau, 20km/32 mi from Aix, ☎ 04–42–53–28–38) on a sunny day. **Sellerie Lou Mazet** (⊠ 13680 Lançon-de-Provence, 27 km/17 miles from Aix off N113, ☎ 04–90–42–89–38) offers horseback excursions of the Camargue that cost from 250 to 400 francs a day.

Shopping

Deliciously fragrant soaps and *calissons d'Aix,* ingeniously sculpted marzipan figures, are two specialities of Aix. One thousand different models of *santons,* the colorful painted clay figures traditionally placed around a Christmas crib, can be found at **Santons Fouque** (⊠ 65 cours Gambetta). Aix has several delightful **markets**—the flower market (⊠ pl. de l'Hôtel-de-Ville) on Tuesday, Thursday, and Saturday mornings; the fruit and vegetable market (⊠ pl. Richel) every morning; the fruit, vegetable, and herb market (⊠ pl. des Prêcheurs) on Tuesday, Thursday, and Saturday mornings; and the antiques market (⊠ pl. de Verdun) on Tuesday, Thursday, and Saturday mornings.

Marseille

35   *31 km (19 mi) south of Aix-en-Provence, 188 km (117 mi) west of Nice.*

Marseille, the Mediterranean's largest port, is not crowded with tourist goodies, nor is its reputation as a big dirty city entirely unjustified, but it still has more going for it than many realize: a craggy mountain hinterland that provides a spectacular backdrop, superb coastal views of nearby islands, and the sights and smells of a Mediterranean melting pot where different peoples have mingled for centuries—ever since the

Phocaean Greeks invaded in around 600 BC. The most recent immigrants come from North Africa.

The sizable, ugly industrial docks virtually rub shoulders with the intimate, picturesque old harbor, the **Vieux Port,** packed with fishing boats and pleasure craft: This is the heart of Marseille, with the Canebière avenue leading down to the water's edge. The **tourist office** is at No. 4 La Canebière. For 6 francs you can cross the harbor on a barge that runs every few minutes. Restaurants line the quays, and fishwives spout incomprehensible Provençal insults as they serve gleaming fresh sardines each morning. The Marseillais can be an irascible lot: Louis XIV built the Fort St-Nicolas, at the entry of the Vieux Port, with the guns facing inland to keep the citizens in order. A short way down the right quay of the Vieux Port (as you look out to sea) is the elegant 17th-century **Hôtel de Ville.**

Running east from the Vieux Port is the legendary **La Canebière**—the "Can O' Beer" to prewar sailors—where stately mansions recall faded glory. The avenue has been on the decline in recent years, but cafés and restaurants continue to provide an upbeat pulse.

Displays of costumes, pictures, and figurines can be found in the the **36** **Musée du Vieux Marseille,** housed in the **Maison Diamantée,** a 16th-century mansion with an elaborate interior staircase just behind the town hall. ⊠ *rue de la Prison,* ☎ *04–91–55–10–19.* ⚏ *12 frs.* ◷ *Tues.–Sun. 11–6 in summer; 10–5 in winter.*

37 Marseille's pompous, striped neo-Byzantine **cathedral** stands a few blocks from the Vieux Port, its various domes looking utterly incongruous against the backdrop of industrial docks. If, however, you climb up rue du Panier behind the city police station, or *archevêché* (archbishop's seat), as it is irreverently known, the cathedral's Oriental silhouette, facing out over the Mediterranean, acquires fresh significance as a symbol of Marseille's role as gateway to the Levant.

The grid of narrow, tumbledown streets leading off rue du Panier is called simply Le Panier (The Basket). There is a claustrophobic feel here, heightened by the lines of washing strung from window to window, sometimes blotting out the sky; you can taste some of the dowdy, Naples-like essence of Marseille. Yet, apart from the colorful, sleazy ambience, the Panier is worth visiting for the elegantly restored 17th-century hos-**38** pice now known as the **Musée de la Vieille-Charité.** Excellent art exhibitions are held here, and the architecture—a shallow-domed chapel in the middle of an arcaded, three-story courtyard—displays the subtlety lacking in the cathedral. ⊠ *2 rue de la Charité,* ☎ *04–91–56–28–38.* ⚏ *12 frs (25 frs for exhibitions).* ◷ *Tues.–Sun. 11–6 in summer; 10–5 in winter.*

39 The **Basilique St-Victor,** on the south side of the Vieux Port, stands in the shadow of the **Fort St-Nicolas** (which can't be visited). With its powerful tower and thick-set walls, the basilica itself resembles a fortress; it boasts one of southern France's oldest doorways (circa 1140), a 13th-century nave, and a 14th-century chancel and transept. Downstairs, you'll find the murky 5th-century underground crypt, with its collection of ancient sarcophagi. ⊠ *rue Sainte.* ⚏ *20 frs.* ◷ *Daily 8–noon and 2–6.*

NEED A   Just up the street from the Basilique St-Victor is the **Four des Navettes** (⊠
BREAK?   136 rue Sainte, ☎ 04-91-33-32-12) bakery, where orange-spiced,
                shuttle-shaped *navette* loaves have been made for more than 200 years.

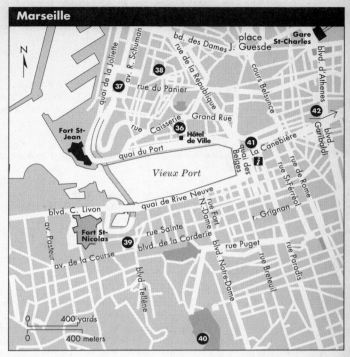

Marseille

A brisk half-mile walk up boulevard Tellène from the Vieux Port, followed by a trudge up a steep flight of steps, will take you to the foot
40 of **Notre-Dame de la Garde.** This church, a flashy 19th-century cousin of the Sacré-Coeur in Paris and Fourvière in Lyon, features a similar hilltop location. The expansive view stretches from the hinterland mountains to the sea via the Cité Radieuse, a controversial 1950s housing project by Swiss-born architect Le Corbusier. The church's interior is generously endowed with bombastic murals, mosaics, and marble, while, at the top of the tower, the great gilded statue of the Virgin stands sentinel over the old port, 500 feet below. If you are not up to the hike, Bus. No. 60 from Le Vieux Port is an easy way out. ⊠ *pl. du Colonel-Edon,* ☎ *04–91–13–40–80.* ◷ *Daily 7–5:30.*

41 Just off the Vieux Port on La Canebiére is the **Musée de la Marine** (Nautical Museum), housed in the big white **Palais de la Bourse** (stock exchange). It gives a history of the port and has an interesting display of model ships. ⊠ *Palais de la Bourse, la Canebière,* ☎ *04–91–39–33–33.* ⊡ *12 frs.* ◷ *Wed.–Mon. 10–noon and 2–6.*

Take a stroll around the **Jardin des Vestiges,** a public park behind the Palais de Bourse that holds the excavated ruins of Greek and Roman fortifications and foundations. Here you will find the little **Musée de l'Histoire de Marseille** (Town Museum), featuring exhibits related to the town's history. One of the highlights is the 60-foot Roman boat. ⊠ *Centre Bourse,* ☎ *04–91–90–42–22.* ⊡ *15 frs.* ◷ *Mon.–Sat. noon–7.*

NEED A BREAK? — Enjoy the Bohemian flavor of one of the sidewalk cafés along the traffic-free **cours Julien.**

42 The **Musée des Beaux-Arts** is in the imposing **Palais Longchamp,** built in 1860 by Henri Espérandieu (1829–74), the architect of Notre-

Dame de la Garde. Its collection of paintings and sculptures includes works by 18th-century Italian artist Giovanni Battista Tiepolo, Rubens, and French caricaturist and painter Honoré Daumier. ✉ *bd. Longchamp,* ☎ *04–91–62–21–17.* ✆ *12 frs.* ☉ *Tues.–Sun. 11–6 in summer, 10–5 in winter.*

Marseille is no seaside resort, but a scenic 5-kilometer (3-mile) coast road—**corniche du Président-J.-F.-Kennedy**—links the Vieux Port to the newly created Prado beaches in the swanky parts of southern Marseille. There are breathtaking views across the sea toward the rocky Frioul Islands, which can be visited by boat.

Ferries leave the Vieux Port hourly in summer and frequently in winter to visit the Château d'If and the Frioul islands; the trip takes 90 minutes and the cost is 40 francs to Château d'If or Frioul and 60 francs to both. The very name of **Château d'If,** the castle where political prisoners were held captive down the ages, speaks of romance and derring-do. Alexandre Dumas condemned his fictional hero, the count of Monte Cristo, to be shut up in a cell here, before the wily count made his celebrated escape through a hole in the wall. ✉ ☎ *04–91–59–02–30.* ✆ *23 frs.* ☉ *June–Sept., daily 8:30–noon and 1:30–6:30; Oct.–May, daily 8:30–noon and 1:30–4.*

Dining and Lodging

$$$ ✗ **Chez Fonfon.** The Marseillais come here for the best bouillabaisse in the world, and past diners lured by the top-quality seafood have included John Wayne and Nikita Khrushchev. You'll also find rock fish soup, grilled lobster and crayfish, and rock octopus served with oil and vinegar and truffles. Chef Alphonse Mounier, known as "Fonfon," is thinking of retiring, but a successor is being trained to his rigorous standards. The restaurant is on corniche J.-F.-Kennedy; the great sea views come gratis. ✉ *140 rue du Vallon des Auffes,* ☎ *04–91–52–14–38. Reservations essential. AE, DC, MC, V. Closed Oct., Dec. 25–Jan. 1, and weekends.*

$$ ✗ **Chez Madie.** Every morning Madie Minassian, the colorful *pa-*
★ *tronne,* bustles along the quayside to trade insults with the fishwives and scour their catch for the freshest specimens. They swiftly end up in her bouillabaisse, fish soup, and *favouilles* sauce (made with tiny local crabs). ✉ *138 quai du Port,* ☎ *04–91–90–40–87. AE, DC, MC, V. Closed Mon., Sun. dinner, and most of Aug.*

$$ ✗ **Dar Djerba.** This is one of the best North African restaurants scattered throughout Marseille, specializing in couscous of all kinds (with lamb, chicken, or even quail) as well as Arab coffees and pastries. ✉ *15 cours Julien,* ☎ *04–91–48–55–36. Reservations essential in summer. DC, MC, V. Closed Tues. and second half of Aug.*

$$$ ✗🏠 **Le Petit Nice.** Only the smallest of signs marks the turnoff from
★ the corniche to the rocky promontory a mile from Le Vieux Port that's the small enclave of Jean-Paul Passédat and his son Gérald, whose fame lies in the many-windowed dining room where regional recipes with a new, lighter twist are served. Though game is available in late fall, the menu concentrates on fish and seafood like grilled *coquille St. Jacques* (scallops) with a light sauce enhanced with baby artichokes. Gérald's enthusiasm and creative flair are at their height in his desserts; the wine list is impressive and pricey; and there's a superb cheese tray. There are smooth stone floors and rich, rare woods and almost no doors or walls in rooms—baths are part of the decor. The "Caesar" suite, for instance, looks out to sea and has a king-size bed at a diagonal with a wood wall at its back. ✉ *anse de Maldormé, Corniche J.F. Kennedy, 13007,* ☎ *04–91–59–25–92,* FAX *04–91–59–28–08. 26 rooms with bath. Restaurant, pool, free parking. AE, DC, MC, V.*

$$$ ✕⌷ **Sofitel.** Mainly because of its idyllic views, the Sofitel has more appeal than most modern chain hotels. Rooms with a balcony are more expensive, but the pleasure of breakfast in the morning sunshine—possible much of the year—is worth a splurge. The top-floor restaurant, Les Trois Forts, has stunning panoramic views and delicious Provençal fare; the red mullet with pepper is superb. ⊠ *36 bd. Charles-Livon, 13007,* ☎ *04–91–52–90–19,* FAX *04–91–31–46–52. 127 rooms and 3 suites with bath. Restaurant, pool. AE, DC, MC, V.*

$$$ ⌷ **Grand Hotel Beauvau.** Right on the Vieux Port, a few steps from the
★ end of La Canebière, the Beauvau, in a totally modernized 200-year-old former coaching inn, is the ideal town hotel. Its charming old-world opulence is enhanced by wood paneling, fine paintings, genuine antique furniture—and exceptional service. The best rooms look out onto the port. ⊠ *4 rue Beauvau, 13001,* ☎ *04–91–54–91–00 (U.S. reservations, 800/223–9868; in the U.K., 0171/621–1962),* FAX *04–91–54–15–76. 71 rooms with bath. Bar, breakfast room. AE, DC, MC, V.*

$$ ⌷ **Lutétia.** There's nothing remarkable about this small hotel, but its rooms are quiet, airy, modernized, and a good value for the money, given the handy setting between La Canebière and St-Charles rail station. ⊠ *38 allée Léon-Gambetta, 13001,* ☎ *04–91–50–81–78,* FAX *04–91–50–23–52. 29 rooms with bath or shower. DC, MC, V.*

Nightlife and the Arts
Marseille's major cabaret-nightclub is still going strong: **Au Son des Guitares** (⊠ 18 rue Corneille). Disco lovers should try **Le Club 95** (⊠ 95 rue St-Jacques. Informal evenings at **Jazz Hot** (⊠ 48 av. La Rose) attract locals.

Shopping
Leading south from La Canebière, the busy rue Paradis, rue St-Ferréol, rue de Rome, and boulevard Garibaldi are good for shopping. The delicately patterned Provençal print fabrics can be found at **Souleïado** (⊠ 101 rue du Paradis). Marseille's famous **fish market** is held on Monday through Saturday mornings at the Vieux Port.

Aubagne

16 km (10 mi) east from Marseille, 36 km (22 mi) south of Aix-en-Provence.

Aubagne is the headquarters of the French Foreign Legion (to get there, take a left off D2 onto D44A just before Aubagne.) The legion was created in 1831 and accepts recruits from all nations, no questions asked. The discipline and camaraderie instilled among its motley team of adventurers, criminals, and mercenaries has helped the legion forge a reputation for exceptional valor—a reputation romanticized by songs and films in which sweaty deeds of heroism are performed under the desert sun. The **Musée du Képi Blanc,** named after the *légionnaires'* distinctive white caps, does its best to polish the image by way of medals, uniforms, weapons, and photographs. ⊠ *Caserne Viénot,* ☎ *04–42–03–03–20.* ☞ *Free.* ☉ *June–Sept., Tues.–Sun. 9–noon and 2–5; Oct.–May, Wed. and weekends, 9–noon.*

☾ The Wild West has invaded Provence at the **O.K. Corral,** a huge amusement park with roller coasters, Ferris wheels, and rootin' tootin' cowboy shows. The less than authentic flavor is more Gallic than *Gunsmoke,* but children love it nonetheless. ⊠ *11 km (7 mi) west of Aubagne on N8, just beyond Cuges-les-Pins,* ☎ *04–42–73–80–05.* ☞ *78 frs.* ☉ *June, daily 10:30–6:30; July–Aug., daily 10:30–7:30; Apr.–May and Sept.–Oct., Wed. and weekends 10:30–6:30.*

Cassis

11 km (7 mi) south of Aubagne, 30 km (19 mi) east of Marseille, 42 km (26 mi) west of Toulon.

Cafés, restaurants, and seafood shops cluster around the harbor and three beaches at Cassis. The fishing village is at the foot of Europe's highest cliff, the 1,300-foot Cap Canaille. Boats leave the harbor from quai St-Pierre to visit the neighboring *calanques* (coves) in the long creeks that weave their way between towering white-stone cliffs. The most spectacular and the farthest of the three calanques visited by boat is En-Vau—you may want to walk back from here along the scenic footpath.

En Route From Cassis, a daring clifftop road runs along the top of Cap Canaille to the shipbuilding base of **La Ciotat,** 13 kilometers (8 miles) away. Stay on D559 for another 19 kilometers (12 miles), through Bandol, to reach **Sanary,** whose old streets and charming seafront invite discovery. At neighboring **Six-Fours-les-Plages,** head right on D616, around the Cap Sicié peninsula, in search of more fine panoramas and a colossal view across the Bay of Toulon.

Six-Fours-les-Plages

28 km (17 mi) east of Cassis.

Six-Fours-les-Plages on the dramatic Cap Sicié peninsula is a sprawling town of limited interest, but three nearby sites deserve a visit. The **Fort of Six-Fours,** at the top of a steep hill, is a private military base that can't be visited, but the views from here across the Bay of Toulon are stupendous. The former parish church of **St-Pierre,** near the fort, features a Romanesque nave and a rich medieval altarpiece by Louis Bréa. Archaeological digs to the right of the entrance have revealed Roman walls on the site.

Just north of Six-Fours (take D63 and turn left following signs marked *Monument Historique*) you'll come to the small stone chapel of **Notre-Dame de Pépiole,** hemmed in by pines and cypresses. It is one of the oldest Christian buildings in France, dating from the 5th century. The simple interior has survived the years in remarkably good shape, although the colorful stained glass that fills the tiny windows is modern—composed mainly of broken bottles! ☉ *Most afternoons.*

En Route From Six-Fours-les-Plages, take D11 5 kilometers (3 miles) to Ollioules, then N8 (direction Le Beausset) through a 5-kilometer (3-mile) route that twists its scenic way beneath awesome chalky rock faces in the spectacular **Gorge d'Ollioules.** A right along D462 will take you to the village of **Evenos,** a patchwork of inhabited and ruined houses dominated by an abandoned cliff-top castle.

Toulon

❹❸ *42 km (26 mi) east of Cassis, 64 km (40 mi) east of Marseille.*

Toulon is France's leading Mediterranean naval base. Leave your car in the underground parking lot at place de la Liberté, head along boulevard de Strasbourg, and turn right after the theater into rue Berthelot. This street leads into the pedestrian streets that constitute the heart of old Toulon. Shops and colorful stalls make it an attractive area by day, but avoid it at night.

NEED A BREAK?	Good-value menus and a cozy setting make **La Ferme** (⌧ 6 pl. Louis-Blanc, ☎ 04–94–42–69–77) a sensible choice for lunch; it's closed Sunday and August.

Avenue de la République, an ugly array of concrete apartment blocks, runs parallel to the waterfront, where yachts and pleasure boats—some available for trips to the Iles d'Hyères or around the bay—add bright splashes of color. At the western edge of the quay is the **Musée Naval,** with large models of ships, figureheads, paintings, and other items related to Toulon's maritime history. ⊠ *pl. Monsenergue,* ☎ *04–94– 02–02–01.* ☞ *22 frs.* ☼ *Wed.–Mon. 9–noon and 2–5.*

Mighty hills surround Toulon. **Mont-Faron,** at 1,600 feet, is the highest of all. You can drive to the top, taking the circular route du Faron in either direction, or make the six-minute ascent by cable car from boulevard de l'Amiral Jean-Vence. ☎ *04–94–92–68–25.* ☼ *Daily 9:15– noon and 2:15–6; closed Mon., Sept.–May.*

Outdoor Activities and Sports

Set out on a sunny day for a game at **Golf de Valcros** (⊠ la Londe—Les Maures, 37 km/23 mi east of Toulouse, ☎ 04–94–66–81–02). The **Wanako Centre du Nautisme** (⊠ av. du Dr-Robin, Hyéres, 19 km/12 mi east of Toulouse, ☎ 04–94–57–77–20) rents sailboats starting at 300 francs for the day and Windsurfers beginning at 320 francs.

Shopping

Stop in at the celebrated fish, fruit, and household-goods **market** (⊠ cours Lafayette) near the harbor from Monday to Saturday mornings.

La Tour-Fondue and the Iles d'Hyères

44 *12 km (7 mi) east of Toulon.*

Boats leave frequently from La Tour-Fondue, at the tip of the narrow Giens peninsula (every half hour in July and August, every 60 or 90 minutes at other times) for the nearby island of Porquerolles. The crossing time takes 20 minutes. Rount-trip fare is 70 francs.

Ile de Porquerolles is the largest of the Iles d'Hyères, an archipelago spanning some 20 miles. Although the village has several small hotels and restaurants, the main reason for coming here is simply to escape from the hustle of the modern world. Filmmakers love the island and use it as a handy base for shooting tropical or South Sea Island–type scenery. You can stroll across from the harbor to the lighthouse (*le phare*) in about 90 minutes, or head east among luxuriant flowers and thick woods.

Boats for two of the other islands leave from Hyères-Plages and, farther along, from Port-de-Miramar and Le Lavandou. **Ile de Port-Cros,** a national park, has delightful, well-marked nature trails. **Ile du Levant** is long and rocky and much less interesting; the French Navy has grabbed part of it, and much of the rest is a nudist camp.

Dining and Lodging

$$$ ✕▥ **Mas du Langoustier.** This luxurious hideout lies amid some stun-
★ ningly lush terrain at the westernmost point of the island, 3 kilometers (2 miles) from the harbor. Mme. Richard will pick you up whether you arrive by yacht or ferry. Rooms are delightful and the views superb. Guests must eat their meals here (no hardship), but the restaurant is open to nonresidents, too. Chef Michel Sarran uses a delicate touch with his seafood dishes; try the fresh sardines in ginger accompanied by the rare island rosé. ⊠ *pointe du Langoustier, 83400 Ile de Porquerolles,* ☎ *04– 94–58–30–09,* ℻ *04–94–58–36–02. 55 rooms with bath. Restaurant, 1 tennis court, beach, billiards. AE, DC, MC, V. Closed Nov.–Apr.*

PROVENCE A TO Z

Arriving and Departing

By Plane

Marseille and Montpellier are served by frequent flights from Paris and London, and daily flights from Paris arrive at the smaller airport at Nîmes. There are direct flights in the summer from the United States to Nice, 160 kilometers (100 miles) from Aix-en-Provence.

By Car

The A6/A7 expressway (toll road) from Paris, known as the Autoroute du Soleil—the Expressway of the Sun—takes you straight to Provence, whereupon it divides at Orange.

By Train

Avignon is less than four hours from Paris's Gare de Lyon by TGV.

Getting Around

By Bus

A moderately good network of bus services links places not served, or badly served, by the railway. If you plan to explore Provence by bus, Avignon is the best base. The town is well served by local buses, and excursion buses and boat trips down the Rhône start from here.

By Car

After the A7 divides at Orange, the A9 heads west to Nîmes and Montpellier (765 kilometers, or 475 miles, from Paris), and continues into the Pyrénées and across the Spanish border. A7 continues southeast from Orange to Marseille on the coast (1,100 kilometers, or 680 miles, from Paris), while A8 goes to Aix-en-Provence (with a spur to Toulon) and then to the Riviera and Italy.

By Train

After the main line divides at Avignon, the westbound link heads to Nîmes, Montpellier (less than five hours from Paris by TGV), and points west. The southeast-bound link takes in Marseille (also under five hours from Paris by TGV), Toulon, and the Riviera.

Contacts and Resources

Bicycling

Bikes can be rented from train stations at Aix-en-Provence, Arles, Avignon, Marseille, Montpellier, Nîmes, and Orange; the cost is about 40 francs per day. Contact the **Comité Départemental de Cyclotourisme** (⊠ les Passadoires, 84420 Piolenc) for a list of scenic bike paths.

Car Rental

Avis (⊠ 11 cours Gambetta, Aix-en-Provence, ☎ 04–42–21–64–16; ⊠ 267 bd. National, Marseille, ☎ 04–91–50–70–11; and ⊠ 92 bd. Rabatau, Marseille, ☎ 04–91–80–12–00), **Europcar** (⊠ 2 bis av. Victor-Hugo, Arles, ☎ 04–90–93–23–24; ⊠ 27 av. St-Ruf, Avignon, ☎ 04–90–82–49–85), and **Hertz** (⊠ Parking des Gares, 18 rue Jules-Ferry, Montpellier, ☎ 04–67–58–65–18; ⊠ 5 bd. de Prague, Nîmes, ☎ 04–66–76–25–91).

Guided Tours

The regional tourist offices' "52 Week" program pools 52 tours offered by various agencies, allowing visitors to choose from a myriad of tours throughout the year, touching on wine tasting, sailing, hang gliding, golfing, gastronomy, and cultural exploration. Contact **Loisirs-Acceuil** (⊠ Domaine de Vergon, 13370 Mallemort, ☎ 04–90–59–18–

05) for details. In addition, local tourist offices can arrange many tours, ranging from one-hour guided walks to excursions that take a week or longer by bus, by bicycle, on horseback, or on foot.

The **Arles Tourist Office** (⊠ 35 pl. de la République, ☎ 04–90–18–41–22) employs 15 guide-lecturers to run excursions of the town and region. The **Comité Départemental du Tourisme** (⊠ 6 rue Jeune-Anacharsis, 13006 Marseille, ☎ 04–91–54–92–66) offers a five-day bus tour called "Découverte de la Provence," which includes full board in two-star hotels and entry to all places of interest. The **Office Municipal de Tourisme** in Marseille features a six-day guided tour on horseback, during which you can stay in simple houses or tents. **S.A.A.F.** (⊠ 110 bd. des Dames, 13002 Marseille, ☎ 04–91–91–10–91) offers a two-day tours of Marseille and Avignon.

Illinois-based **Euro-Bike Tours** (⊠ box 990, DeKalb, IL 60115, ☎ 800/321–6060) runs nine-day cycling tours of Provence in May, June, and September.

Cheval Nomade (⊠ col du Pointu, Bonnieux, ☎ 04–90–74–40–48) specializes in tours on horseback. Or contact the **Association de Tourisme Equestre** (⊠ Chemin St-Julien, 30133 Les Angles, ☎ 04–90–25–38–91) for details.

Hiking
Contact the **Comité Départemental de la Randonnée Pédestre** (⊠ 307 av. Foch, Orange, ☎ 04–90–51–14–86) for a detailed list of trails and outfitters.

Travel Agencies
Wagons-Lits (⊠ 2 rue Olivier, Avignon, ☎ 04–90–82–20–56; ⊠ 225 av. du Prado, Marseille, ☎ 04–91–79–30–80; ⊠ 3 rue des Cordeliers, Aix-en-Provence, ☎ 04–42–96–31–88). **Midi-Libre Voyages** (⊠ 40 bd. Victor-Hugo, Nîmes, ☎ 04–66–67–45–34).

Visitor Information
Provence's regional tourist offices accept written inquiries only. **Comité Régional du Tourisme du Languedoc-Roussillon** (⊠ 20 rue de la République, 34000 Montpellier, ☎ 04–67–22–81–00) will provide information on all towns west of the River Rhône, while the remainder of towns covered in this chapter are handled by the **Comité Régional du Tourisme de Provence-Alpes-Côte d'Azur** (⊠ 14 rue Ste-Barbe, Espace Colbert, 13001 Marseille, ☎ 04–91–39–38–00) and the **Chambre Départementale de Tourisme de Vaucluse** (⊠ la Balance, pl. Campana, B.P. 147, 84008 Avignon cedex, ☎ 04–90–86–43–42).

Local tourist offices for major towns covered in this chapter are as follows: **Aix-en-Provence** (⊠ 2 pl. du Général-de-Gaulle, ☎ 04–42–16–11–61), **Arles** (⊠ Esplanade Charles-de-Gaulle, ☎ 04–90–18–41–21), **Avignon** (⊠ 41 cours Jean-Jaurès, ☎ 04–90–82–65–11), **Marseille** (⊠ 4 La Canebière, ☎ 04–91–13–89–00), **Montpellier** (⊠ pl. René-Devic, ☎ 04–67–58–67–58), **Nîmes** (⊠ 6 rue Auguste, ☎ 04–66–67–29–11), and **Toulon** (⊠ pl. des Riaux, ☎ 04–94–18–53–00).

3 The Riviera

St-Tropez to Monaco

The fabled Riviera is France's open door to the color and emotion of Southern Europe and the Mediterranean—no Pyrenees, no Alps in the way, just an easy slide into Monaco and Italy, across the border. From the medieval hill towns of Provence to the beaches and tiny streets of St-Tropez to the ochre and pastel hues of old Nice, there is a distinct light and feeling here that attracted and inspired artists from Renoir to Matisse to Picasso.

THE RIVIERA CONJURES UP images of fabulous yachts and villas, movie stars and palaces, and budding starlets sunning themselves on ribbons of golden sand. But the truth is that most beaches, at least east of Cannes, are small and pebbly, and that, in summer, hordes of visitors are stuffed into concrete high-rises and roadside campsites—on weekends it can take two hours to drive the last six miles into St-Tropez. Yes, the film stars are here—but in their private villas. When the merely wealthy come, they come off-season, in the spring and fall.

Updated by
George Semler

That said, we can still recommend the Riviera, even in summer, as long as you're selective about the places you choose to visit. A few miles inland are fortified medieval towns perched on mountaintops, high above the sea. The light that Renoir and Matisse came to capture is as magical here as ever and fields of roses and lavender still send their heady perfume up to these fortified towns, where craftspeople make and sell their wares, as their predecessors did in the Middle Ages.

It's impossible to be bored along the Riviera. You can try a different beach or restaurant every day. When you've had enough of the sun, you can visit pottery towns like Vallauris, where Picasso worked, or the perfumeries at Grasse. You can drive along dizzying gorges, almost as deep as the Grand Canyon. You can disco or gamble the night away in Monte Carlo and shop for the best in Cannes or Nice. Only minutes from the beaches are some of the world's most famous modern art museums, featuring the works of artists who were captivated by the light and color of the Côte d'Azur.

Pleasures and Pastimes

Dining
Though prices often scale Parisian heights, the Riviera shares its cuisine with Provence—vegetable and fish dishes prepared with vivid seasonings. The most famous is bouillabaisse, a fish stew. Local fish is scarce, however, so dishes like *loup flambé* (sea bass with fennel and anise liqueur), braised tuna, and even fresh sardines are priced accordingly. *Estocaficada* (a stockfish stew with garlic and olives) is a Nice specialty as is *pan bagna* (salad in a bun) and *poulpe à la niçoise* (octopus in tomato sauce). With Italy so close, it's no surprise that many menus feature such specialties as ravioli and potato gnocchi. Try vegetable *soupe au pistou* (a seasoned, aromatic soup) or *pissaladière* (a version of pizza with olives, anchovies, and onions). Anise-flavored pastis is the Riviera's number one drink.

CATEGORY	COST*
$$$$	over 500 frs
$$$	250–500 frs
$$	150–250 frs
$	under 150 frs

per person for a three-course meal, including tax (20.6%) and tip but not wine.

Lodging
Hotels on the Riviera can push opulence to the sublime—or the ridiculous. Pastel colors, gilt, and plush are the decorators' staples in the hotels catering to the beau monde. The glamour comes hand in hand with hefty price tags, however, and although inexpensive hotels do exist, they're found mainly on dull outskirts of big centers and in less fash-

ionable "family" resort towns. But less expensive inns can also be found in the hilltop villages above the coast.

CATEGORY	COST*
$$$$	over 1,000 frs
$$$	600–1,000 frs
$$	300–600 frs
$	under 300 frs

All prices are for a standard double room for two, including tax (20.6%) and service charge.

Exploring the Riviera

Also known as the Côte d'Azur, the French Riviera is a narrow stretch of Mediterranean coastline, 75 miles long, extending from St-Tropez to the Italian border. It's best to begin exploring the region on the western end of the coast at St-Tropez. Make Cannes and Antibes your next targets, then head inland to the medieval *villages perchés* (hilltop villages) of Grasse, Vence, and St-Paul-de-Vence. Lastly, visit the area to the east that includes Cagnes, Nice, and Monaco.

Great Itineraries

The towns along the Mediterranean are quite close together—Antibes is practically a suburb of Cannes and St-Paul-de-Vence is just a ten-minute drive inland from Nice—so you can see many places in a short amount of time (the only problem is that you may want to stay forever). In three days, it is possible, and even advisable, to rush along the Riviera, just to see it all. Five days is time enough to visit all of the major spots. With seven to ten days you can thoroughly explore the coast and inland sights, as well as the Riviera's major cities.

IF YOU HAVE 3 DAYS
Numbers in the text and in the margins correspond to numbers on The Riviera: St-Tropez to Cannes; The Riviera: Cannes to Menton; Nice; and Monaco maps.

Start in **St-Tropez** ①: Wander along the quayside cafés and the picturesque backstreets of town. In the afternoon, loop through the ancient villages of **Ramatuelle** ② and **Gassin** ③, then drive along the Corniche de l'Esterel through **Fréjus** ⑥, an old Roman town, and **La Napoule** ⑨, with a stop, if you have time, at the Chateau de La Napoule Art Foundation; get to world-famous 🖪 **Cannes** ⑩ by evening. On day two explore Cannes's ancient upper town—Le Suquet—and walk along the beachfront before driving to **Antibes** ⑬. The perfume-producing town of **Grasse** ⑯ is just twenty minutes inland; from there you can drive through some hill country on your way to the medieval hilltop villages of **Vence** ⑱ and 🖪 **St-Paul de Vence** ⑲ for the night. The next day drive to **Cagnes-sur-Mer** ⑳ and see the Renoir museum, then head to the faded but graceful city of 🖪 **Nice** ㉒–㊳.

IF YOU HAVE 5 DAYS
You can follow the three day tour at a more relaxed pace: Spend a night in 🖪 **St-Tropez** ① and 🖪 **Antibes** ⑬ and stop in the medieval town of **Eze** ㊸ on your way to Monte Carlo.

IF YOU HAVE 7 DAYS
Follow the five day itinerary, but stop for lunch in **Cagnes-sur-Mer** ⑳ on your way to 🖪 **Nice** ㉒–㊳ for a night and day of leisurely exploration. On the sixth day, drive along the Moyenne Corniche, stopping at **Eze** ㊸, on your way to 🖪 **Monte Carlo** ㊹. Visit 🖪 **Roquebrune** ㊾ and spend the night in 🖪 **Menton** ㊿ or even across the border in Italy, on

day seven. Extra days would allow for a run inland to the Corniche Sublime (D71) overlooking the spectacular Grand Canyon du Verdon.

When to Tour the Riviera

October, May, and June are the optimal times to be on the Riviera. Summer is too hot and too crowded, unless you want to be part of the banks of sunbathers watching each other on the beach. From early November through Easter, many of the most famous places are closed. But the ones that do stay open off-season are guaranteed to be good. During any time of the year, it pays to get up early to see the light of the Riviera.

ST-TROPEZ, CANNES, AND ANTIBES

The headlands or *caps* (capes) of St-Tropez and Antibes look across the Corniche de l'Esterel at each other with little but the Iles de Lérins between them. The 60 kilometers (37 miles) of towns, beaches, and the small but vibrant city of Cannes comprise an intense combination of riches that have made this coast into one of France's most sought-after destinations.

St-Tropez

❶ *73 km (45 mi) east of Toulon and southwest of Cannes.*

Old money never came to St-Tropez, but Brigitte Bardot did—with her director Roger Vadim in 1956 to film *And God Created Woman,* and the town has never been the same. Actually, the village was first "discovered" by the writer Guy de Maupassant (1850–93) and again, later, by the French painter Paul Signac (1863–1935), who came in 1892 and brought his friends—Matisse, Pierre Bonnard, and others, too. The writer Colette moved into a villa here between the two world wars and contributed to its notoriety. What attracted them was the pure, radiant light and the serenity and colors of the landscape.

Anything associated with the distant past almost seems absurd in St-Tropez. Still, the place has a history that predates the invention of the bikini, and people have been finding reasons to come here for centuries. First, in AD 68 there was a Roman soldier from Pisa named Torpes who was beheaded for professing his Christian faith in the presence of the emperor Nero. The headless body was put in a boat between a dog and a cock and sent drifting out to sea. The body eventually floated ashore, perfectly preserved, still watched over by the two animals. The buried remains became a place of pilgrimage, which by the 4th century was called St-Tropez. In the late 15th century, under the Genovese, St-Tropez became a small independent republic. Since then, people—and celebrities—have come for the sun and the sea. In summer, the population swells from 7,000 to 64,000.

Off-season is the time to come, but even in summer there are reasons to stay. The soft, sandy beaches are the best on the coast. Take an early morning stroll along the harbor or down the narrow medieval streets—the rest of the town will still be sleeping—and you'll see just how pretty St-Tropez is, with its tiny squares and rich, pastel-color houses. There are trendy boutiques to explore and many cute cafés, where you can sit under colored awnings. Five minutes from town, you'll be in a green world of vineyards, fields, and mountains crowned with medieval villages. Perhaps it's the soft light, perhaps the rich fields and faded pastels, but nowhere else along the coast will you experience so completely the magic of the Riviera.

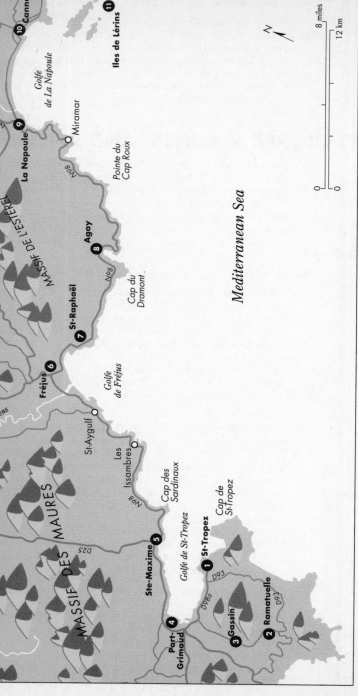

The Riviera: St-Tropez to Cannes

Mediterranean Sea

8 miles

12 km

N

Cannes ⑪

⑩

Îles de Lérins ⑪

D805

Mandelieu

N7

A8

Golfe
de La Napoule

Miramar

La Napoule ⑨

N98

Pointe du
Cap Roux

MASSIF DE L'ESTÉREL

Agay ⑧

N98

Cap du
Dramont

N7

St-Raphaël ⑦

A8

Fréjus ⑥

Argens

Golfe
de Fréjus

St-Aygulf

Les
Issambres

N98

Cap des
Sardinaux

MASSIF DES MAURES

D25

Ste-Maxime ⑤

Golfe de St-Tropez

Cap de
St-Tropez

St-Tropez ①

D93

D98a

Gassin ③

**Port-
Grimaud** ④

Ramatuelle ②

D93

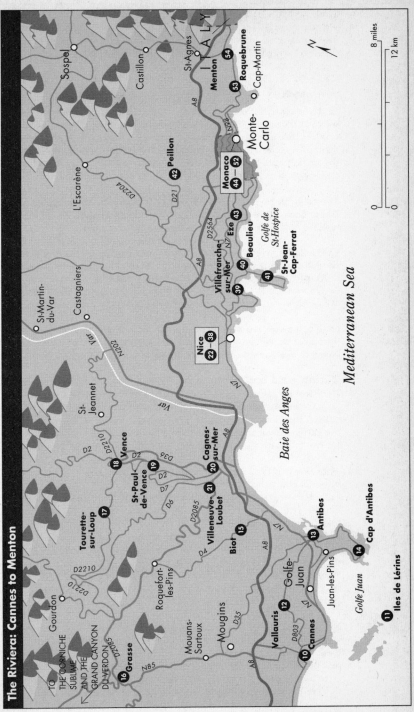

45

The Riviera: Cannes to Menton

I T A L Y

8 miles
12 km

Mediterranean Sea

Sospel
Castillon
St-Agnès
54 Menton
Roquebrune
Cap-Martin
53

L'Escarène
Peillon 42
Monte-Carlo

Monaco
44 — 52

43 Èze
Beaulieu
Golfe de
St-Hospice
St-Martin-
du-Var
Castagniers
Villefranche-
sur-Mer
40
39
St-Jean-
Cap-Ferrat
41

Nice
22 — 38

St-
Jeannet

Vence 18
Cagnes-
sur-Mer
20
19
St-Paul-
de-Vence
21
Baie des Anges

Tourette-
sur-Loup 17
Villeneuve-
Loubet
Biot 15

Gourdon
Roquefort-
les-Pins
Antibes
13
Cap d'Antibes
14

Grasse 16
Mouans-
Sartoux
Mougins
Vallauris
12
Golfe-
Juan
Juan-les-Pins
Golfe Juan

Cannes
10

Iles de Lérins 11

TO
THE CORNICHE
SUBLIME
AND THE
GRAND CANYON
DU VERDON

N

★ Walk along the harbor, filled with pleasure boats, and along the break-water (the Môle), to the **Musée de l'Annonciade,** a church converted into a major art museum. The collection of Impressionist paintings is filled with views of St-Tropez by Matisse, Bonnard, Paul Signac, Maurice de Vlaminck, and others. ⊠ *quai de l'Epi,* ☎ *04–94–97–04–01.* 🎫 *25 frs.* ⊙ *June–Sept., Wed.–Mon. 10–noon and 3–7; Oct.–May, Wed.–Mon. 10–noon and 2–6.*

At the center of the half-moon quay surrounding the **old port,** is the **tourist office** at the corner of rue de la Citadelle. Less than 20 yards from the tourist office up rue de la Citadelle on the left is a covered **fish market**—it's small, but has a marvelous array of *fruits de mer* (seafood). Pass through the market and you'll find a delightful tiny square with produce stalls and shops, which supply the myriad St-Tropez restaurants.

NEED A BREAK?
> Two cafés on the harbor provide dress-circle seats for admiring the St-Tropez scene: **Le Gorille** (⊠ quai Suffren) and **Sénéquier's** (⊠ quai Jaurès), the café with the big terrace beyond the tourist office.

Commanding views across the bay to Ste-Maxime can be found at the **citadelle,** a 16th-century fortress. The keep is home to the **Musée de la Marine,** stocked with marine paintings and ship models. ⊠ *rue de la Citadelle,* ☎ *04–94–97–59–43.* 🎫 *30 frs.* ⊙ *Nov.–Easter, Wed.–Mon. 10–5; Easter–Oct., 10–noon and 2–4:30.*

NEED A BREAK?
> Food at the **Café des Arts** (⊠ pl. Carnot) may be ordinary, but the café is popular with the in-crowd; its closed October–March. For a year-round café that bubbles with activity, try the **Café de Paris** (⊠ quai Suffren).

Dining and Lodging

$$ ✕ **Bistrot des Lices.** You'll find a mix of celebrities and locals at this popular bistro, where interesting food is served by a staff as fashionable as the clientele. Bronzed men and glamorous women lounge in the garden or eat in the pastel dining room. The barman is renowned for his way with a cocktail shaker. ⊠ *3 pl. des Lices,* ☎ *04–94–97–29–00. MC, V.* ⊙ *Closed Jan.–Mar., Nov.–Christmas.*

$$ ✕ **Le Girelier.** Fish enthusiasts—especially those with a taste for garlic—will enjoy the hearty, heavily spiced dishes at this bustling restaurant on the quay. The fish soup and the giant shrimp are local favorites. ⊠ *quai Jean-Jaurès,* ☎ *04–94–97–03–87. AE, DC, MC, V. Closed mid-Jan.–early Mar.*

$$ ✕ **Lou Revelen.** This smart restaurant has outside tables in a tiny square during the summer and an open fire in the dining room in winter. It serves good Provençal cooking, with menus beginning at 125 francs. Roasted shoulder of rabbit with a strong scent of thyme and a wide selection of fish, many with a robust, tomato-based sauce, are good choices. ⊠ *bd. d'Aumale,* ☎ *04–94–97–41–76. MC, V.*

$$$$ ✕🏨 **Byblos.** The Byblos resembles a Provençal village, with cottage-like suites grouped around courtyards. Inside, the atmosphere is distinctly Casbah, with lots of heavy damask, a leopard-skin bar, and Persian carpets on the dining room ceiling. If you can't afford to stay here, at least go to use the pool (for a steep fee). The restaurant, Les Arcades, is lucky to have the talented Philippe Audibert as chef; his grilled sardines are memorable. ⊠ *av. Paul Signac, 83990,* ☎ *04–94–56–68–00,* FAX *04–94–56–68–01. 58 rooms, 48 suites, all with bath. Restaurant, pool, exercise room, nightclub. AE, DC, MC, V. Closed mid-Oct.–mid-Mar.*

$$$–$$$$ ✕🏨 **Le Mas de Chastelas.** This pink-toned old farmhouse, offset by white shutters, was once a silkworm farm. Inside, white walls, mod-

ern furniture, and sculpture by the owner's sister combine to create a cool retreat. The restaurant is usually filled with a mélange of celebrities and well-heeled travelers, attracted by chef Patrick Cartier's traditional regional cuisine, such as asparagus with sea urchins. ⊠ *quartier Bertaud, Grande Bastide, 83580 Gassin,* ☎ *04–94–56–09–11,* FAX *04–94–56–11–56. 15 rooms and 12 duplexes, all with bath. Restaurant, pool. AE, DC, MC, V. Closed Nov.–Easter.*

$$$ 🏠 **Ermitage.** This hotel near the heart of St-Tropez has old-fashioned
★   charm. The rooms' white walls are offset by strong primary colors on the beds and windows; ask for one overlooking the garden and the town. The friendly bar seems always open and owner Annie Bolloreis is more than willing to chat (in English) on the virtues and vices of her hometown. ⊠ *av. Paul-Signac, 83990,* ☎ *04–94–97–52–33,* FAX *04–94–97–10–43. 28 rooms with bath. AE, DC, MC, V.*

$–$$ 🏠 **Lou Cagnard.** This in-town farmhouse is one of the few inexpensive hotels in St-Tropez, just a two-minute walk from place des Lices, so book well ahead. Don't expect great style or comfort, but the rooms are clean and not too cramped. ⊠ *18 av. Paul-Roussel, 83990,* ☎ *04–94–97–04–24.* FAX *04–94–97–09–44. 19 rooms with bath. AE, DC, MC, V. Closed Nov.–Christmas.*

Nightlife and the Arts

NIGHTLIFE

At night, the hottest place in St-Tropez is **Les Caves du Roy** in the Byblos Hotel (⊠ av. Signac); the decor is stunningly vulgar, but the *très chic* clientele doesn't seem to mind. Look your best if you want to get in.

THE ARTS

St-Tropez's major concert hall, which doubles as a cinema, is the **Salle de la Renaissance** (⊠ pl. des Lices, ☎ 04–94–97–48–16).

Outdoor Activities and Sports

The best **beaches** are scattered along a 3-mile stretch reached by the Routes des Plages (beach road); the most fashionable are Moorea, Tahiti Plage, and Club 55. You'll see lots of topless bathers; some beaches allow total nudity. Those close to town—Plage des Greniers and the Bouillabaisse—are great for families, but French vacationers snub them, preferring the 10-kilometer (6-mile) sandy crescent at Les Salins and Pampellone, 3 kilometers (2 miles) from town. **Bicycles** are an ideal way to get to the beach; try **M. Mas** (⊠ rte. des Tamaris, ☎ 04–94–97–00–60) or **Holiday Bikes** (⊠ R.N. 98, ☎ 04–94–79–87–75). If you want to get in some **sailing,** Sportmer (⊠ 8 pl. Blanqui) rents boats.

Shopping

Trendy **boutiques** are on rue Sibilli. At **Soleido** (⊠ av. du 8-mai-1945) you can find very French, printed fabrics and clothes.

Delicious handmade chocolates are sold at **Georget** (⊠ 11 rue Allard). Great produce and daily games of *boules* (like boccie), can be found at the **market** (⊠ pl. Carnot) on Tuesday and Saturday. Tuesday and Saturday are also the days for the **clothing and antiques market** (⊠ pl. des Lices).

Ramatuelle

❷ *12 km (7 mi) southwest of St-Tropez.*

The old Provence market town of Ramatuelle is a twenty-minute drive south of St-Tropez through fields and vineyards. The ancient houses are huddled together on the slope of a rocky spur 440 feet above the sea and the central square has a 17th-century church and a huge 300-year-old elm. Surrounding the square are narrow, twisting streets with medieval archways and vaulted passages.

En Route   From Ramatuelle, follow signs to the ancient hilltop village of Gassin. The ride through vineyards and woods is lovely, and takes you over the highest point of the peninsula (1,070 feet).

Gassin

❸   *7 km (4 mi) north of Ramatuelle.*

The perched village of Gassin, with its venerable old houses and 12th-century Romanesque church, has managed to maintain its medieval appearance. When it gets really hot at the beaches, people come up here to have a drink and contemplate the view and the vineyards.

Port-Grimaud

❹   *6 km (3¾ mi) north of Gassin.*

On your way along the coast, stop at Port-Grimaud, a modern architect's idea of a Provençal fishing village-cum-Venice, built into the gulf for the yachting crowd—each house with its own mooring. Particularly appealing are the harmonious pastel colors, which have weathered nicely, and the graceful bridges over the canals.

Ste-Maxime

❺   *8 km (5 mi) east of Port-Grimaud.*

Fun and lively Ste-Maxime is a family resort with fine sandy beaches that face St-Tropez across the gulf. Surrounded by the high red mountains of the Massif des Maures, the town has the same relaxed feeling and creature comforts as its neighbor across the water, but is less expensive.

En Route   The coastline between Ste-Maxime and Cannes consists of a succession of bays and beaches. Minor resorts—curious mixtures of lush villas, campsites, and fast-food stands—have sprung up wherever nature permits.

Fréjus

❻   *19 km (12 mi) northeast of St-Maxime, 14 km (9 mi) northeast of St-Tropez.*

Fréjus was founded by Julius Caesar as Forum Julii in 49 BC, and it is thought that the Roman city grew to 40,000 people—10,000 more than the population today. The Roman remains are unspectacular, and consist of part of the theater, an arena, an aqueduct, and city walls.

Fréjus Cathedral dates from the 10th century, although the richly worked choir stalls belong to the 15th century. The baptistry alongside it, square on the outside and octagonal inside, is thought to date from AD 400, making it one of France's oldest buildings. The cloisters have an unusual combination of round and pointed arches.

En Route   The rugged **Massif de l'Estérel,** between Fréjus and Cannes, is a hiker's joy, made up of volcanic rocks (porphyry) carved by the sea into dreamlike shapes. The harshness of the landscape is softened by patches of lavender, cane apple, and gorse. Drivers can take N7, the mountain route to the north or stay on the N98 coast road past tiny rust-color beaches and sheer rock faces plunging into the sea.

St-Raphaël

❼ *4 km (2 mi) east of Fréjus.*

St-Raphaël, next door to Fréjus, is another family resort town with sandy beaches, marinas, an 18-hole golf course, and a casino. It is best known as the railway stop for St-Tropez. It was here that the Allied forces landed in their offensive against the Germans in August 1944.

Agay

❽ *10 km (6 mi) east of St-Raphaël.*

Agay has the best protected anchorage along the Esterel coast and was once used as a deep-water anchorage by traders from ancient Greece. It was near here that writer Antoine de Saint-Exupéry (*The Little Prince*) was shot down in July 1944, having just flown over his family castle on his last mission.

La Napoule

❾ *24 km (15 mi) northeast of Agay.*

La Napoule forms a unit with the older, inland village of Mandelieu. The village explodes with color during the Fête du Mimosa in February and offers extensive sports facilities.

Art lovers will want to stop at the **Château de La Napoule Art Foundation** to see the eccentric work of the American sculptor Henry Clews. A cynic and reputed sadist, Clews had, as one critic remarked, a knowledge of anatomy worthy of Michelangelo and the bizarre imagination of Edgar Allen Poe. ✉ *av. Henry-Clews,* ☎ *04–93–49–95–05.* ▨ *30 frs. Guided visits Mar.–Nov., Wed.–Mon. at 3, 4, and 5; Dec.–Feb., at 3 and 4.*

Dining and Lodging

$$$ ✕▨ **Royal Hôtel Casino.** With plenty of marble, plush, and gilt, this is a pocket edition of the Loews at Monte Carlo. Rooms have sea views and balconies and are decorated in pink and blue, with blond wood furniture. Those overlooking the main road can be noisy. Diners at the restaurant can gaze out over a floodlit swimming pool and deliberate among such textbook delicacies as caviar, lobster, and champagne. Unfortunately, the preparation is relatively uninspiring for the price. ✉ *605 av. Général-de-Gaulle, 06210,* ☎ *04–92–97–70–00.* FAX *04–93–49–51–50. 211 rooms with bath. 2 restaurants, bar, pool, sauna, 18-hole golf, 2 tennis courts, cabaret, casino, travel services. AE, DC, MC, V.*

$$$ ▨ **Le Domaine d'Olival.** There's not the slightest hint of mass production at this charming hotel, whose rooms have been individually designed by the architect-owner. It's small, so make reservations far in advance. Rooms have balconies. Some suites sleep six, which brings the price down to $$. ✉ *778 av. de la Mer, 06210,* ☎ *04–93–49–31–00,* FAX *04–92–97–69–28. 18 apartments with bath. Air-conditioning, kitchenettes, tennis court. AE, DC, MC, V. Closed Nov.–mid-Jan.*

Outdoor Activities and Sports

Ask for the "Star du Siècle" brochure at the tourist office for details about canoeing, cycling, riding, climbing, rambling, hang gliding, and rafting. There are also facilities for boating, golf, horseback riding, and tennis, and eight beaches with waterskiing, jet-skiing, deep-sea diving, and windsurfing. The **Club Nautique de L'Esterel** (✉ port de la Rague, ☎ 04–93–49–74–33) gives deep-sea diving lessons to anyone over age eight. The **Plongée International Center** (⊠ port Cannes Marina, ☎ 04–93–49–01–01) also has diving gear. Boats and other water sports equipment can be rented from **Maison de la Mer** (⊠ av. du Général de Gaulle). For windsurfing, try **Sillages** (⊠ av. Henry-Clews). Golf can be played at the **Riviera Golf Club** (⊠ av. des Amazones, ☎ 04–92–97–67–67). The **Poney Club du Soleil** (⊠ Domaine de Barbossi), just a couple of miles inland from Mandelieu-La Napoule on N7, rents horses and offers lessons to children and adults.

Cannes

🔟 *73 km (45 mi) northeast of St-Tropez, 30 km (19 mi) southwest of Nice.*

Cosmopolitan, sophisticated, smart—these are words that describe the most lively and flourishing town on the Riviera. Cannes is a resort town—unlike Nice, which is a city—that exists only for the pleasure of its guests. It's a tasteful and expensive breeding ground for the up-scale, a sybaritic heaven for those who believe that life is short and sin has something to do with the absence of a tan.

★ Alongside the narrow beach runs a broad, elegant promenade called **La Croisette,** bordered by palm trees and flowers. All along the promenade are cafés, boutiques, and luxury hotels. Speedboats and waterskiers glide by; little waves lick the beach, lined with prostrate bodies. Behind the promenade lies the town, filled with shops, restaurants, and hotels, and behind the town, the hills with the villas of the very rich.

At one end of La Croisette, is a **winter casino** and a modern harbor for some of the most luxurious yachts in the world. Before you reach Port Canto, you'll come across the **Parc de la Roserie,** where some 14,000 roses nod their heads in the wind. At the other end of La Croisette is the modern **Palais des Festivals** (Festival Hall), where the famous film festival is held. Just past the Festival Hall is **place du Général de Gaulle** and the **old port** where pleasure boats are moored.

Straight beyond the port on Allées de la Liberté, you'll reach a tree-shaded area, where flowers are sold in the morning, boules is played in the afternoon, and a flea market is held on Saturday. If instead of continuing straight from the square you turn inland, you'll quickly come to rue Meynadier, the old main street. The many 18th-century houses lining the street are now boutiques and specialty food shops. Rue Louis Blanc, off rue Meynadier, is home to the colorful Forville vegetable and general produce market. The **Eglise Miséricorde** with its tiny bell tower, is farther down rue Louis Blanc. The **Hôtel de Ville** (Town Hall), an ornate structure with an elegant stairway, is on rue Felix Faure, parallel to rue Meynadier.

NEED A BREAK? Stop for restoration at one of the outdoor kiosks in the leafy open space off the Allées de la Liberté; the best is the **Kiosque des Sports** on the inland left corner of the Allées.

To get to **Le Suquet,** known as *le berceau,* or cradle, of Cannes, take a right turn off rue Félix Faure into rue St-Antoine and continue spiraling up through rue du Suquet to the top of a 60-meter (197-foot) hill where there is a 12th-century tower overlooking the rooftops of Cannes. The medieval tower in Le Suquet houses the **Musée de la Castre,** filled with Provençal paintings, ethnological artifacts, and medieval archaeological finds. ⊠ *pl. de la Castre.* ☎ *04–93–39–17–49.* 🔳 *15 frs.* ☉ *Daily 10–12, 2–6.*

NEED A
BREAK?

For a coffee, don't miss the wonderfully normal (no tourist prices or tacky decor) **Cristal Bar** (⊠ 1 rue Félix-Faure, on the corner of rue Dr. Pierre Gazagnaire diagonally across from the Hôtel de Ville). For an ice cream, the **Café Poët** (⊠ 7 rue Félix-Faure) is the spot. Don't expect to find the place thick with bards and poets, though—Poët is the name of the owner.

Dining and Lodging

$$ ✕ **Chez Astoux.** For seafood, this stands out among the other restaurants on the block. The ambience is simple but elegant, both on the terrace and inside. Locals go to the seafood stall and restaurant next door, Astoux & Brun, for their own kitchens and their pockets. ⊠ 43 rue Felix-Faure, ☎ 04–93–39–06–22. AE, DC, MC, V.

$$ ✕ **La Mère Besson.** Locals come to this quiet family restaurant, for its authentic Provençal fare. Go on Friday for the aïoli, a heaped platter of fish, seafood, and vegetables in a thick garlic mayonnaise. The lapin farci (stuffed rabbit) is equally superb. The decor is classical. ⊠ 13 rue des Frères-Pradignac, ☎ 04–93–39–59–24. AE, DC, MC, V. Closed Sat. lunch and Sun.

$ ✕ **Au Bec Fin.** Devoted regulars will attest to the quality of this family-
★   run restaurant near the train station. The spirited local clientele and the homey food distinguish this cheerful bistro. The prix-fixe menus are a fantastic value; choucroute (sauerkraut and sausage) and fish are often the main dish. Also try the fish cooked with fennel or the salade niçoise (tuna and potatoes on mixed greens). ⊠ 12 rue du 24-Août, ☎ 04–93–38–35–86. AE, DC, MC, V. Closed Sat. dinner, Sun., and mid-Dec.–mid-Jan.

$$$$ ✕🏨 **Carlton Intercontinental.** Built at the turn of the century right on the seafront, the gleaming white Carlton is elegantly old-fashioned and opulent. Service, though, is not what it used to be, and some rooms are cramped. Those in the west wing are quieter and have terrific views. The restaurant, La Côte, serves haute cuisine in an imposingly formal atmosphere (it's closed Tuesday, Wednesday, and November to December); La Belle Otéro has a terrace overlooking La Croisette; and the Grill Room is simpler but still impressive. The bar is one of the places in town. ⊠ 58 bd. de la Croisette, 06400, ☎ 04–93–68–91–68, FAX 04–93–38–20–90. 325 rooms with bath. 3 restaurants, bar, health club, beach, casino. AE, DC, MC, V.

$$$$ ✕🏨 **Gray d'Albion.** This striking contemporary hotel is the last word in state-of-the-art luxury. Its white facade is austere; inside, the atmosphere is ultra-sophisticated. Rooms are fitted with slick, modern accessories. Comfort is the key word, making up for the lack of sea views. There are a number of restaurants; the Royal Gray is one of Cannes's most fashionable; it's closed Sunday, Monday, and February. ⊠ 38 rue des Serbes, 06400, ☎ 04–92–99–79–79, FAX 04–93–99–26–10. 174 rooms with bath. 3 restaurants, beach, dance club. AE, DC, MC, V.

$$$$ ✕🏨 **Majestic.** Unlike the other "palaces" that line La Croisette, this has a more discreet, less blatantly luxurious charm. Rooms are spacious and traditional in decor. Service is impeccable. The restaurant offers excellent and reasonably priced fare all year. ⊠ 14 bd. de la Croisette, 06400, ☎ 04–92–98–77–00, FAX 04–93–38–97–90. 262 rooms, 25 apartments with bath. Air-conditioning, pool, golf course, tennis courts, parking (fee). AE, DC, MC, V. Closed early Nov.–mid-Dec.

$$$$ ✕🏨 **Martinez.** The Art Deco Martinez still manages to retain an at-
★   mosphere of indulgence. Rooms are decorated in cool blues and salmons, with wooden furniture. One of the hotel's biggest assets is the Palme d'Or restaurant, where chef Christian Willer draws lavish praise for his modern cuisine; it's closed Monday and Tuesday lunch, mid-November to mid-December, and February. ⊠ 73 bd. de la Croisette, 06400, ☎ 04–92–98–73–00, FAX 04–93–39–67–82. 418

rooms and 12 apartments with bath. 3 restaurants, bar, pool, 7 tennis courts, beach. Closed mid-Nov.–mid-Jan. AE, DC, MC, V.

$$$$ ✕ ⌂ **Noga Hilton.** On the site of the old Palais des Festivals, the Noga has "*Palais Croisette*" unashamedly emblazoned on its gleaming white-and-glass facade. Service and comfort are as you'd expect from the luxury Hilton chain. Chef Jean-Yves Méraud oversees the hotel's four restaurants, including a Caviar House, a round-the-clock brasserie, a beach diner across the road, and the upscale, Italian La Scala. ⌂ *50 bd. de la Croisette, 06400,* ☎ *04–92–99–70–00,* FAX *04–92–99–70–11. 229 rooms with bath and 45 suites, some with Jacuzzis. 4 restaurants, 3 bars, pool, health club, beach. AE, DC, MC, V.*

$$$ ⌂ **Le Fouquet's.** If you're looking for a comfortable base from which to explore in a quiet residential neighborhood, this is the place. The ambience is welcoming—from the brightly lit archway, plants, and mirrors to the large rooms, decorated in warm shades and decked out with lots of French flounce. ⌂ *2 Rond-Point Duboys-d'Angers, 06400,* ☎ *04–93–38–75–81,* FAX *04–92–98–03–39. 10 rooms with bath. AE, DC, MC, V. Closed Nov.–Dec.*

$$ ⌂ **Le Mondial.** A three-minute walk from the beach takes you to this six-story hotel, a haven of unpretentious lodging. Many rooms offer sea views and most have small terraces, though the hotel is in the heart of the commercial center, 250 yards from the train station. ⌂ *77 rue d'Antibes, 06400,* ☎ *04–93–68–70–00,* FAX *04–93–99–39–11. No credit cards. Closed Nov.*

$–$$ ⌂ **Beverly.** Halfway between the train station and La Croisette, this little hotel offers some of the best value in central Cannes. The quieter rooms (some with small balconies) are at the back. ⌂ *14 rue Hoche, 06400,* ☎ *04–93–39–10–66,* FAX *04–92–98–65–63. 19 rooms, 16 with shower. AE, MC, V. Closed Dec.*

$–$$ ⌂ **Touring Hôtel.** This simple but elegant little hotel in an ancient Cannes town house is just five minutes from the beach and two minutes from the train station. The place manages to retain a distinct old-world flavor thanks to its high ceilings, solid furnishings, floor-to-ceiling windows and small balconies. ⌂ *11 rue Hoche, 06400,* ☎ *04–93–38–34–40,* FAX *04–93–38–73–34. 30 rooms with bath. AE, DC, MC, V.*

Nightlife and the Arts

Studio-Circus (⌂ 48 bd. de la République) is one of the top night spots in Cannes. **Jimmy'z** (⌂ Palais des Festivals) admits celebrities, stars, and starlets, but not necessarily everyone else; the cabaret shows are legendary. For insomniacs and gamblers, the Carlton Intercontinental and Noga Hilton hotels (☞ Lodging, *above*) both have **casinos.** There's also one in Palm Beach, at the eastern end of La Croisette.

The Riviera's cultural calendar is splashy and star-studded, and never more so than during the **Cannes Film Festival** in May.

Outdoor Activities and Sports

One of Cannes's most fashionable **beaches** belongs to the Carlton Hotel. If you're not lying on the beach, tool around town or take a scenic ride to Cap Ferrat on a **bike** from the train station (⌂ pl. de la Gare). If you want to sail the blue waters of the Mediterranean contact the **Yacht Club de Cannes** (⌂ Palm Beach Port) or **Camper & Nicholson's** (⌂ Port Canto). Windsurfing equipment can be rented from **Le Club Nautique La Croisette** (⌂ plage Pointe Palm-Beach) and the **Centre Nautique Municipal** (⌂ 9 rue Esprit-Violet).

Golf courses in town include, **Golf de Biot** (✉ La Bastide du Roy, ☎ 04–93–65–08–48) and **Golf Cannes-Mandelieu** (✉ rte. du Golf, ☎ 04–93–49–55–39).

Shopping

Cannes is one of the Riviera's top spots for chic clothing. Some of the most exclusive shops are **Alexandra** (✉ Rond-Point Duboys-d'Angers), **Cacharel** (✉ 16 rue des Belges), **Chanel** (✉ 5 la Croisette), **Révillon** (✉ 45 la Croisette), and **Yves St-Laurent** (✉ 44 la Croisette). For well-cut menswear, try **Cerruti** (✉ 15 rue des Serbes), **Christian Dior** (✉ 38 rue des Serbes), and **Francesco Smalto** (✉ 38 rue des Serbes). For clothes in printed fabrics and helpful service try **Soleido** (✉ 17 la Croisette). For anyone with a sweet tooth, **Schwartz** (✉ 75 bd. de la République), is renowned for candy and macaroons.

During the **market** (✉ Allées de la Liberté) on Saturday you can by anything from strings of garlic to secondhand gravy boats. On the first and third Saturday of each month, an array of old books, posters, and postcards are on sale at the **Marché du Livre Ancien et des Vieux Papiers** (✉ pl. de la Justice).

Iles de Lérins

⓫ *15–30-min boat ride from Cannes Harbor.*

You may want to visit the peaceful Iles de Lérins (Lerin Islands) off the coast of Cannes to escape the crowds. The ferry (☎ 04–93–39–11–82) leaves from Cannes's harbor (near the Palais des Festivals) and takes 15 minutes and costs 45 francs to reach **Ste-Marguerite,** an island of wooded hills and a tiny main street lined with fishermen's houses. It takes 30 minutes and costs 50 francs to get to its sister island, the wilder and quieter **St-Honorat,** named for the monk who started a monastery on the island. A ticket to both islands costs 60 francs. Boats leave approximately every hour.

Vallauris

⓬ *5 km (3 mi) from Cannes on D803, 6 km (4 mi) from Antibes.*

In the pottery-making center of Vallauris, ceramics are on sale throughout the village, and several workshops can be visited. Picasso spurred a resurgence of activity when he settled here in 1947 and created some whimsically beautiful pieces. The fresco in the tunnel-like medieval chapel of the former priory—now the **Musée National Picasso**—was done by Picasso. ✉ *pl. de la Libération,* ☎ *04–93–64–18–05.* 🎫 *15 frs.* ⌚ *Mid-Dec.–Oct., Wed.–Mon. 10–noon and 2–6 (until 5 in winter).*

Antibes

⓭ *11 km (7 mi) northeast of Cannes.*

Founded as a Greek trading port in the 4th century BC, Antibes is now a resort town, fishing port, and, until recently, an important rose-growing center. Antibes officially forms one town (dubbed "Juan-tibes") with the newer, Juan-les-Pins to the south, where beach and nightlife attract a younger and less affluent crowd. In the summer, the mood is especially frenetic.

Avenue de l'Amiral-Grasse runs along the seafront from the harbor to the marketplace, a colorful sight most mornings. The church of the **Immaculate Conception,** also on the avenue, has intricately carved portals (dating from 1710) and a 1515 altarpiece by Nice artist Louis Bréa (c. 1455–1523).

★ The **Château Grimaldi**, built in the 12th century by the ruling family of Monaco and extensively rebuilt in the 16th century, is reached by steps near the church of the Immaculate Conception. Tear yourself away from the sunbaked terrace overlooking the sea to go inside to the **Picasso Museum**. There are stone Roman remains on exhibit, but the works of Picasso—who occupied the château during his most cheerful and energetic period—hold center stage. ✉ *pl. du Château*, ☎ *04–93–34–91–91*. ⬛ *25 frs.* ⊙ *Dec.–Oct., Wed.–Mon. 10–noon and 2–6 (3–7 July–Sept.).*

The **St-André Bastion**, constructed by the military engineer Sébastien de Vauban in the late 17th century is home to the **Musée Archéologique**. Here 4,000 years of local history are illustrated in continually expanding displays. ✉ *av. de l'Amiral-Grasse*, ☎ *04–93–34–48–01*. ⬛ *15 frs.* ⊙ *Dec.–Oct., weekdays 9–noon and 2–6.*

☾ The **Jungle des Papillons**, opposite Marineland, hosts a fluttering "Butterfly Ballet" that must be seen to be believed. Visitors are requested to wear colored clothing because this apparently stimulates the butterflies into a wing-flapping frenzy. ✉ *309 av. de Mozart*, ☎ *04–93–33–55–77*. ⬛ *30 frs.* ⊙ *Daily 10–5.*

Dining and Lodging

$$–$$$ ✕ **La Bonne Auberge.** Chef Philippe Rostang creates such specialties as lamb in thyme with kidneys, lobster ravioli, and airy soufflés—though the menu changes seasonally. The dining room is a flower-filled haven of exposed beams, dim lantern lighting, and rose-color walls; huge glass windows allow diners a view of the inspired work in the kitchen. ✉ *quartier de la Brague*, ☎ *04–93–33–36–65. Jacket required. AE, MC, V. Closed Mon. (except for dinner mid-Apr.–Sept.), Wed. lunch (July–Aug.), and mid-Nov.–mid-Dec.*

$$ ✕ **Le Brulot.** This bistro is one of the busiest in Antibes. Burly Chef
★ Christian Blancheri horses anything from suckling pigs to apple pies in and out of his roaring wood oven, and it's all delicious. The decor is rustic and chaotic and the seating so close it's almost unavoidable to become part of one large unruly mob at this popular spot. ✉ *3 rue Frédéric Isnard, 06600*, ☎ *04–93–34–17–76. MC, V. Closed Sun., Mon lunch, late Dec.–mid-Jan., last three weeks of Aug.*

$$$$ ✕🖾 **Hôtel du Cap Eden-Roc.** The "no credit cards" here doesn't mean the simple, inexpensive kind of place this sort of listing usually implies. Payment here is an international banking matter, possibly an affair of state. Crystal chandeliers, gilt mirrors, gleaming antique furniture, and lots of marble make it a glorious testimony to the opulence of another age. Rooms are enormous and feature the same impressive decor. The glass-fronted Pavillon Eden Roc is the place for lobster thermidor, accompanied by champagne. ✉ *bd. Kennedy, 06600 Antibes*, ☎ *04–93–61–39–01*, 🇫🇦🇽 *04–93–67–76–04. 112 rooms with bath. Restaurant, pool, 5 tennis courts. No credit cards. Closed Nov.–Easter.*

$$$$ ✕🖾 **Juana.** This luxuriously renovated '30s hotel sits opposite the casino, a couple of blocks from the beach. Pine trees tower over the grounds and the white marble pool. Rooms are large and individually decorated. Chef Christian Morisset wins praise for his fine seafood at La Terrasse, one of the best restaurants on the Côte d'Azur. Eat outside on the terrace, overlooking the palm trees in the landscaped garden. ✉ *av. Georges-Gallice, 06160 Juan-les-Pins*, ☎ *04–93–61–08–70*, 🇫🇦🇽 *04–93–61–76–60. 45 rooms with bath. Restaurant, bar, pool. No credit cards. Closed late Oct.–mid-Apr.*

$$–$$$ ✕🖾 **Auberge de l'Esterel.** The affable Denis Latouche runs the best moderately priced restaurant in Juan-les-Pins, lending a nouvelle twist to local dishes; try the monkfish and, for dessert, the lemon tart. The secluded garden is a romantic setting for dinner under the stars. Rooms are in the small attached hotel. ⊠ *21 rue des Iles, Juan-les-Pins,* ☎ *04–93–61–74–11. 15 rooms, 6 with bath. MC, V. Closed mid-Nov.–mid-Dec., part of Feb., Sun. dinner, and Mon.*

$$ ✕🏠 **Auberge Provençale.** The six rooms in this one-time abbey, com-
★ plete with exposed beams, canopied beds, and lovely antique furniture, seem straight from some romantic Victor Hugo novel. The dining room and the covered garden are decorated with the same impeccable taste; the cuisine features fresh seafood, lamb, and duck grilled over wood coals. The bouillabaisse is excellent. Monsieur Martin is an excellent host. The restaurant is closed Monday and Tuesday lunch. ⊠ *61 pl. Nationale, 06600,* ☎ *04–93–34–13–24,* 𝔽𝔸𝕏 *04–93–34–89–88. 6 rooms with bath. Restaurant. AE, DC, MC, V.*

$$ ✕🏠 **Le Mas Djoliba.** There are only 14 rooms in this converted Provençal farmhouse. The salon features an airy bamboo-shoot motif, while the rooms, painted in a range of pastel shades, have antique furnishings. Choose between views of the park or the sea. The restaurant is open for dinner only and is closed October to March. ⊠ *29 av. de Provence, 06600 Antibes,* ☎ *04–93–34–02–48,* 𝔽𝔸𝕏 *04–93–34–05–81. 14 rooms with bath. Restaurant. AE, DC, MC, V. Closed Jan.*

Nightlife and the Arts

The **Eden Casino** (⊠ bd. Baudoin, Juan-les-Pins, ☎ 04–92–93–71–71) draws a young crowd. For raging 'til dawn, **La Siesta** (⊠ rte. du Bord de Mer) is an enormous setup, with dance floors, bars, and roulette, bars; it's open summer only.

Outdoor Activities and Sports

Bikes can be rented from **Juan Midi Location** (⊠ 93 bd. Wilson, ☎ 04–92–93–05–06) and **Holiday Bikes** (⊠ 93 bd. Wilson, ☎ 04–93–61–51–51).

Cap d'Antibes

★ ⓮ *2 km (1 mi) from Antibes.*

The Cap d'Antibes peninsula is rich and residential, with beaches, views, and large villas hidden in luxurious vegetation. Barely two miles long by a mile wide, it offers a perfect day's outing from Antibes.

An ideal walk is along the **Sentier des Douaniers,** the customs officers' path. From **Pointe Bacon** there is a striking view over the Baie des Anges (Bay of Angels) toward Nice. Climb up to the **Plateau de la Garoupe** for a sweeping view inland over the Esterel massif and the Alps. The **Sanctuaire de la Garoupe** (Sailors' Chapel) has a 14th-century icon, a statue of Our Lady of Safe Homecoming, and numerous frescoes and votive offerings.

The **phare** (lighthouse) alongside the sailor's chapel on the Plateau de la Garoupe has a powerful beam that carries more than 40 miles out to sea. ⊠ *Plateau de la Garoupe.* 🎫 *Free.* ☉ *Nov.–Mar., daily 10:30–12:30 and 2:30–5; Apr.–Oct., daily 10:30–12:30 and 2–7:30.*

A lovely place to spend an hour is in the **Jardin Thuret,** established by botanist Gustave Thuret (1817–75) in 1856 as France's first garden for subtropical plants and trees. Now run by the Ministry of Agriculture, the garden remains a haven for rare, exotic plants. ⊠ *bd. du Cap.* 🎫 *Free.* ☉ *Weekdays 8–12:30 and 2–5:30.*

At the southwest tip of the peninsula, opposite the luxurious Grand Hôtel du Cap d'Antibes, is the **Musée Naval & Napoléonien,** a former battery, where you can spend an interesting hour scanning Napoleonic proclamations and viewing scale models of oceangoing ships. ☒ *Batterie du Grillon, av. Kennedy,* ☎ *04–93–61–45–32.* ☒ *20 frs.* ☾ *Apr.–Sept., weekdays 10–noon and 3–7, Sat. 10–noon; Nov.–Mar., weekdays 9:30–noon and 2:15–4, Sat. 9:30–noon.*

Dining and Lodging

$$$–$$$$ ✕ **Restaurant de Bacon.** This is the Riviera's top spot for bouillabaisse
★   and other fish dishes. The prices generally match the quality, except
for the bargain 250-franc menu. The Sordellos have owned Bacon since
1948, and don't regard a fish as fresh unless it's still twitching. Ask
for a table outside on the airy terrace overlooking the old port and the
bay. ☒ *bd. de Bacon,* ☎ *04–93–61–50–02. Reservations essential.
Jacket required. AE, DC, MC, V. Closed Mon. and mid-Nov.–Jan.*

$$ 🏠 **Manoir Castel Garoupe Axa.** This old inn is known locally as Motel
Axa, after owner Madame Axa. She speaks little English, but smiles
and a minimal grasp of French will do. Not deluxe by any means, it's
a friendly place and only two-minutes from the beach. Rooms have
balconies with countryside views. Breakfast is served. ☒ *959 bd. de
la Garoupe, 06600 Cap d'Antibes,* ☎ *04–93–61–36–51,* FAX *04–93–
67–74–88. 22 rooms with bath. Kitchenettes, pool, 1 tennis court. MC,
V. Closed Jan.*

Biot

15 *4 km (3 mi) northeast of Antibes on N7 and D4.*

Mimosa and roses for the cut-flower market are grown in the charming old village of Biot and glass is made here. The **Verrerie de Biot** (glassworks) at the edge of Biot welcomes visitors to observe its glassblowers. ☒ *5 chemin des Combes,* ☎ *04–93–65–05–85.* ☾ *Mon.–Sat. 9–6:30, Sun. 10:30–1 and 2:30–6:30.*

Artist Fernand Léger (1881–1955) lived in Biot, and hundreds of his paintings, ceramics, and tapestries are on display at the **Musée National Fernand Léger,** a strikingly designed museum, which opened in 1960. Léger's stylistic evolution is traced from his early flirtation with cubism to his ultimate preference for flat expanses of primary color and shades of gray, separated by thick black lines. ☒ *Chemin du Val de Pomme,* ☎ *04–93–65–63–61.* ☒ *32 frs.* ☾ *Apr.–Oct., Wed.–Mon. 10–noon and 2–6; Nov.–Mar., Wed.–Mon. 10–noon and 2–5.*

CANNES TO MENTON

Beginning in the medieval hill towns of Provence, dipping down through Nice and Monaco to balmy Menton (close to the Italian border), the eastern part of the Riviera offers an extraordinary range of sights. From the Grand Canyon du Verdon, France's Grand Canyon, to the casinos at Monte Carlo, there is much to experience in France's southeastern corner.

Mougins

8 km (5 mi) north of Cannes, 12 km (7 mi) northwest of Antibes.

Quaint, fortified, hilltop Mougins, with its cluster of ancient houses, offers splendid views of Cannes and the Golfe de Napoule. The **Notre-Dame-de-Vie** hermitage and the **Chapelle St-Barthelmy** are the village's most interesting sights.

Dining and Lodging

$$$$ ✕🏨 **Moulin de Mougins.** A 16th-century olive mill houses one of the
★ country's top restaurants and a small inn. Chef Roger Vergé's reper-
toire of traditional and innovative cuisine changes seasonally. The intimate beamed dining rooms, with oil paintings, plants, and porcelain
tableware, are perfect for world-class fare. In summer, dine outside under
the awnings. Reservations are essential for the restaurant, which is closed
Monday and Thursday for lunch. Rooms are elegantly rustic. ✉ *Notre-
Dame-de-Vie, 06250,* ☎ *04–93–75–78–24,* FAX *04–93–90–18–55.
3 rooms and 2 tiny apartments. Restaurant. AE, DC, MC, V. Closed
Feb.–Mar.*

Grasse

🔟 *10 km (6 mi) northwest of Mougins, 17 km (10½ mi) northwest of
Cannes, 22 km (14 mi) northwest of Antibes.*

If touring a perfume factory in a tacky modern town is your idea of pleasure, by all means visit Grasse. If you had visited four centuries ago,
when the town specialized in leather, you would have come for gloves.
In the 16th century, when scented gloves became the rage, the town began
cultivating flowers and distilling essences. That was the beginning of
the perfume industry. Today some three-fourths of the world's essences
are made here from wild lavender, jasmine, violets, daffodils, and other
sweet-smelling flowers. Five thousand producers supply some 20 factories and six cooperatives. If you've ever wondered why perfume is so
expensive, consider that it takes 10,000 flowers to produce 2.2 pounds
of jasmine petals and that nearly one ton of petals is needed to distill
1½ quarts of essence. Sophisticated Parisian perfumers mix Grasse
essences into their own secret formulas; perfumes made and sold in Grasse
are considerably less subtle. You can, of course, buy Parisian perfumes
in Grasse at Parisian prices.

Several **perfume houses** welcome visitors—daily 9–noon and 2–6, free—
for a whiff of their products and an explanation of how the perfumes
are made: **Galimard** (✉ 73 rte. de Cannes, ☎ 04–93–09–20–00); **Moli-
nard** (✉ 60 bd. Victor-Hugo, ☎ 04–93–36–01–62); and **Fragonard**
(✉ 20 bd. Fragonard, ☎ 04–93–36–44–65), which is conveniently
central and has its own museum.

A perfume museum, the **Musée International de la Parfumerie,** explains
the history and manufacturing process of perfume. Old machinery, pots,
and flasks can be admired; toiletry, cosmetics, and makeup accessories
are on display. ✉ *8 pl. du Cours,* ☎ *04–93–36–80–20.* 🎫 *14 frs.* ☉
Oct.–May, daily 10–noon and 2–5; June–Sept., daily 10–7.

The artist Jean-Honoré Fragonard (1732–1806) was born in Grasse,
and many of his pictures, etchings, drawings, and sketches—plus others
by his son Alexandre-Evariste and his grandson Théophile—are hung
in the 17th-century **Musée Fragonard.** ✉ *23 bd. Fragonard,* ☎ *04–
93–36–01–61.* 🎫 *10 frs.* ☉ *Wed.–Sun. 10–noon and 2–5.*

The **Musée d'Art et d'Histoire de Provence,** 150 yards away from the
Musée Fragonard, in an 18th-century mansion, houses a collection of
china and Provençal furniture, folk art, and tools. ✉ *2 rue Mirabeau,*
☎ *04–93–36–01–61.* 🎫 *10 frs.* ☉ *Apr.–Oct., Mon.–Sat. 10–noon
and 2–6; Dec.–Mar., Mon.–Sat. 10–noon and 2–5.*

Dining and Lodging

$$ 🏨 **Panorama.** This tidy modern hotel has a pleasant, helpful staff and
well-appointed, soundproof, air-conditioned rooms. Snacks can be

served on request. ✉ *2 pl. Cours, 06130,* ☎ *04–93–36–80–80,* 🅵🅰🆇
04–93–36–92–04. 36 rooms with bath. MC, V.

En Route   One of the most famous roads in France is the **Route Napoléon,** taken
by Napoléon Bonaparte in 1815 after his escape from imprisonment
on the Mediterranean island of Elba. Napoléon landed at Golfe-Juan,
near Cannes, on March 1, and forged northwest to Grasse and through
dramatic, hilly countryside to Castellane, Digne, and Sisteron. In
Napoléon's day, most of this "road" (now N85) was little more than
a winding dirt track. Commemorative plaques bearing the imperial eagle
stud the route, inspired by Napoléon's remark that, "The eagle will
fly from steeple to steeple until it reaches the towers of Notre-Dame."
That prediction came true. Napoléon covered the 110 miles from the
coast to Sisteron in just four days, romped north through Grenoble and
Burgundy, and entered Paris in triumph on May 20.

The Corniche Sublime and the Grand Canyon du Verdon

*From Grasse, take Route Napoléon (N85), turn left after 43 km (27
mi) along D21, which becomes D71 at Comps-sur-Artuby.*

The Route Napoléon leads to one of the most spectacular roads in
France—the Corniche Sublime (D71), which runs along the south side
of the Grand Canyon du Verdon, France's answer to the Grand Canyon.
The Corniche Sublime is not a road for anyone who is afraid of heights.
The narrow lane—just wide enough for two cars to scrape by—snakes
its way for 25 miles along the cliffside, 3,000 feet above the tiny River
Verdon. At times the river disappears from view beneath the sheer rock
face. At the far end of the gorge you'll arrive at the sparkling blue Lac
de Ste-Croix.

Trigance

72 km (45 mi) north of Grasse.

Trigance, a tiny village of stone houses and some 60 souls, is arranged
in rampartlike rings around the château. Chapelle St-Roch stands sentinel to the labyrinth of narrow alleys winding to the ancient bell
tower and the Eglise St-Michel.

Dining and Lodging

$$–$$$ ✗🏨 **Château de Trigance.** Not much remains of the 9th-century orig-
inal, except for the barrel vaulting in the lounge and dining room. Hos-
pitable Monsieur Thomas, the owner, has spent the last decade
reconstructing the fortress and offers comfortable, pleasantly simple
rooms. The setting, on top of a bluff above a small village, gives commanding views of the surrounding hills. The dining atmosphere is
wonderful; the culinary art, average. ✉ *83840 Trigance,* ☎ *04–94–
76–91–18,* 🅵🅰🆇 *04–94–85–68–99. 8 rooms and 2 apartments with
bath. Restaurant, helipad. AE, DC, MC, V. Closed mid-Nov.–mid-Mar.*

Tourrettes-sur-Loup

⑰   *20 km (12 mi) east of Grasse on D2085/D2210.*

The outer houses of Tourrettes-sur-Loup form a rampart on a rocky
plateau, 1,300 feet above a valley full of violets. The town is much less
commercialized than many others in the area; its shops are filled not
with postcards and scented soaps but with the work of dedicated artisans. A rough stone path takes you on a circular route around the
rim of the town, past their workshops: Ask for a map that locates each

of the shops. Also worth visiting is the single-nave 14th-century church with its notable wooden altar.

Vence

⑱ *5 km (3 mi) east of Tourrettes-sur-Loup.*

When you arrive in Vence, leave your car on avenue Foch and climb up to the **Vieille Ville,** the medieval town. The Romans were the first to settle on the 1,000-foot hill; the cathedral (built between the 11th and 18th centuries), rising above the medieval ramparts and traffic-free streets, was erected on the site of a temple to Mars. Of special note is a Marc Chagall mosaic of Moses in the bulrushes and the ornate 15th-century wooden choir stalls.

At the foot of the hill, on the outskirts of Vence, is the **Chapelle du Rosaire,** a small chapel decorated with beguiling simplicity and clarity by Matisse between 1947 and 1951. The walls, floor, and ceiling are gleaming white and there are small stained-glass windows in cool greens and blues. "Despite its imperfections I think it is my masterpiece . . . the result of a lifetime devoted to the search for truth," wrote Matisse, who designed and dedicated the chapel when he was in his eighties and nearly blind. ⊠ *av. Henri-Matisse,* ☎ *04–93–58–03–26.* ⊡ *Free.* ☉ *Tues. and Thurs. 10–11:30 and 2–5:30.*

Dining and Lodging

$$$$ ✕☷ **Château St-Martin.** The secluded, elite St-Martin stands on the site
★ of a Templar castle, surrounded by tall, shady trees. Rooms are exquisitely decorated with antiques and brocade; those in the tower are smaller and less expensive. The excellent restaurant serves Provençal-inspired dishes. ⊠ *rte. de Coursegoules, 06140,* ☎ *04–93–58–02–02,* FAX *04–93–24–08–91. 25 rooms with bath. Restaurant, pool, 2 tennis courts. AE, DC, MC, V. Closed mid-Oct.–early May.*

$$ ✕☷ **La Roseraie.** Although there's no rose garden, a giant magnolia spreads its venerable branches over the terrace. Chef Maurice Ganier hails from the southwest, as do most of his dishes. Polished service, sophisticated menus, and a warm welcome prove that you don't have to be rich to enjoy life in this part of France. All rooms have sunny southern exposure and, like the entire hotel, are furnished with antiques. The restaurant is closed Tuesday lunch and Wednesday. ⊠ *51 av. Henri-Giraud, 06140,* ☎ *04–93–58–02–20,* FAX *04–93–58–99–31. 12 rooms with bath. Restaurant, pool. AE, MC, V. Closed Jan.*

St-Paul de Vence

★ **⑲** *4 km (2½ mi) south of Vence on D2.*

St-Paul-de-Vence is a perfectly preserved medieval town. Not even the hordes of tourists—to which the village now caters—can destroy its ancient charm. You can walk the narrow, cobbled streets in perhaps 15 minutes, but you'll probably need another hour to explore the shops. Your best bet is to visit in the late afternoon, when the tour buses are gone, and enjoy a drink among the Klees and Picassos in the Colombe d'Or (☞ Dining and Lodging, *below*). Be sure to stop into the remarkable 12th-century Gothic church. The treasury is rich in 12th- to 15th-century pieces, including processional crosses, reliquaries, and an enamel Virgin and Child.

★ At the northwest edge of the village is the **Fondation Maeght** (founded in 1964 by art dealer Aimé Maeght), one of the world's most famous small museums of modern art. Monumental sculptures are scattered around its pine tree park, and a courtyard full of Alberto Giacometti's creations separates the two museum buildings. The rooms inside show-case the works of Miró, Braque, Kandinsky, Bonnard, Matisse, and others. There is also a library, movie theater, and auditorium. ☎ 04–93–32–81–63. ⊞ 40 frs. ☉ July–Sept., daily 10–7; Oct.–June, daily 10–12:30 and 2:30–6.

Dining and Lodging

$$$ ✕▥ **Colombe d'Or.** Although you'll have to pay for your room or meal
★   with cash or credit cards, Picasso, Klee, Dufy, Utrillo—all friends of the former owner—paid to stay and eat at this country-feeling inn with the paintings that now decorate the walls. The restaurant has a very good reputation. The Colombe d'Or is certainly on the tourist trail, but many of those who stay are rich and famous—if that's any con-solation. ⊠ pl. Général-de-Gaulle, 06570 St-Paul-de-Vence, ☎ 04–93–32–80–02, ℻ 04–93–32–77–78. 24 rooms with bath. Restaurant, pool. AE, DC, MC, V. Closed mid-Nov.–late Dec.

$$ ✕▥ **Les Ramparts.** This simple, rustic inn built into the town ramparts is a handy alternative if you feel less than compelled to blow a lot of francs for a night's sleep. Excellent Provençal cuisine is served in the restaurant. The corner table in the dining porch is one of the finest perches in Provence. ⊠ 72 rue Grande, 06570. ☎ 04–93–32–09–88. 16 rooms with bath. Restaurant. AE, DC, MC, V. Closed late Nov.–late Dec.

Cagnes-sur-Mer

⑳ 6 km (4 mi) south of St-Paul-de-Vence on D2.

An attractive castle and a Renoir museum make Cagnes-sur-Mer worth a visit. Once a medieval fortress, the **château** is perched on a hilltop, within the walls of Haut-de-Cagnes. Much of it's Renaissance deco-ration—frescoes, plasterwork, and fireplaces—remains intact, and the third floor hosts an art gallery devoted to Mediterranean artists, in-cluding Chagall and Raoul Dufy. ⊠ pl. Grimaldi, ☎ 04–93–20–85–57. ⊞ 6 frs. ☉ Easter–mid-Oct., daily 10–noon and 2:30–7; mid-Nov.–Easter, Wed.–Mon. 10–noon and 2–5.

The painter Auguste Renoir (1841–1919) spent the last 12 years of his life at Cagnes. His home at Les Collettes has been preserved as a **Musée Renoir,** and you can see his studio, as well as some of his work. A bronze statue of Venus nestles amid the fruit trees in the colorful gar-den. ⊠ av. des Collettes, ☎ 04–93–20–61–07. ⊞ 22 frs. ☉ June–Oct., daily 10–noon and 2–6; Nov.–May, Wed.–Mon. 10–noon and 2–5.

Villeneuve-Loubet

㉑ 1 ½ km (1 mi) west of Cagnes.

The tiny village of Villeneuve-Loubet is best known for its gourmet shrine. The **Fondation Escoffier** is a museum dedicated to Auguste Escoffier (1846–1935), one of Europe's top chefs. As kitchen overlord at the London Carlton and the Paris Ritz, he invented, among other dishes, peach melba. This museum, in the house where he was born, displays some elaborate pièces montées in sugar and marzipan and boasts a col-lection of 15,000 lip-smacking menus. ⊠ 3 rue Escoffier, ☎ 04–93–20–80–51. ⊞ 15 frs. ☉ Dec.–Oct., Tues.–Sun. 2–6.

Nice

㉒ 12 km (7 mi) from Cagnes-sur-Mer on N7.

The congested road from Cagnes to Nice at the wrong time of day or year can be enough to put you off the Riviera for life. Tedious con-crete constructions assault the eye; the railroad on one side and the stony shore on the other offer scant respite. Soon, however, you'll arrive at the Queen of the Riviera—Nice.

Less glamorous, less sophisticated, and less expensive than Cannes, Nice is also older and more weathered. A big, sprawling city of 350,000 people—five times as many as Cannes—it has a life and vitality that survive when tourists pack their bags and go home.

Nice is worth a visit, but should you stay here? On the negative side, its beaches are cramped and pebbly. Many of its hotels are either run-down or being refurbished. On the positive side, Nice is likely to have hotel space, at prices you can afford. It's also a convenient base from which to explore Monte Carlo and the medieval towns in the interior. It does have its share of first-class restaurants and boutiques, and an evening stroll through the old town or along the Promenade des Anglais is something to savor.

㉓ We suggest that you divide your visit to Nice into three short walks, using the arcaded **place Masséna,** the city's main square, as the starting point. First, head west through the fountains and gardens of the
㉔ **Jardin Albert I** to the **Promenade des Anglais,** built, as the name indicates, by the English community in 1824. Traffic on this multilane highway can be heavy, but once you have crossed to the seafront, there are fine views, across private beaches, of the Baie des Anges.

NEED A
BREAK?
Walk west as far as the Neptune Plage and cross over to the **Negresco** (✉ 37 promenade des Anglais) for a cup of coffee—think of it as an admission charge to the palatial hotel.

㉕ The **Palais Masséna,** just up rue de Rivoli from the Negresco, is a museum concerned principally with the Napoleonic era and, in particular, with the life of local-born general André Masséna (1756–1817). Bonaparte rewarded the general for his heroic exploits during the Italian campaign with the sonorous sobriquet *l'Enfant chéri de la victoire* (the Cherished Child of Victory). Sections of the museum evoke the history of Nice and its carnival; there are also some fine Renaissance paintings and objects. ✉ *65 rue de France,* ☎ *04–93–88–11–34.* ▧ *Free.* ☽ *Dec.–Oct., Tues.–Sun. 10–noon and 2–5 (3–6 May–Sept.).*

㉖ Head west along rue de France, then turn right up avenue des Baumettes to the **Musée des Beaux-Arts Jules-Chéret,** Nice's fine-arts museum, built in 1878 as a palatial mansion for a Russian princess. The rich collection of paintings includes works by Auguste Renoir, Edgar Degas, Claude Monet, and Raoul Dufy; sculptures by Auguste Rodin; and ceramics by Pablo Picasso. Jules Chéret (1836–1932) is best known for his belle epoque posters; several of his oils, pastels, and tapestries can be admired here. ✉ *33 av. des Baumettes,* ☎ *04–93–62–18–12.* ▧ *Free.* ☽ *May–Sept., Tues.–Sun. 10–noon and 3–6; Oct. and Dec.–Apr., Tues.–Sun. 10–noon and 2–5.*

㉗ From the north side of place Masséna, take avenue Jean-Médecin, Nice's main shopping street, to avenue Thiers: Take a left, pass the train station, turn right on boulevard Gambetta, then make the first left onto boulevard du Tzarewitch. As the name suggests, the **Russian Orthodox Cathedral**—a famously unorthodox Nice landmark, with its colorful ceramics, onion domes, and iconed interior—is right around the corner. It was built largely with money from Czar Nicholas II (early this century, the Riviera was popular with Russian top brass, too). But within six years of its 1912 grand opening, Czar Nicholas and the "Czarevitch"—his son Alexis—were dead and the Romanov dynasty overthrown.

Nice

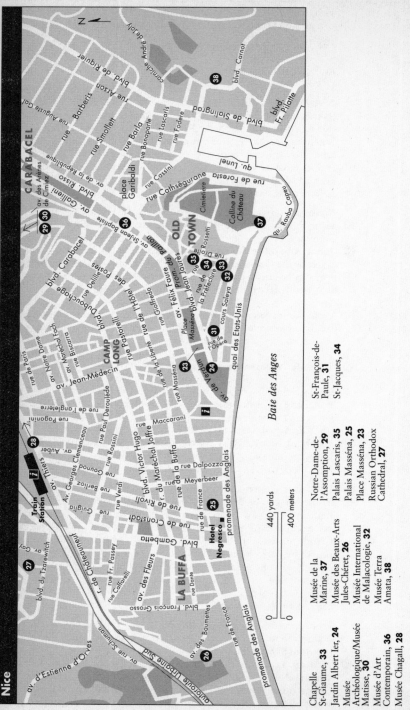

Chapelle
St-Giaume, **33**
Jardin Albert Ier, **24**
Musée
Archéologique/Musée
Matisse, **30**
Musée d'Art
Contemporain, **36**
Musée Chagall, **28**

Musée de la
Marine, **37**
Musée des Beaux-Arts
Jules-Chéret, **26**
Musée International
de Malacologie, **32**
Musée Terra
Amata, **38**

Notre-Dame-de-
l'Assomption, **29**
Palais Lascaris, **35**
Palais Masséna, **25**
Place Masséna, **23**
Russian Orthodox
Cathedral, **27**

St-François-de-
Paule, **31**
St-Jacques, **34**

440 yards

400 meters

㉘ Pass the train station on avenue Thiers, turn left onto avenue Malausséna, cross the railway tracks, and take the first right down to the **Musée Chagall,** built to show off the paintings of Marc Chagall (1887–1985) in natural light. The Old Testament is the primary subject of the works, which include 17 huge canvases, 195 preliminary sketches, several sculptures, and nearly 40 gouaches. ✉ *av. du Dr-Ménard,* ☎ *04–93–81–75–75.* ▣ *27 frs.* ☉ *July–Sept., Wed.–Mon. 10–7; Oct.–July, Wed.–Mon. 10–12:30 and 2–5:30.*

Boulevard de Cimiez, just east of the Chagall museum, runs northeast to the residential quarter of Nice—the hilltop site of **Cimiez,** occupied by the Romans 2,000 years ago. The foundations of the Roman town can be seen, along with vestiges of the arena, less spectacular than those at Arles or Nîmes but still in use (notably for a summer jazz festival).

㉙ The Franciscan monastery of **Notre-Dame-de-l'Assomption,** in Cimiez, has some outstanding late-medieval religious pictures; guided tours include the small museum and an audio-visual show on the life and work of the Franciscans. ✉ *pl. du Monastère,* ☎ *04–93–81–00–04.* ▣ *Free.* ☉ *Mon.–Sat. 10–noon and 3–6.*

㉚ A 17th-century Italian villa amid the Roman remains in Cimiez contains the **Musées Archéologique et Matisse.** The archaeology museum contains a plethora of ancient objects; the Matisse museum contains paintings and bronzes by Henri Matisse (1869–1954), illustrating the different stages of his career. ✉ *164 av. des Arènes-de-Cimiez. Musée Archéologique:* ▣ *free.* ☉ *10–noon and 2–5 Tues.–Sat., and 2–5 Sunday, Dec.–Oct. Musée Matisse:* ▣ *25 frs.* ☉ *Weds.–Mon. 1–7 Apr.–Sept. and 10–5 Oct.–Mar.*

★ The **old town** of Nice is one of the delights of the Riviera. Cars are forbidden on streets that are so narrow that their buildings crowd out the sky. The winding alleyways are lined with faded 17th- and 18th-century buildings. Flowers cascade from window boxes on soft-pastel-colored walls.

㉛ The 18th-century church of **St-François-de-Paule** (✉ rue St-Francois-de-Paule) is renowned for its ornate Baroque interior and sculpted decoration.

NEED A BREAK? Enjoy an ice cream at **Henri Auer** (✉ 7 rue St-François-de-Paule), a cozy tearoom where the best crystallized fruits in Nice are sold.

㉜ Rue St-François-de-Paule widens to become the pedestrian-only cours Saleya, which has a colorful morning market selling seafood, flowers, and orange trees in tubs. At the far end of cours Saleya is the **Musée International de Malacologie,** with a collection of seashells from all over the world (some for sale) and a small aquarium of Mediterranean sea life. ✉ *3 cours Saleya,* ☎ *04–93–85–18–44.* ▣ *25 frs.* ☉ *Dec.–Oct., Tues.–Sat. 10:30–1 and 2–6.*

㉝ Pop into the **Chapelle St-Giaume** (✉ rue la Poissonnerie), one block north of the cours Saleya, to admire its gleaming Baroque interior and grand
㉞ altarpieces. **St-Jacques** (✉ rue de Jésus), around the corner from St-Giaume, features an explosion of painted angels on the ceiling.

㉟ The elegant **Palais Lascaris,** built in the mid-17th century and decorated with paintings and tapestries, has a particularly grand staircase and a reconstructed 18th-century pharmacy. ✉ *15 rue Droite.* ▣ *25 frs.* ☉ *Dec.–Oct., Tues.–Sun. 9:30–noon and 2–6.*

㊱ The state-of-the-art **Musée d'Art Contemporain** has four marble-fronted towers overlooking a sculpture-laden concourse. Its collection of French and international abstract and figurative art from the late 1950s onward is outstanding. ⊠ *Promenade des Arts,* ☎ *04–93–62–61–62.* ⊡ *25 frs.* ⊙ *Wed.–Mon. 11–6, Fri. 11–10.*

Old Nice is dominated by the **Colline du Château** (Castle Hill), a romantic cliff fortified many centuries before Christ. The ruins of the 6th-century castle and the surrounding garden are fun to explore.

③⑦ The small **Musée de la Marine** (Naval Museum), on Castle Hill, is in the 16th-century **Tour Bellanda** (tour). It contains models, instruments, and documents charting the history of the port of Nice. The elevator between Tour Bellanda and the quayside operates daily 9 until 7 in summer and 2 until 6 in winter. ⊠ *rue du Château,* ☎ *04–93–80–47–61.* ⊡ *25 frs.* ⊙ *June–Sept., Wed.–Mon. 10–noon and 2–7; Oct.–mid-Nov. and Jan.–May, Wed.–Mon. 10–noon and 2–5.*

Relics of a local settlement that was active 400,000 years ago, can be
③⑧ seen in the **Musée Terra Amata,** across the water from Castle Hill. Recorded commentaries in English and films explain the lifestyle of prehistoric dwellers. ⊠ *25 bd. Carnot,* ☎ *04–93–55–59–93.* ⊡ *25 frs.* ⊙ *Oct.–mid-Sept. Tues.–Sun. 9–noon and 2–6.*

**OFF THE
BEATEN PATH**   **CORSICA** – If you have a day or two to spare, a high-speed ferry will whisk you to Corsica: 2½ hours to Calvi or 3½ hours to Bastia. These ferries, operated by SNCM Ferryterranée, depart from Nice twice a day.

Dining and Lodging

$$$$ ✕ **L'Ane Rouge.** This old favorite in Nice's *vieux port* has been famous for generations as *the* place to go to for Nice's best fish and seafood. The reputation of Chef Michel Devilliers, who prepped at the Michelin three-star Troisgrois, is beyond question, but the feeling here is too serious and too expensive despite the fine cuisine. Celebrities frequent the place, so if that's what whets your appetite, give it a try. ⊠ *7 quai des Deux-Emmanuel,* ☎ *04–93–89–49–63. Reservations essential. AE, DC, MC, V. Closed Wed. in winter.*

$$ ✕ **Grand Cafe de Turin.** This booming place on place Garibaldi is one
★   of Nice's top shellfish emporiums. Eat on the terrace or under the arcaded porticoes of the square. Brown bread and a dozen oysters is a standard order. Ask for *fines de claires,* especially good Atlantic-bred oysters. ⊠ *5 pl. Garibaldi, 06300,* ☎ *04–93–62–29–52.* ⊙ *8 AM–10 PM, 8–11 in summer. AE, DC, MC, V. Closed June.*

$$ ✕ **La Mérenda.** This tiny gem is worth squeezing into for fine, authentic
★   local cooking. Although rumors indicate that the Giustis may retire, they assure us that a like-minded successor is waiting in the wings. Everything on the menu is excellent, especially the stockfish or the *boeuf en daube* (veal in wine sauce). ⊠ *4 rue de la Terrasse. No phone. No credit cards. Closed Sat.–Mon., Feb. and Aug.*

$$ ✕ **L'Olivier.** Franck Musso bakes his own bread and serves up sturdy Provençal dishes (fish soup, snail ravioli) and homemade desserts, while his brother Christian provides guests with a chirpy welcome to the small, cozy dining room that locals love. ⊠ *2 pl. Garibaldi,* ☎ *04–93–26–89–09. Reservations essential. AE, MC, V. Closed Sun., Mon. lunch, and Aug.*

$–$$ ✕ **La Cambuse.** This little bistro on the cours Saleya next to the lovely
★   Chapelle de la Miséricorde is a winner. Aptly named for a ship's storeroom, this sunny place serves fresh seafood and wonderful steamed vegetable dishes on elevated platters to save space on the tables. The resulting proximity of diners and dinner can only be described as erotic. ⊠ *5 cours Saleya, 06300,* ☎ *04–93–80–12–31. MC, V. Closed Sun.*

$ ✕ **Le Tire Bouchon.** In the heart of old Nice, this small, popular restaurant is made to seem wider by mirrors on the wall. It serves good simple fare at very reasonable prices. The salade niçoise is an obvious choice; less obvious is the salad with smoked duck. Other dishes include curries, entrecôte, and grilled fish. ⊠ *19 rue de la Préfecture, 06300,* ☎ *04–63–92–63–64. MC, V. Closed Sun.*

$$$$ ✕ ⊞ **Elysée Palace.** This glass-fronted addition to the Nice hotel scene lies close to the seafront; rooms have views of the Mediterranean. The interior is spacious and ultramodern, with plenty of marble. The large restaurant is a sound bet for nouvelle cuisine, enjoyed amid contemporary art. ⊠ *59 Promenade des Anglais (entrance at 117 rue de France), 06000,* ☎ *04–93–86–06–06,* FAX *04–93–44–50–40. 143 rooms with bath. Restaurant, bar, pool, sauna, health club. AE, DC, MC, V.*

$$$$ ✕ ⊞ **Negresco.** Henri Negresco wanted to out-Ritz all the Ritzes when
★ he built this place. There were eight kings at the opening ceremony in 1912, grouped on the 560,000-franc gold Aubusson carpet beneath the 1-ton crystal chandelier in the great oval salon. No two rooms are the same, though each floor has its own motif based on an epoch from the 16th to the 20th century. The third floor, for example, has 19th-century antiques, and the second floor is decorated with opulent contemporary designs. Chef Dominique Le Stanc has made the restaurant one of France's finest. The menu translated into Japanese hints that prices are high. The brasserie, decorated with charming carousel horses, serves informal, lighter, less expensive fare. ⊠ *37 promenade des Anglais, 06000,* ☎ *04–93–16–64–00,* FAX *04–93–88–35–68. 148 rooms with bath. 2 restaurants, bar, beach.*

$$$–$$$$ ✕ ⊞ **Beau Rivage.** Occupying an imposing late 19th-century town
★ house near the cours Saleya, this hotel is just a few steps from the best parts of old Nice and the beach. Rooms are decorated in soothing pastels. The hotel's fine restaurant, Le Relais, is expertly directed by the affable Armand. Try the hot goat cheese salad. ⊠ *24 rue St-François-de-Paule, 06000,* ☎ *04–93–80–80–70,* FAX *04–93–80–55–77. 106 rooms with bath. Restaurant, beach. AE, DC, MC, V.*

$$ ⊞ **Florence.** This old-yet-modernized hotel, just off rue Jean-Médecin (Nice's major shopping street), is recommended for friendly service, comfort (air-conditioning) and style (marble bathrooms). ⊠ *3 rue Paul-Déroulède, 06000,* ☎ *04–93–88–46–87,* FAX *04–93–88–43–65. 56 rooms with bath or shower. Air-Conditioning. AE, DC, MC, V.*

$$ ⊞ **Mirabeau.** This stylishly renovated palm-tree-fronted hotel lies 200 yards from the train station on busy avenue Malausséna, a good 15-minute walk from the beach. Plants, flowers, and leather armchairs brighten up the lobby-breakfast area; rooms, with floral-pattern quilts and functional modern furniture, are scarcely large enough for a lengthy stay. ⊠ *15 av. Malausséna, 06000,* ☎ *04–93–88–33–67,* FAX *04–93–16–14–08. 42 rooms with shower. Bar, air-conditioning. AE, MC, V.*

$ ⊞ **Little Palace.** Monsieur and Madame Carlier run the closest thing to a boarding house hotel in Nice. The old-fashioned decor, the jumble of bric-a-brac, and the heavy wooden furniture lend an old-world air. ⊠ *9 av. Baquis, 06000,* ☎ *04–93–88–70–49,* FAX *04–93–88–78–89. 36 rooms, 31 with bath and 5 with shower. MC, V.*

$ ⊞ **La Mer.** This small hotel is close to the old town and seafront. Rooms are spartan (and carpets are sometimes frayed), but the location and prices are good. Overall, the staff is pleasant. Ask for a room away from the square to be sure of a quiet night. ⊠ *4 pl. Masséna,*

06000, ☎ 04–93–92–09–10, ꜰᴀx 04–93–85–00–64. *12 rooms with bath or shower. AE, MC, V.*

Nightlife and the Arts

NIGHTLIFE

Not much more needs to be said about the **casino** (⊠ Promenade des Anglais) other than it's expensive and sophisticated. After dark, the **Offshore** (⊠ 29 rue Alphonse-Karr), Nice's trendiest spot, comes alive—but you'll have to dress sharply to get past the doorman. If you don't make it into the Offshore, try the young, lively **Bin's Discothèque** (⊠ 71 bd. Jean-Béhra).

THE ARTS

Nice hosts a **jazz festival** during July, drawing international performers from around the world. Classical music and ballet can be found at Nice's **Acropolis** (⊠ Palais des Congrès, Esplanade John F. Kennedy, ☎ 04–93–92–80–00). The Nice **Opéra's** (⊠ 4 rue St-François-de-Paul, ☎ 04–93–85–67–31) season extends from September to June. Try the **Théâtre Municipal Francis-Gag** (⊠ 4 rue St-Joseph, ☎ 04–93–62–00–03) for dramatic productions. Plays are also performed at the **Théâtre de Nice** (⊠ Promenade des Arts, ☎ 04–93–13–90–90). Jazz and pop concerts are frequently held at the **Théâtre de Verdure** (⊠ Jardin Albert Ier, ☎ 04–93–82–38–68), which relocates to the **Arènes de Cimiez** in summer.

Outdoor Activities and Sports

Nice's **beaches** extend along the Baie des Anges (the Bay of Angels); Ruhl Plage is one of the most popular, with a good restaurant and facilities for waterskiing, windsurfing, and children's swimming lessons. Not to be outdone, Neptune Plage has all that plus a sauna. If you're not on the beach, take a bike trip to Cap d'Antibes; **bikes** can be rented from the **train station** (⊠ 17 av. Thiers, ☎ 04–36–35–35–35).

In winter, **skiing** is the sport of choice: Nice is just 60 miles from Valberg (4,600 feet), Auron (5,250 feet), and Isola 2000 (6,500 feet) in the Alps.

Shopping

Nice's main shopping street, **avenue Jean-Médecin,** runs inland from place Masséna; all needs and most tastes are catered to in its big department stores (Nouvelles Galeries, Prisunic, and the split-level Etoile mall). At **Soleido** you can buy lovely clothes in very French print fabrics (⊠ 1 bis rue du Paradis).

Crystallized fruit is a Nice specialty; there's a terrific selection at **Henri Auer** (⊠ 7 rue St-François-de-Paule). Locals and visitors alike buy olive oil by the gallon from tiny **Alziari,** just down the street at No. 14; the cans sport colorful, old-fashioned labels. From November to April you can visit Alziari's "oil mill" (⊠ 318 bd. de la Madeleine).

Seafood of all kinds is displayed and sold at the **fish market** (⊠ pl. St-François). The **flea market** (⊠ pl. Robilante) by the Old Port is held Tuesday through Saturday and every first Sunday of the month. In addition to plants, Nice's famous **flower market** (⊠ cours Saleya) also features mounds of fruits and vegetables.

En Route   There are three scenic roads at various heights above the coast between Nice and Monte Carlo, a distance of about 19 kilometers (12 miles). All are called "corniches"—literally, a projecting molding along the top of a building or wall. The **Basse** (lower) **Corniche** is the busiest and slowest route because it passes through all the coastal towns. The **Moyenne** (middle) **Corniche** is high enough for views and close enough for details. It passes the perched village of Eze. The **Grande** (upper)

Corniche winds some 1,300 to 1,600 feet above the sea, offering sweeping views of the coast. It follows the Via Aurelia, the great Roman military road that brought Roman legions from Italy to Gaul (France). In 1806, Napoléon rebuilt the road and sent Gallic troops into Italy. The best advice is to take the Moyenne Corniche one way and the Grande Corniche the other. The view from the upper route is best in the early morning or evening.

Villefranche-sur-Mer

39 *4 km (2½ mi) east of Nice.*

The popular, pretty Basse Corniche (N98) connects Nice to Villefranche-sur-Mer. If you're staying in Nice, include Villefranche on a tour of Cap Ferrat. The harbor town is a miniature version of old Marseille, with steep narrow streets—one, rue Obscure, is actually a tunnel winding down to the sea. The town is a stage set of brightly colored houses—orange buildings with lime-green shutters, yellow buildings with ice-blue shutters. Be sure to visit the 17th-century **Eglise St-Michel** (⊠ pl. Poullan) with its strikingly realistic Christ, carved of boxwood by an unknown convict.

Try to get to the **Cocteau Chapel,** the chapel of St-Pierre-des-Pêcheurs, near the port. It's a small Romanesque chapel, once used for storing fishing nets, which the French writer and painter Jean Cocteau decorated in 1957. Visitors walk through the flames of the Apocalypse (represented by staring eyes on either side of the door) and enter a room filled with frescoes of St. Peter, Gypsies, and the women of Villefranche. ⊠ *pl. Pollanais.* 🖭 *15 frs.* ✆ *May–Oct., Tues.–Sun. 9–noon and 2:30–7; Dec.–Apr., Tues.–Sun. 9:30–noon and 2:30–5.*

Beaulieu

40 *6 km (4 mi) east of Villefranche-sur-Mer, 10 km (6 mi) east of Nice.*

Beaulieu was a turn-of-the-century high society haunt. Stop and walk along the promenade, sometimes called Petite Afrique (Little Africa) because of its magnificent palm trees, to get a flavor of how things used to be.

The one thing to do in Beaulieu is visit the **Villa Kérylos.** In the early part of the century, a rich amateur archaeologist named Théodore Reinach asked an Italian architect to build an authentic Greek house for him. The villa, now open to the public, is a faithful reproduction, made from cool Carrara marble, alabaster, and rare fruitwoods. The furniture, made of wood inlaid with ivory, bronze, and leather, was copied from drawings of Greek interiors found on ancient vases and mosaics. ⊠ *rue Gustave-Eiffel,* ☎ *04–93–01–01–44.* 🖭 *35 frs.* ✆ *July–Aug., weekdays 3–7, weekends 10:30–12:30 and 3–7; Sept.–June, Tues.–Fri. 2–5:30, weekends 10:30–12:30 and 2–5:30.*

St-Jean-Cap-Ferrat

41 *1 km (½ mi) south of Beaulieu on D25.*

From Beaulieu, make a detour around the lush peninsula of St-Jean-Cap-Ferrat and visit the 17-acre gardens and the richly varied art museum. The **Musée Ephrussi de Rothschild** reflects the sensibilities of its former owner, Madame Ephrussi de Rothschild, sister of Baron Edouard de Rothschild. An insatiable collector, she surrounded herself with an eclectic but tasteful collection of Impressionist paintings, Louis XIII furniture, rare Sèvres porcelain, and objets d'art from the Far East. ⊠ *Villa Ile-de-*

France, ☎ 04–93–01–33–09. ⌨ 38 frs. Guided tours 17 frs extra. ☉
June–Sept., daily 10–6; Oct.–May, weekdays 2–6, weekends 10–6.

Peillon

㊷ 19 km (12 mi) northeast of Nice on D2204 to D21, then right up the
mountain.

Of all the perched villages along the Riviera, the fortified medieval town
of Peillon, on a craggy mountaintop more than 1,000 feet above the
sea, is the most spectacular and the least spoiled. Unchanged since the
Middle Ages, the village has only a few narrow streets and many steps
and covered alleys. There's really nothing to do here but look—which
is why the tour buses stay away, leaving Peillon uncommercialized for
the 50 families who live there—including professionals summering
away from Paris and artists who want to escape the craziness of the
world below. Visit the **Chapel of the White Penitents** (key available at
the Auberge); spend a half hour exploring the ancient streets, then head
back down the mountain to Nice.

NEED A   Have lunch at the charming **Auberge de la Madone** (⊠ pl. Arnulf), a
BREAK?   short walk from the chapel.

Eze

㊸ 2 km (1 mi) east of Beaulieu, 12 km (7 mi) east of Nice, 8 km (5 mi)
west of Monte-Carlo.

Almost every tour from Nice to Monaco includes a visit to the medieval
hill town of Eze, perched on a rocky spur near the Middle Corniche,
some 1,300 feet above the sea. (Don't confuse Eze with the beach town
of **Eze-sur-Mer,** which is down by the water.) Although Eze has its share
of serious craftspeople, most of its vendors cater to the crowds of tourists.

Enter the town through the fortified 14th-century gate and wander down
the narrow, cobbled streets with vaulted passageways and stairs. The
church is 18th century, but the small **Chapel of the White Penitents**
dates from 1306 and contains a 13th-century gilded wooden Spanish
Christ and some notable 16th-century paintings. Tourist and crafts shops
line the streets leading to the ruins of the castle, which has a scenic
belvedere.

Near the top of the village is the **Jardin Exotique,** a garden with exotic
flowers and cacti. It's worth the admission price, but if you have time
for only one exotic garden, visit the one in Monte Carlo. ⊠ rue du
Château, ☎ 04–93–41–10–30. ⌨ 12 frs. ☉ 9–8 June–Sept. and 9–
noon and 2–5 Oct.–May.

If you're not going to Grasse, the perfume capital of the world (☞ above),
consider visiting a branch of a Grasse perfumerie, **La Parfumerie Fragonard,** in front of the public gardens. ⊠ Moyenne Corniche, ☎ 04–
93–41–05–05. ⌨ free. ☉ 8:30–6:30.

Dining and Lodging

$$$$ ✕🏨 **Château de la Chèvre d'Or.** A member of the Relais & Châteaux
  ★   group, this hotel comprises a number of ancient houses whose mellow
stone walls are set off by terra-cotta pots brimming with geraniums.
The small rooms are decorated with antiques; ask for room 9. The views
from the poolside terrace are sensational. The bar is in a medieval room
with stone walls, a tall fireplace, and Louis XIII furniture. The restaurant is dignified, but be prepared for the prices. When you've swal-

lowed those, settle in to enjoy the beautifully presented cuisine, scented, as chef Mazot likes to say, with the perfumes of Provence. ⊠ *rue du Barri, 06360,* ☎ *04–93–41–12–12,* FAX *04–93–41–06–72. 28 rooms with bath. Restaurant, bar, café, pool. AE, DC, MC, V. Closed mid-Nov.–early Mar.*

Monaco

44 *8 km (5 mi) east of Eze on the Moyenne Corniche.*

From Eze it's just a short—albeit spectacular—drive up the coast to Monaco. The Principality of Monaco covers just 473 acres and would fit comfortably inside New York's Central Park or a family farm in Iowa. Its 5,000 citizens would fill only a small fraction of the seats in Yankee Stadium. The country is so tiny that residents have to go to another country to play golf.

The present ruler, Rainier III, traces his ancestry to Otto Canella, who was born in 1070. The Grimaldi dynasty began with Otto's great-great-great-grandson, Francesco Grimaldi, also known as Frank the Rogue. Expelled from Genoa, Frank and his cronies disguised themselves as monks and seized, in 1297, the fortified medieval town known today as the Rock. Except for a short break under Napoléon, the Grimaldis have been here ever since, which makes them the oldest reigning family in Europe. On the Grimaldi coat of arms are two monks holding swords (look up and you'll see them above the main door as you enter the palace).

Back in the 1850s, a Grimaldi named Charles III made a decision that turned the Rock into a giant blue chip. Needing revenues but not wanting to impose additional taxes on his subjects, he contracted with a company to open a gambling facility. The first spin of the roulette wheel was on December 14, 1856. There was no easy way to reach Monaco then—no carriage roads or railroads—so no one came. Between March 15 and March 20, 1857, one person entered the casino—and won two francs. In 1868, however, the railroad reached Monaco, filled with wheezing Englishmen who came to escape the London fog. The effects were immediate. Profits were so great that Charles eventually abolished all direct taxes.

Almost overnight, a threadbare principality became an elegant watering hole for European society. Dukes (and their mistresses) and duchesses (and their gigolos) danced and dined their way through a world of spinning roulette wheels and bubbling champagne—preening themselves for nights at the opera, where such artists as Vaslav Nijinsky, Sarah Bernhardt, and Enrico Caruso came to perform.

Monte Carlo—the modern gambling town with elegant shops, man-made beaches, high-rise hotels, and a few Belle Epoque hotels—is actually only one of four parts of Monaco. The second part of Monaco is **Old Monaco,** the medieval town on the Rock, 200 feet above the sea. It's here that Prince Rainier lives. The third area of Monaco is **La Condamine,** the commercial harbor area with apartments and businesses. **Fontvieille,** the fourth area of Monaco, is an industrial district on 20 acres of reclaimed land.

Start exploring Monte Carlo at the **tourist office** (⊠ av. de la Costa) just north of the casino gardens (ask for the useful English booklet *Getting Around in the Principality*). The **Casino** is a must-see, even if you don't bet a cent. You may find it fun to count the Jaguars and Rolls-Royces parked outside and breathe on the windows of shops selling Yves Saint-Laurent dresses and fabulous jewels. Into the gold-leaf

★ **45**

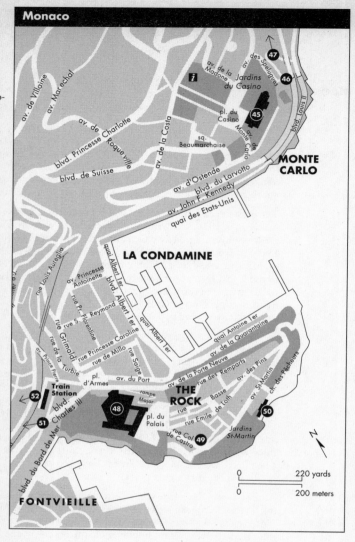

splendor of the casino, where fortunes have been won and shirts have been lost, the hopeful traipse from tour buses to tempt fate at slot machines beneath the gilt-edged rococo ceiling.

The main gambling hall, once called the European Room, has been renamed the **American Room** and fitted with 150 one-armed bandits from Chicago. Adjoining it is the **Pink Salon**, now a bar where unclad nymphs float about on the ceiling smoking cigarillos. The **Salles Privées** (Private Rooms) are for high rollers. ⊠ *pl. du Casino.* ☉ *noon–the last die is thrown. Jacket and tie in the back rooms, which open at 4* PM. *Bring your passport (under-21s not admitted).*

Place du Casino is the center of Monte Carlo, and, in the true spirit of the town, it seems that the **Opera House,** with its 18-ton gilt-bronze chandelier, is part of the casino complex. The designer, Charles Garnier, also built the Paris Opera.

46 The serious gamblers, some say, play at **Loew's Casino,** nearby. It opens weekdays at 4 PM and weekends at 1 PM. You may want to try parking here, since parking near the old casino is almost impossible.

47 From place des Moulins there is an escalator down to the Larvotto beach complex, artfully created with imported sand, and the **Musée National,** housed in a Garnier villa within a rose garden. This museum has a beguiling collection of 18th- and 19th-century dolls and mechanical automatons, most in working order. ⊠ *17 av. Princesse Grace,* ☎ *93–30–91–26.* 🎟 *28 frs.* ⊙ *Daily except holidays 10–12:15 and 2:30–6:30.*

48 Prince Rainier spends much of the year in his grand Italianate **Palace** on the Rock. The changing of the guard takes place here each morning at 11:55, and the State Apartments can be visited in summer. ☎ *93–25–18–31.* 🎟 *35 frs. Joint ticket with Musée Napoléon: 40 frs.* ⊙ *June–Oct., daily 9:30–6:30.*

One wing of the palace, open throughout the year, is taken up by the **Musée Napoléon,** filled with Napoleonic souvenirs and documents related to Monaco's history. 🎟 *25 frs. Joint ticket with palace apartments as above.* ⊙ *Tues.–Sun. 9:30–6:30.*

49 The **cathedral** (⊠ rue Col de Castro), just a short stroll though the medieval alleyways near the Napoléon museum, is a neo-Romanesque monstrosity (1875–84), with several important paintings of the Nice school.

50 One of Monaco's most outstanding showpieces, the **Musée Océanographique,** is an important research institute headed by celebrated underwater explorer and filmmaker Jacques Cousteau (his films are shown in the museum cinema). Prince Rainier's great-grandfather Albert I (1848–1922), an accomplished marine biologist, founded the institute in 1910. It now boasts two exploration ships, laboratories, and a staff of 60 scientists. Nonscientific visitors may wish to go straight to the well-arranged and generously stocked aquarium in the basement. Other floors are devoted to Prince Albert's collection of seashells and whale skeletons and to Cousteau's diving equipment. ⊠ *av. St-Martin,* ☎ *93–15–36–00.* 🎟 *70 frs.* ⊙ *July–Aug., daily 9–8; Sept.–June, daily 9:30–7 (6 in winter).*

NEED A BREAK?
Take the Oceonographic Museum's elevator to the roof terrace for a fine view and a restorative drink.

51 Six hundred varieties of cacti and succulents cling to a sheer rock face at the **Jardin Exotique** (Tropical Gardens), a brisk half-hour walk west from the palace.

52 The **Museum of Prehistoric Anthropology,** on the grounds of the tropical gardens, contains bones, tools, and other artifacts. Shapes of the stalactites and stalagmites in the cavernous grotto (entered from the gardens) resemble the cacti outside. ⊠ *bd. du Jardin Exotique,* ☎ *93–15–80–06.* 🎟 *39 frs.* ⊙ *Daily 9–7 (dusk in winter).*

Dining and Lodging

$$–$$$ ✕ **Port.** Harbor views from the terrace and top-notch Italian food make the Port a good choice. The large, varied menu includes shrimp, lasagna, fettuccine, and fish risotto. ⊠ *quai Albert-Ier,* ☎ *93–50–77–21. AE, DC, MC, V. Closed Mon. and Nov.*

$–$$ ✕ **Polpetta.** This popular little trattoria is close enough to the Italian
★ border to pass for the real McCoy. If it's on the menu, go for the vegetable soupe au pistou and the *risotto al porcini* (risotto with wild mush-

rooms). ⊠ *2 rue Paradis,* ☎ *93–50–67–84. Reservations essential in summer. MC, V. Closed Tues. and Sat. lunch and Feb.*

$$$$ ✕🏨 **Hermitage.** Even if you're not staying, come to see the glass-dome Art Nouveau vestibule at the avenue d'Ostende entrance and the white-stucco rococo corridor leading to the lavish dining room, where pink marble columns hold up a gilded, frescoed ceiling. The adjacent terrace, with a tinkling pianist in summer, has a view of the harbor. Rooms are comfortable but far less stylish. ⊠ *Square Beaumarchais, BP 277, 98005 cedex,* ☎ *92–16–40–00,* 🄵🄰🄷 *93–50–47–12. 25 apartments, 216 rooms with bath. Restaurant, bar, pool. AE, DC, MC, V.*

$$$$ ✕🏨 **Hôtel de Paris.** Though discreetly modernized, the Hôtel de Paris
  ★   still exudes the gold-plate splendor of an era in which kings and grand dukes were regulars. The spacious rooms are decorated in light colors with white oak furniture. The restaurant, the Louis XV, stuns you with royal decor and superb food—chef Alain Ducasse, now running Joël Robuchon's former restaurant in Paris as well, is one of Europe's most celebrated chefs. Try his ravioli de foie gras. Le Côte Jardin is good for lunch on the terrace and Le Grill serves Mediterranean-style cuisine on a rooftop overlooking the harbor. Restaurant Louis XV is closed Tuesday and Wednesday (except dinner July to August), mid-February to early March, and late November to late December. ⊠ *pl. du Casino, 98000,* ☎ *92–16–30–00,* 🄵🄰🄷 *92–16–38–49. 143 rooms, 41 suites, and 19 junior suites. 4 restaurants, indoor and outdoor pool, spa. AE, DC, MC, V.*

$$$$ ✕🏨 **Loews.** Big, brash, and more than a touch vulgar, Loews has a plush extravagance on a scale Donald Trump would envy. Contemporary rooms are decorated in ice cream shades and celebrities mix with sheikhs in the bars, casino, and restaurants. Diehard football fans can watch the Super Bowl by satellite; those in search of live entertainment can head for the Folie Russe cabaret. ⊠ *12 av. des Spélugues, 98000,* ☎ *93–50–65–00,* 🄵🄰🄷 *93–30–01–57. 69 apartments, 650 rooms with bath. 3 restaurants, pool, hot tub, health club, casino. AE, DC, MC, V.*

$$ 🏨 **Alexandra.** Shades of the Belle Epoque linger in this comfortable hotel's spacious lobby and airy rooms. Tan and rose colors dominate the newer rooms. If you're willing to do without a private bath, this place sneaks into the $ category. The friendly proprietress, Madame Larouquie, makes foreign visitors feel right at home. ⊠ *35 bd. Princesse-Charlotte, 98000,* ☎ *93–50–63–13,* 🄵🄰🄷 *92–16–06–48. 55 rooms, 46 with bath. AE, DC, MC, V.*

Nightlife and the Arts

NIGHTLIFE

There's no need to go to bed before dawn in Monte Carlo when you can go to its renowned **casino** (⊠ pl. du Casino). **Jimmy'z** (⊠ pl. du Casino from Sept.–June, ⊠ av. Princesse Grace from July–Oct.) is almost as fun as the casino. If you can't get in to Jimmy'z, try at the neighboring, chic, and slightly younger **Parady'z** (⊠ av. Princesse Grace). **The Living Room** (⊠ 7 av. des Spélugues) is a popular, crowded bar open year-round. **Tiffany's** (⊠ 3 av. des Spélugues) is another year-round hot spot. **Harry's** piano bar (⊠ 19 av. Charles-III) often attracts good jazz singers.

THE ARTS

Monte Carlo's spring arts festival, **Printemps des Arts** takes place from early April to mid-May, and includes the world's top ballet, operatic, symphonic, and chamber performers. The **Salle Garnier** (⊠ pl. du

Casino, ☎ 93−50−76−54) offers both classical music and ballet.
Théâtre Princesse Grace (✉ 12 av. d'Ostende, ☎ 93−25−32−27)
stages a number of plays during the spring festival; off-season, there's
usually a new show each week.

Outdoor Activities and Sports

The best **beaches** in Monte Carlo are Monte Carlo Beach and Plage
du Larvotto, the public beach. Both are off avenue Princesse Grace and
both offer a variety of water sports facilities. Diving equipment can be
rented from the **Under Water Diving Club** (✉ quai des Sanbarbani, ☎
92−05−91−78). Sailboats are available at the **Monaco Yacht Club** (✉
16 quai Antoine 1er, ☎ 93−30−63−63).

Golf can be played at the spectacular 18-hole course on the slopes of
Mont-Agel at nearby La Turbie.

For sports fans, the Monte Carlo **tennis tournament** is held during the
Spring Arts Festival. When the tennis stops, the racing begins: The
Grand Prix de Monaco (☎ 93−15−26−00 for information) takes place
in mid-May.

Roquebrune

53 *5 km (3 mi) east of Monaco.*

The engaging hilltop village of Roquebrune has a Carolingian castle,
medieval houses, covered steps, and narrow streets. The adjacent Cap-
Martin peninsula is colonized by wealthy villa dwellers. Near the tip,
on avenue Winston-Churchill, is the start of a coastal path—promenade
Le Corbusier—that leads hardy walkers to Monte Carlo in 1½ hours.

Menton

54 *9 km (5 ½ mi) east of Monaco.*

Next door to Roquebrune is Menton, a comparatively quiet all-year
resort town with the warmest climate on the Riviera. Lemon trees flourish here, as do senior citizens, enticed by a long strand of beaches. Menton likes to call itself the Pearl of the Riviera—beautiful, respectable,
and not grossly expensive.

Walk eastward from the casino along promenade du Soleil to the harbor. There is a small 17th-century fort here, where writer, artist, and
filmmaker Jean Cocteau (1889–1963) once worked. The fort now houses
the **Cocteau Museum** of fantastic paintings, drawings, stage sets, and
a large mosaic. ✉ *Bastion du Port, 111 quai Napoléon-III,* ☎ *04−
93−57−72−30.* 🎟 *Free.* 🕐 *Apr.–Oct., Wed.–Sun. 10–noon and 2–
6; Nov.–Mar., Wed.–Sun. 10–noon and 3–6.*

The quaint **Vieille Ville** (Old Town) above the jetty has an Italian feel
to it. Visit the **Eglise St-Michel** (✉ rue St-Michel) for its ornate
Baroque interior and altarpiece of St. Michael slaying a dragon. Concerts of chamber music are held in the square on summer nights.
Walk up through the old town and you come to the **Vieux Cimetière**
(Old Cemetery), with a magnificent view of the old town and coast.
Here lie Victorian foreigners who hoped (in vain, as the dates on the
tombstones reveal) that Menton's balmy climate would reverse the rav-
ages of tuberculosis.

In the center of town, on avenue de la République, which runs parallel to the pedestrian rue St-Michel, is the **Hôtel de Ville** (Town Hall).
The room in which civil marriage ceremonies are conducted has vibrant allegorical frescoes by Cocteau; a tape in English helps to in-

terpret them. ⊠ *17 rue de la République.* 🖾 *5 frs.* ☉ *Weekdays 8:30–12:30 and 1:30–5.*

On the west side of Menton is the **Palais Carnolès,** an 18th-century villa once used as a summer retreat by the princes of Monaco. The gardens are beautiful, and the collection of European paintings (13th to 18th century) is extensive. ⊠ *3 av. de la Madone,* ☎ *04–93–35–49–71.* 🖾 *Free.* ☉ *Wed.–Sun. 10–noon and 2–6; closed holidays.*

At the east end of Menton, above the Garavan harbor, lie the **Colombières Gardens,** where follies and statues lurk among 15 acres of hedges, yew trees, and Mediterranean flowers. ⊠ *Chemin de Valleya.* 🖾 *20 frs.* ☉ *Feb.–Sept., daily 9–noon and 3–8 (or sunset if earlier).*

Dining and Lodging

$$ ✕🖾 **Londres.** This small, central hotel, close to the beach and casino, has its own restaurant, serving solid, traditional French cuisine, and a small garden for outdoor summer dining. The restaurant is closed Wednesday. ⊠ *15 av. Carnot, BP 73, 06502 cedex,* ☎ *04–93–35–74–62,* ꜰᴀx *04–93–41–77–78. 26 rooms with shower or bath. Restaurant, bar. AE, MC, V.*

Nightlife and the Arts

NIGHTLIFE

Top-class cabaret is offered at **Club 06,** at the casino (⊠ promenade de Soleil).

THE ARTS

Menton hosts two **music festivals** during the year: The **chamber music festival** in August at the Eglise St-Michel and the **September music festival** at the Palais d'Europe (⊠ av. Boyer).

OFF THE
BEATEN PATH

VENTIMIGLIA AND SAN REMO – The Italian border is just 1½ kilometers (1 mile) east of Menton, and the first Italian towns are Ventimiglia (Vintimille in French), 9 kilometers (5½) away, and San Remo, 6 kilometers (4 miles) farther. Both Ventimiglia and San Remo are known for their colorful Friday flower markets. If you visit on market day, take the train or bus; there will be no place to park. The old town of San Remo is an atmospheric warren of alleyways leading up to the piazza Castello, from which there's a splendid view.

THE RIVIERA A TO Z

Arriving and Departing

By Plane

The area's only international airport is at Nice (☎ 04–93–21–30–12).

By Train

Mainline trains from Paris stop at most of the major towns; the trip to Nice takes about seven hours.

By Car

If you're traveling from Paris by car, you can avoid a lengthy drive by taking the overnight motorail (*train-auto-couchette*) service to Nice, which departs from Paris's Gare de Bercy, five minutes from the Gare de Lyon. Otherwise, leave Paris by A6 (becoming A7 after Lyon), which continues down to Avignon. Here A8 branches off east toward Italy, with convenient exit/entry points for all major towns (except St-Tropez).

Getting Around

By Bus

Local buses cover a network of routes along the Riviera and stop at many out-of-the-way places that can't be reached by train. Timetables are available from tourist offices, train stations, and the local bus depots (*gares routières*).

By Car

If you prefer to avoid the slower, albeit spectacularly scenic, coastal roads, opt for the Italy-bound A8.

By Train

The train is a practical and inexpensive way of getting around the Riviera and stops at dozens of stations. Note that the pretty Nice-Digne line is not run by the SNCF but by the Chemin de Fer de Provence (⊠ Gare du Sud, 33 av. Malausséna, Nice, ☎ 04–93–88–28–56).

Guided Tours

Bus

A variety of tours (most starting from the bus station, or gare routière, on Promenade du Paillon in Nice (but sometimes with pickups in Menton, Cannes, or Antibes) are organized by **Santa Azur** (⊠ 11 av. Jean-Médecin, 06000 Nice, ☎ 04–93–85–46–81, FAX 04–93–87–90–08). Full- or half-day minibus tours for up to eight passengers, with English-speaking driver-guides, are organized by **Joe's Sight-Seeing** (⊠ 15 rue Alberti, BP 194, 06000 Nice cedex 1, ☎ 04–93–88–97–11, FAX 04–93–82–44–93), which promises a 10% discount on normal prices to Fodor's readers.

Boat

Gallus Excursions 80 (⊠ 24 quai Lunel, 06000 Nice, ☎ 04–93–55–33–33) offers an enjoyable day-long jaunt to the Iles de Lérins; the cost is about 175 francs.

Special-Interest

Any tourist office will produce a sheaf of suggestions on gourmandizing, golfing, and walking tours, among others. **Novatour** (⊠ 9 rue de Lille, 06400 Cannes, ☎ 04–93–69–47–47) offers tailor-made packages for its clients, though museum tours are a specialty.

Important Addresses and Numbers

Travel Agencies

American Express (⊠ 8 rue des Belges, Cannes, ☎ 04–93–38–15–87; ⊠ 11 promenade des Anglais, Nice, ☎ 04–93–16–53–53); **Wagons-Lits** (⊠ 2 av. Monte-Carlo, Monaco, ☎ 04–93–25–01–05).

Car Rental

Avis (⊠ 9 av. d'Ostende, Monaco, ☎ 04–93–30–17–53; and ⊠ av. du 8-Mai-1945, St-Tropez, ☎ 04–94–97–03–10), **Europcar** (⊠ 9 av. Thiers, Menton, ☎ 04–93–28–21–80), and **Hertz** (⊠ 147 rue d'Antibes, Cannes, ☎ 04–93–99–04–20; and ⊠ 12 av. de Suède, Nice, ☎ 04–93–87–11–87).

Visitor Information

The Riviera's regional tourist office is the **Comité Régional du Tourisme de Riviera-Côte d'Azur** (⊠ 55 promenade des Anglais, 06000 Nice; written inquiries only). Local tourist offices in major towns covered in this chapter are as follows: **Antibes** (⊠ 11 pl. Général-de-Gaulle, ☎ 04–92–90–53–00), **Cannes** (⊠ Palais des Festivals, 1 La Croisette, ☎ 04–93–39–24–53), **Fréjus** (⊠ 325 rue Jean-Jaurès, ☎ 04–94–17–19–19),

Grasse (⊠ 22 Cours Honoré-Cresp, ☎ 04–93–36–03–56), **Juan-les-Pins** (⊠ 51 bd. Charles-Guillaumont, ☎ 04–93–61–04–98), **La Napoule** (⊠ 272 av. Henry-Clews, ☎ 04–93–49–95–31), **Menton** (⊠ Palais de l'Europe, av. Boyer, ☎ 04–93–57–57–00), **Monte Carlo** (⊠ 2a bd. des Moulins, ☎ 92–16–61–66), **Nice** (⊠ av. Thiers, ☎ 04–93–87–07–07), **St-Tropez** (⊠ quai Jean-Jaurès, ☎ 04–94–97–45–21), and **Vence** (⊠ pl. du Grand-Jardin, ☎ 04–93–58–06–38).

4 Portraits of Provence & the Riviera

Provence & the Riviera at a Glance:
A Chronology

Postcards from Summer

PROVENCE & THE RIVIERA AT A GLANCE: A CHRONOLOGY

ca. 600 BC Greek colonists found Marseille.

after 500 BC Celts appear in France.

58–51 BC Julius Caesar conquers Gaul; writes up the war in *De Bello Gallico*.

52 BC Lutetia, later to become Paris, is built by the Gallo-Romans.

46 BC Roman amphitheater built at Arles.

14 BC The Pont du Gard aqueduct at Nîmes is erected.

AD 406 Invasion by the Vandals (Germanic tribes).

The Merovingian Dynasty

486–511 Clovis, king of the Franks (481–511), defeats the Roman governor of Gaul and founds the Merovingian Dynasty. Great monasteries, such as those at Tours, Limoges, and Chartres, become centers of culture.

497 Franks converted to Christianity.

567 The Frankish kingdom is divided into three parts—the eastern countries (Austrasia), later to become Belgium and Germany; the western countries (Neustria), later to become France; and Burgundy.

The Carolingian Dynasty

768–78 Charlemagne (768–814) becomes king of the Franks (768); conquers northern Italy (774); and is defeated by the Moors at Roncesvalles, Spain, after which he consolidates the Pyrénées border (778).

800 The pope crowns Charlemagne Holy Roman Emperor in Rome. Charlemagne expands the French kingdom far beyond its present borders and establishes a center for learning at his capital, Aix-la-Chapelle (Aachen, in present-day Germany).

814–987 Death of Charlemagne. The Carolingian line continues through a dozen or so monarchs, with a batch called Charles (the Bald, the Fat, the Simple) and a sprinkling of Louises. Under the Treaty of Verdun (843), the empire is divided in two—the eastern half becoming Germany, the western half France. Provence is given to Lothair I. Kingdom of Provence founded in 879; join Arles in 933.

The Capetian Dynasty

987 Hugh Capet (987–996) is made king of France and establishes the principle of hereditary rule for his descendants.

1066 Norman conquest of England by William the Conqueror (1028–87).

ca. 1100 Development of European vernacular verse: *Chanson de Roland*. The Gothic style of architecture begins to appear.

1112–1245 Provence ruled by the counts of Barcelona.

ca. 1150 Struggle between the Anglo-Norman kings (Angevin Empire) and the French; when Eleanor of Aquitaine switches husbands (from Louis VII of France to Henry II of England), her extensive lands pass to English rule.

1245–1481 Provence ruled by the dukes of Anjou.

1270 Louis IX (1226–70), the only French king to achieve sainthood, dies in Tunis on the seventh and last Crusade.

1302–07 Philippe IV the Fair (1285–1314), calls together the first States-General, predecessor to the French Parliament. He disbands the Knights Templars to gain their wealth (1307).

1309 Pope, under pressure, leaves a corrupt and disorderly Rome for Avignon in southern France, seat of the papacy for nearly 70 years.

The Valois Dynasty

1337–1453 Hundred Years' War between France and England: fighting for control of those areas of France gained by the English crown following the marriage of Eleanor of Aquitaine and Henry II.

1348–50 The Black Death rages in France.

1428–31 Joan of Arc (1412–31), the Maid of Orléans, sparks the revival of French fortunes in the Hundred Years' War but is captured by the English and burned at the stake at Rouen.

1453 France finally defeats England, terminating the Hundred Years' War and English claims to the French throne.

1494 Italian wars: beginning of Franco-Hapsburg struggle for hegemony in Europe.

1515–47 Reign of François I, who imports Italian artists, including Leonardo da Vinci (1452–1519), and brings the Renaissance to France. The château of Fontainebleau is begun (1528).

1562–98 Wars of Religion: Catholics versus Huguenots (French Protestants).

The Bourbon Dynasty

1589 The first Bourbon king, Henri IV (1589–1610), is a Protestant who converts to Catholicism and achieves peace in France. He signs the Edict of Nantes, giving limited freedom of worship to Protestants.

ca. 1610 Scientific revolution in Europe begins, marked by the discoveries of mathematician and philosopher René Descartes (1596–1650).

1643–1715 Reign of Louis XIV, the Sun King, a monarch who builds the Baroque power base of Versailles and presents Europe with a glorious view of France. With his first minister, Colbert, Louis makes France, by force of arms, the most powerful nation-state in Europe. He persecutes the Huguenots, who emigrate in great numbers, nearly ruining the French economy.

1660 Classical period of French culture: Dramatists Pierre Corneille (1606–84), Jean-Baptiste Molière (1622–73), and Jean Racine (1639–99), and painter Nicolas Poussin (1594–1665).

ca. 1715 Rococo art and decoration develop, typified by the painter Antoine Watteau (1684–1721) and, later, François Boucher (1703–70) and Jean-Honoré Fragonard (1732–1806).

1700–onward Writer and pedagogue François-Marien Voltaire (1694–1778) is a central figure in the French Enlightenment, along with Jean-Jacques Rousseau (1712–78) and Denis Diderot (1713–84), who, in 1751, compiles the first modern encyclopedia. The ideals of the Enlightenment—for reason and scientific method and against social and political injustices—pave the way for the French Revolution. In the arts, painter Jacques-Louis David (1748–1825) reinforces revolutionary creeds in his neoclassical works.

1756–63 The Seven Years' War results in France's losing most of its overseas possessions and in England becoming a world power.

1776 The French assist in the American War of Independence. Ideals of liberty cross the Atlantic with the returning troops to reinforce new social concepts.

The French Revolution

1789–1804 The Bastille is stormed on July 14, 1789. Following upon early Republican ideals comes the Reign of Terror and the administration of the Directory under Robespierre. There are widespread political executions—Louis XVI and Marie Antoinette are guillotined in 1793. Reaction sets in, and the instigators of the Terror are themselves executed (1794). Napoléon Bonaparte enters the champion of the Directory (1795–99) and is installed as First Consul during the Consulate (1799–1804).

1790 The departments of Bocuhes-du-Rhône, Var, and Basses-Alpes, and parats of Drôme, Alpes-Maritimes, and Vaucluse are formed from Provence.

The First Empire

1804 Napoléon crowns himself emperor of France at Notre-Dame in the presence of the pope.

1805–12 Napoléon conquers most of Europe. The Napoléonic Age is marked by a neoclassical artistic style called Empire as well as by the rise of Romanticism—characterized by such writers as François-Auguste-René de Chateaubriand (1768–1848) and Marie-Henri Stendhal (1783–1842), and the painters Eugène Delacroix (1798–1863) and Théodore Géricault (1791–1824)—which is to dominate the arts of the 19th century.

1812–14 Winter cold and Russian determination defeat Napoléon outside Moscow. The emperor abdicates and is transported to Elba.

Restoration of the Bourbons

1814–15 Louis XVIII, brother of the executed Louis XVI, regains the throne after the Congress of Vienna settles peace terms.

1815 The Hundred Days: Napoléon returns from Elba and musters an army on his march to the capital, but lacks national support. He is defeated at Waterloo (June 18) and exiled to the island of St. Helena in the south Atlantic.

1821 Napoléon dies in exile.

1830 Bourbon king Charles X, locked into a prerevolutionary state of mind, abdicates. A brief upheaval (Three Glorious Days) brings Louis-Philippe, the Citizen King, to the throne.

1840 Napoléon's remains are brought back to Paris.

1846–48 Severe industrial and farming depression contributes to Louis-Philippe's abdication (1848).

Second Republic and Second Empire

1848–52 Louis-Napoléon (nephew and step-grandson of Napoléon I) is elected president of the short-lived Second Republic. He makes a successful attempt to assume supreme power and is declared emperor of France, taking the title Napoléon III.

ca. 1850 The ensuing period is characterized in the arts by the emergence of realist painters—Jean-François Millet (1814–75), Honoré Daumier (1808–79), Gustave Courbet (1819–77)—and late-Romantic writers—Victor Hugo (1802–85), Honoré de Balzac (1799–1850), and Charles Baudelaire (1821–87).

1863 Napoléon III inaugurates the Salon des Refusés in response to critical opinion. It includes work by Édouard Manet (1832–83), Claude Monet (1840–1926), and Paul Cézanne (1839–1906) and is commonly regarded as the birthplace of Impressionism and of modern art in general.

The Third Republic

1870–71 The Franco-Prussian War sees Paris besieged by and fall to the Germans. Napoléon III takes refuge in England.

1871–1914 Before World War I, France expands its industries and builds vast colonial empires in North Africa and Southeast Asia. Sculptor Auguste Rodin (1840–1917), composers Maurice Ravel (1875–1937) and Claude Debussy (1862–1918), and poets such as Stéphane Mallarmé (1842–98) and Paul Verlaine (1844–96) set the stage for Modernism.

1874 Emergence of the Impressionist school of painting: Monet, Pierre Auguste Renoir (1841–1919), and Edgar Degas (1834–1917).

1894–1906 Franco-Russian Alliance (1894). Dreyfus affair: The spy trial and its anti-Semitic backlash shock France.

1904 The Entente Cordiale: England and France become firm allies.

1914–18 During World War I, France fights with the Allies, opposing Germany, Austria-Hungary, and Turkey. Germany invades France.

1918–39 Between wars, France attracts artists and writers, including Americans Ernest Hemingway (1899–1961) and Gertrude Stein (1874–1946). The country nourishes major artistic and philosophical movements: Constructivism, Dadaism, Surrealism, and Existentialism.

1939–45 At the beginning of World War II, France fights with the Allies until invaded and defeated by Germany in 1940. The French government, under Marshal Philippe Pétain (1856–1951), moves to Vichy and cooperates with the Nazis. French overseas colonies split between allegiance to the legal government of Vichy and declaration for the Free French Resistance, led (from London) by General Charles de Gaulle (1890–1970).

1944 D-Day, June 6: The Allies land on the beaches of Normandy and successfully invade France. Additional Allied forces land in Provence. Paris is liberated in August 1944, and France declares full allegiance to the Allies.

1944–46 A provisional government takes power under General de Gaulle; American aid assists French recovery.

The Fourth Republic

1946 France adopts a new constitution; French women gain the right to vote.

1946–54 In the Indochinese War, France is unable to regain control of its colonies in Southeast Asia. The 1954 Geneva Agreement establishes two governments in Vietnam: one in the north, under the Communist leader Ho Chi Minh, and one in the south, under the emperor Bao Dai. U.S. involvement eventually leads to French withdrawal.

1954–62 The Algerian Revolution achieves Algeria's independence from France. Other French African colonies gain independence.

1957 The Treaty of Rome establishes the European Economic Community (now known as the European Union—EU) with France as one of it's members.

The Fifth Republic

1958–68 De Gaulle is the first president under a new constitution; he resigns in 1968 after widespread disturbances begun by student riots in Paris.

1976 The first supersonic transatlantic passenger service begins with the Anglo-French Concorde.

1981 François Mitterrand (1916–1996) is elected the first Socialist president of France since World War II.

1988 Mitterrand is elected for a second term.

1990 TGV (*Trains à Grande Vitesse*) train clocks a world record—515 kph (322 mph)—on a practice run. Channel Tunnel link-up between France and England begun.

1994 On November 21, the Channel Tunnel becomes operational.

1995 Jacques Chirac, mayor of Paris, is elected president.

1996 Mitterrand dies.

POSTCARDS FROM SUMMER

IT HAS TAKEN US three years to accept the fact that we live in the same house, but in two different places.

What we think of as normal life starts in September. Apart from market days in the towns, there are no crowds. Traffic on the back roads is sparse during the day— a tractor, a few vans—and virtually nonexistent at night. There is always a table in every restaurant, except perhaps for Sunday lunch. Social life is intermittent and uncomplicated. The baker has bread, the plumber has time for a chat, the postman has time for a drink. After the first deafening weekend of the hunting season, the forest is quiet. Each field has a stooped, reflective figure working among the vines, very slowly up one line, very slowly down the next. The hours between noon and two are dead.

And then we come to July and August.

We used to treat them as just another two months of the year; hot months, certainly, but nothing that required much adjustment on our part except to make sure that the afternoon included a siesta.

We were wrong. Where we live in July and August is still the Lubéron, but it's not the same Lubéron. It is the Lubéron *en vacances,* and our past efforts to live normally during abnormal times have been miserably unsuccessful. So unsuccessful that we once considered cancelling summer altogether and going somewhere grey and cool and peaceful, like the Hebrides.

But if we did, we would probably miss it, all of it, even the days and incidents that have reduced us to sweating, irritated, overtired zombies. So we have decided to come to terms with the Lubéron in the summer, to do our best to join the rest of the world on holiday and, like them, to send postcards telling distant friends about the wonderful time we are having. Here are a few.

Saint-Tropez
Cherchez les nudistes! It is open season for nature lovers, and there is likely to be a sharp increase in the number of applicants wishing to join the Saint-Tropez police force.

The mayor, Monsieur Spada, has flown in the face of years of tradition (Saint-Tropez made public nudity famous, after all) and has decreed that in the name of safety and hygiene there will be no more naked sunbathing on the public beaches. *"Le nudisme intégral est interdit,"* says Monsieur Spada, and he has empowered the police to seize and arrest any offenders. Well, perhaps not to seize them, but to track them down and fine them 75 francs, or as much as 1,500 francs if they have been guilty of creating a public outrage. Exactly where a nudist might keep 1,500 francs is a question that is puzzling local residents.

Meanwhile, a defiant group of nudists has set up headquarters in some rocks behind *la plage de la Moutte.* A spokeswoman for the group has said that under no circumstances would bathing suits be worn. Wish you were here.

The Melon Field
Faustin's brother Jacky, a wiry little man of 60 or so, grows melons in the field opposite the house. It's a large field, but he does all the work himself, and by hand. In the spring I have often seen him out there for six or seven hours, back bent like a hinge, his hoe chopping at the weeds that threaten to strangle his crop. He doesn't spray— who would eat a melon tasting of chemicals?—and I think he must enjoy looking after his land in the traditional way.

Now that the melons are ripening, he comes to the field at 6 every morning to pick the ones that are ready. He takes them up to Ménerbes to be packed in shallow wooden crates. From Ménerbes they go to Cavaillon, and from Cavaillon to Avignon, to Paris, everywhere. It amuses Jacky to think of people in smart restaurants paying *une petite fortune* for a simple thing like a melon.

If I get up early enough I can catch him before he goes to Ménerbes. He always has a couple of melons that are too ripe to travel, and he sells them to me for a few francs.

As I walk back to the house, the sun clears the top of the mountain and it is suddenly hot on my face. The melons, heavy and satisfying in my hands, are still cool from the night air. We have them for breakfast, fresh and sweet, less than 10 minutes after they have been picked.

Behind the Bar

There is a point at which a swimming pool ceases to be luxury and becomes very close to a necessity, and that point is when the temperature hits 100 degrees. Whenever people ask us about renting a house for the summer, we always tell them this, and some of them listen.

Others don't, and within two days of arriving they are on the phone telling us what we told them months before. It's so *hot*, they say. Too hot for tennis, too hot for cycling, too hot for sightseeing, too hot, too hot. Oh, for a pool. You're so lucky.

There is a hopeful pause. Is it my imagination, or can I actually hear the drops of perspiration falling like summer rain on the pages of the telephone directory?

I suppose the answer is to be callous but helpful. There is a public swimming pool near Apt, if you don't mind sharing the water with a few hundred small brown dervishes on their school holidays. There is the Mediterranean, only an hour's drive away; no, with traffic it could take two hours. Make sure you have some bottles of Evian in the car. It wouldn't do to get dehydrated.

Or you could close the shutters against the sun, spend the day in the house, and spring forth refreshed into the evening air. It would be difficult to acquire the souvenir suntan, but at least there would be no chance of heatstroke.

These brutal and unworthy suggestions barely have time to cross my mind before the voice of despair turns into the voice of relief. Of course! We could come over in the morning for a quick dip without disturbing you. Just a splash. You won't even know we've been.

They come at noon, with friends. They swim. They take the sun. Thirst creeps up on them, much to their surprise, and that's why I'm behind the bar. My wife is in the kitchen, making lunch for six. *Vivent les vacances.*

The Night Walk

The dogs cope with the heat by sleeping through it, stretched out in the courtyard or curled in the shade of the rosemary hedge. They come to life as the pink in the sky is turning to darkness, sniffing the breeze, jostling each other around our feet in their anticipation of a walk. We take the flashlight and follow them into the forest.

It smells of warm pine needles and baked earth, dry and spicy when we step on a patch of thyme. Small, invisible creatures slither away from us and rustle through the leaves of the wild box that grows like a weed.

Sounds carry: *cigales* and frogs, the muffled thump of music through the open window of a faraway house, the clinks and murmurs of dinner drifting up from Faustin's terrace. The hills on the other side of the valley, uninhabited for 10 months a year, are pricked with lights that will be switched off at the end of August.

We get back to the house and take off our shoes, and the warmth of the flagstones is an invitation to swim. A dive into dark water, and then a last glass of wine. The sky is clear except for a jumble of stars; it will be hot again tomorrow. Hot and slow, just like today.

Knee-Deep in Lavender

I had been cutting lavender with a pair of pruning shears and I was making a slow, amateurish job of it, nearly an hour to do fewer than a dozen clumps. When Henriette arrived at the house with a basket of aubergines, I was pleased to have the chance to stop. Henriette looked at the lavender, looked at the pruning shears, and shook her head at the ignorance of her neighbor. Didn't I know how to cut lavender? What was I doing with those pruning shears? Where was my *faucille?*

She went to her van and came back with a blackened sickle, its needle-sharp tip embedded in an old wine cork for safety. It was surprisingly light, and felt sharp enough to shave with. I made a few passes with it in the air, and Henriette shook her head again. Obviously, I needed a lesson.

She hitched up her skirt and attacked the nearest row of lavender, gathering the long stems into a tight bunch with one arm and slicing them off at the bottom with a single smooth pull of the sickle. In five minutes she had cut more than I had in an hour.

It looked easy; bend, gather, pull. Nothing to it.

"*Voilà!*" said Henriette. "When I was a little girl in the Basses-Alpes, we had hectares of lavender, and no machines. Everyone used the *faucille.*"

She passed it back to me, told me to mind my legs, and went off to join Faustin in the vines.

It wasn't as easy as it looked, and my first effort produced a ragged, uneven clump, more chewed than sliced. I realized that the sickle was made for right-handed lavender cutters, and had to compensate for being left-handed by slicing away from me. My wife came out to tell me to mind my legs. She doesn't trust me with sharp implements, and so she was reassured to see me cutting away from the body. Even with my genius for self-inflicted wounds there seemed to be little risk of amputation.

I had just come to the final clump when Henriette came back. I looked up, hoping for praise, and sliced my index finger nearly through to the bone. There was a great deal of blood, and Henriette asked me if I was giving myself a manicure. I sometimes wonder about her sense of humor. Two days later she gave me a sickle of my very own, and told me that I was forbidden to use it unless I was wearing gloves.

The Alcoholic Tendencies of Wasps

The Provençal wasp, although small, has an evil sting. He also has an ungallant, hit-and-run method of attack in the swimming pool. He paddles up behind his unsuspecting victim, waits until an arm is raised, and—*tok!*—strikes deep into the armpit. It hurts for several hours, and often causes people who have been stung to dress in protective clothing before they go swimming. This is the local version of the Miss Wet T-shirt contest.

I don't know whether all wasps like water, but here they love it—floating in the shallow end, dozing in the puddles on the flagstones, keeping an eye out for the unguarded armpit and the tender extremity—and after one disastrous day during which not only armpits but inner thighs received direct hits (obviously, some wasps can hold their breath and operate under water), I was sent off to look for wasp traps.

When I found them, in a *droguerie* in the back alleys of Cavaillon, I was lucky enough to find a wasp expert behind the counter. He demonstrated for me the latest model in traps, a plastic descendant of the old glass hanging traps that can sometimes be found in flea markets. It had been specially designed, he said, for use around swimming pools, and could be made irresistible to wasps.

It was in two parts. The base was a round bowl, raised off the ground by three flat supports, with a funnel leading up from the bottom. The top fitted over the lower bowl and prevented wasps who had made their way up the funnel from escaping.

But that, said the wasp expert, was the simple part. More difficult, more subtle, more artistic, was the bait. How does one persuade the wasp to abandon the pleasures of the flesh and climb up the funnel into the trap? What could tempt him away from the pool?

After spending some time in Provence, you learn to expect a brief lecture with every purchase, from an organically grown cabbage (two minutes) to a bed (half an hour or more, depending on the state of your back). For wasp traps, you should allow between 10 and 15 minutes. I sat on the stool in front of the counter and listened.

Wasps, it turned out, like alcohol. Some wasps like it *sucré,* others like it fruity, and there are even those who will crawl anywhere for a drop of *anis.* It is, said the expert, a matter of experimentation, a balancing of flavors and consistencies until one finds the blend that suits the palate of the local wasp population.

He suggested a few basic recipes: sweet vermouth with honey and water, diluted *crème de cassis,* dark beer spiked with *marc,* neat *pastis.* As an added inducement, the funnel can be lightly coated with honey, and a small puddle of water should always be left immediately beneath the funnel.

The expert set up a trap on the counter, and with two fingers imitated a wasp out for a stroll.

He stops, attracted by the puddle of water. The fingers stopped. He approaches the water, and then he becomes aware of something delicious above him. He climbs up the funnel to investigate, he jumps into his cocktail, *et voilà!*—he is unable to get out, being too drunk to crawl back down the funnel. He dies, but he dies happy.

I bought two traps, and tried out the recipes. All of them worked, which leads me to believe that the wasp has a serious drinking problem. And now, if ever a guest is overcome by strong waters, he is described as being as pissed as a wasp.

Maladie du Lubéron

Most of the seasonal ailments of summer, while they may be uncomfortable or painful or merely embarrassing, are at least regarded with some sympathy. A man convalescing after an explosive encounter with one *merguez* sausage too many is not expected to venture back into polite society until his constitution has recovered. The same is true of third-degree sunburn, *rosé* poisoning, scorpion bites, a surfeit of garlic, or the giddiness and nausea caused by prolonged exposure to French bureaucracy. One suffers, but one is allowed to suffer alone and in peace.

There is another affliction, worse than scorpions or rogue sausages, which we have experienced ourselves and seen many times in other permanent residents of this quiet corner of France. Symptoms usually appear some time around mid-July and persist until early September: glazed and bloodshot eyes, yawning, loss of appetite, shortness of temper, lethargy, and a mild form of paranoia that manifests itself in sudden urges to join a monastery.

This is the *maladie du Lubéron,* or creeping social fatigue, and it provokes about the same degree of sympathy as a millionaire's servant problems.

If we examine the patients—the permanent residents—we can see why it happens. Permanent residents have their work, their local friends, their unhurried routines. They made a deliberate choice to live in the Lubéron instead of one of the cocktail capitals of the world because they wanted, if not to get away from it all, to get away from most of it. This eccentricity is understood and tolerated for 10 months a year.

Try to explain that in July and August. Here come the visitors, fresh from the plane or hot off the *autoroute,* panting for social action. Let's meet some of the locals! To hell with the book in the hammock and the walk in the woods. To hell with soli-

tude; they want people—people for lunch, people for drinks, people for dinner—and so invitations and counterinvitations fly back and forth until every day for weeks has its own social highlight.

As the holiday comes to an end with one final multibottle dinner, it is possible to see even on the visitors' faces some traces of weariness. They had no idea it was so lively down here. They are only half-joking when they say they're going to need a rest to get over the whirl of the past few days. Is it always like this? How do you keep it up?

It isn't, and we don't. Like many of our friends, we collapse in between visitations, guarding empty days and free evenings, eating little and drinking less, going to bed early. And every year, when the dust has settled, we talk to other members of the distressed residents' association about ways of making summer less of an endurance test.

We all agree that firmness is the answer. Say no more often than yes. Harden the heart against the surprise visitor who cannot find a hotel room, the deprived child who has no swimming pool, the desperate traveler who has lost his wallet. Be firm; be helpful, be kind, be rude, but above all *be firm.*

And yet I know—I think we all know—that next summer will be the same. I suppose we must enjoy it. Or we would, if we weren't exhausted.

Place du Village

Cars have been banned from the village square, and stalls or trestle tables have been set up on three sides. On the fourth, a framework of scaffolding, blinking with colored lights, supports a raised platform made from wooden planks. Outside the café, the usual single row of tables and chairs has been multiplied by 10, and an extra waiter has been taken on to serve the sprawl of customers stretching from the butcher's down to the post office. Children and dogs chase each other through the crowd, stealing lumps of sugar from the tables and dodging the old men's sticks that are waved in mock anger. Nobody will go to bed early tonight, not even the children, because this is the village's annual party, the *fête votive.*

It begins in the late afternoon with a *pot d'amitié* in the square and the official opening of the stalls. Local artisans, the men's faces shining from an afternoon shave, stand behind their tables, glass in hand, or make final adjustments to their displays. There is pottery and jewelry, honey and lavender essence, hand-woven fabrics, iron and stone artifacts, paintings and wood carvings, books, postcards, tooled leatherwork, corkscrews with twisted olive-wood handles, patterned sachets of dried herbs. The woman selling pizza does brisk business as the first glass of wine begins to make the crowd hungry.

People drift off, eat, drift back. The night comes down, warm and still, the mountains in the distance just visible as deep black humps against the sky. The three-man accordion band tunes up on the platform and launches into the first of many *paso dobles* while the rock group from Avignon that will follow later rehearses on beer and *pastis* in the café.

The first dancers appear—an old man and his granddaughter, her nose pressed into his belt buckle, her feet balanced precariously on his feet. They are joined by a mother, father, and daughter dancing *à trois*, and then by several elderly couples, holding each other with stiff formality, their faces set with concentration as they try to retrace the steps they learned 50 years ago.

The *paso doble* session comes to an end with a flourish and a ruffle of accordions and drums, and the rock group warms up with five minutes of electronic tweaks that bounce off the old stone walls of the church opposite the platform.

The group's singer, a well-built young lady in tight black Lycra and a screaming orange wig, has attracted an audience before singing a note. An old man, the peak of his cap almost meeting the jut of his chin, has dragged a chair across from the café to sit directly in front of the microphone. As the singer starts her first number, some village boys made bold by his example come out of the shadows to stand by the old man's chair. All of them stare as though hypnotized at the shiny black pelvis rotating just above their heads.

The village girls, short of partners, dance with each other, as close as possible to the backs of the mesmerized boys. One of the waiters puts down his tray to caper in front of a pretty girl sitting with her parents. She blushes and ducks her head, but her mother nudges her to dance. Go on. The holiday will soon be over.

After an hour of music that threatens to dislodge the windows of the houses around the square, the group performs its finale. With an intensity worthy of Piaf on a sad night, the singer gives us *"Comme d'habitude,"* or "My Way," ending with a sob, her orange head bent over the microphone. The old man nods and bangs his stick on the ground, and the dancers go back to the café to see if there's any beer left.

Normally, there would have been *feux d'artifice* shooting up from the field behind the war memorial. This year, because of the drought, fireworks are forbidden. But it was a good *fête*. And did you see how the postman danced?

—Peter Mayle

In his second popular book on life in Provence, *Toujours Provence*, British writer Peter Mayle wittily evokes the charms of locals and visitors alike.

FRENCH VOCABULARY

One of the trickiest French sounds to pronounce is the nasal final *n* sound (whether or not the *n* is actually the last letter of the word). You should try to pronounce it as a sort of nasal grunt—as in "huh." The vowel that precedes the *n* will govern the vowel sound of the word, and in this list we precede the final *n* with an *h* to remind you to be nasal.

Another problem sound is the ubiquitous but untransliterable *eu,* as in *bleu* (blue) or *deux* (two), and the very similar sound in *je* (I), *ce* (this), and *de* (of). The closest equivalent might be the vowel sound of "stood."

Words and Phrases

English	French	Pronunciation
Basics		
Yes/no	Oui/non	wee/nohn
Please	S'il vous plaît	seel voo play
Thank you	Merci	mair-**see**
You're welcome	De rien	deh ree-**ehn**
That's all right	Il n'y a pas de quoi	eel nee ah pah de kwah
Excuse me, sorry	Pardon	pahr-**dohn**
Sorry!	Désolé(e)	day-zoh-**lay**
Good morning/ afternoon	Bonjour	bohn-**zhoor**
Good evening	Bonsoir	bohn-**swahr**
Goodbye	Au revoir	o ruh-**vwahr**
Mr. (Sir)	Monsieur	muh-**syuh**
Mrs. (Ma'am)	Madame	ma-**dam**
Miss	Mademoiselle	mad-mwa-**zel**
Pleased to meet you	Enchanté(e)	ohn-shahn-**tay**
How are you?	Comment allez-vous?	kuh-mahn-tahl-ay-**voo**
Very well, thanks	Très bien, merci	tray bee-ehn, mair-**see**
And you?	Et vous?	ay voo?
Numbers		
one	un	uhn
two	deux	deuh
three	trois	twah
four	quatre	**kaht**-ruh
five	cinq	sank
six	six	seess
seven	sept	set
eight	huit	wheat
nine	neuf	nuf
ten	dix	deess
eleven	onze	ohnz

twelve	douze	dooz
thirteen	treize	trehz
fourteen	quatorze	kah-torz
fifteen	quinze	kanz
sixteen	seize	sez
seventeen	dix-sept	deez-**set**
eighteen	dix-huit	deez-**wheat**
nineteen	dix-neuf	deez-**nuf**
twenty	vingt	vehn
twenty-one	vingt-et-un	vehnt-ay-**uhn**
thirty	trente	trahnt
forty	quarante	ka-**rahnt**
fifty	cinquante	sang-**kahnt**
sixty	soixante	swa-**sahnt**
seventy	soixante-dix	swa-sahnt-**deess**
eighty	quatre-vingts	kaht-ruh-**vehn**
ninety	quatre-vingt-dix	kaht-ruh-vehn-**deess**
one-hundred	cent	sahn
one-thousand	mille	meel

Colors

black	noir	nwahr
blue	bleu	bleuh
brown	brun/marron	bruhn/mar-**rohn**
green	vert	vair
orange	orange	o-**rahnj**
pink	rose	rose
red	rouge	rouge
violet	violette	vee-o-**let**
white	blanc	blahnk
yellow	jaune	zhone

Days of the Week

Sunday	dimanche	dee-**mahnsh**
Monday	lundi	luhn-**dee**
Tuesday	mardi	mahr-**dee**
Wednesday	mercredi	mair-kruh-**dee**
Thursday	jeudi	zhuh-**dee**
Friday	vendredi	vawn-druh-**dee**
Saturday	samedi	sahm-**dee**

Months

January	janvier	zhahn-vee-**ay**
February	février	feh-vree-**ay**
March	mars	marce
April	avril	a-**vreel**
May	mai	meh
June	juin	zhwehn
July	juillet	zhwee-**ay**
August	août	ah-**oo**
September	septembre	sep-**tahm**-bruh
October	octobre	awk-**to**-bruh
November	novembre	no-**vahm**-bruh
December	décembre	day-**sahm**-bruh

Useful Phrases

Do you speak English?	Parlez-vous anglais?	par-lay **voo** ahn-**glay**
I don't speak	Je ne parle pas	zhuh nuh parl pah
French	français	frahn-**say**
I don't understand	Je ne comprends pas	zhuh nuh kohm-**prahn** pah
I understand	Je comprends	zhuh kohm-**prahn**
I don't know	Je ne sais pas	zhuh nuh say **pah**
I'm American/ British	Je suis américain/ anglais	zhuh sweez a-may-ree-**kehn**/ahn-**glay**
What's your name?	Comment vous ap-pelez-vous?	ko-mahn voo za-pell-ay-**voo**
My name is . . .	Je m'appelle . . .	zhuh ma-**pell** . . .
What time is it?	Quelle heure est-il?	kel air eh-**teel**
How?	Comment?	ko-**mahn**
When?	Quand?	kahn
Yesterday	Hier	yair
Today	Aujourd'hui	o-zhoor-**dwee**
Tomorrow	Demain	duh-**mehn**
This morning/	Ce matin/cet	suh ma-**tehn**/set
afternoon	après-midi	ah-pray-mee-**dee**
Tonight	Ce soir	suh **swahr**
What?	Quoi?	kwah
What is it?	Qu'est-ce que c'est?	kess-kuh-**say**
Why?	Pourquoi?	poor-**kwa**
Who?	Qui?	kee
Where is . . .	Où est . . .	oo ay
the train station?	la gare?	la gar
the subway station?	la station de métro?	la sta-**syon** duh may-**tro**
the bus stop?	l'arrêt de bus?	la-**ray** duh **booss**
the terminal (airport)?	l'aérogare?	lay-ro-**gar**
the post office?	la poste?	la post
the bank?	la banque?	la bahnk
the . . . hotel?	l'hôtel . . .?	lo-**tel**
the store?	le magasin?	luh ma-ga-**zehn**
the cashier?	la caisse?	la **kess**
the . . . museum?	le musée . . .?	luh mew-**zay**
the hospital?	l'hôpital?	lo-pee-**tahl**
the elevator?	l'ascenseur?	la-sahn-**seuhr**
the telephone?	le téléphone?	luh tay-lay-**phone**
Where are the restrooms?	Où sont les toilettes?	oo sohn lay twah-**let**
Here/there	Ici/là	ee-**see**/la
Left/right	A gauche/à droite	a goash/a drwaht

Straight ahead	Tout droit	too drwah
Is it near/far?	C'est près/loin?	say pray/lwehn
I'd like . . .	Je voudrais . . .	zhuh voo-**dray**
a room	une chambre	ewn **shahm**-bruh
the key	la clé	la clay
a newspaper	un journal	uhn zhoor-**nahl**
a stamp	un timbre	uhn **tam**-bruh
I'd like to buy . . .	Je voudrais acheter . . .	zhuh voo-**dray** ahsh-**tay**
a cigar	un cigare	uhn see-**gar**
cigarettes	des cigarettes	day see-ga-**ret**
matches	des allumettes	days a-loo-**met**
dictionary	un dictionnaire	uhn deek-see-oh-**nare**
soap	du savon	dew sah-**vohn**
city plan	un plan de ville	uhn plahn de **veel**
road map	une carte routière	ewn cart roo-tee-**air**
magazine	une revue	ewn reh-**vu**
envelopes	des enveloppes	dayz ahn-veh-**lope**
writing paper	du papier à lettres	dew pa-pee-**ay** a let-ruh
airmail writing paper	du papier avion	dew pa-pee-**ay** a-vee-**ohn**
postcard	une carte postale	ewn cart pos-**tal**
How much is it?	C'est combien?	say comb-bee-**ehn**
It's expensive/ cheap	C'est cher/pas cher	say share/pa share
A little/a lot	Un peu/beaucoup	uhn peuh/bo-**koo**
More/less	Plus/moins	plu/mwehn
Enough/too (much)	Assez/trop	a-say/tro
I am ill/sick	Je suis malade	zhuh swee ma-**lahd**
Call a	Appelez un	a-play uhn
doctor	docteur	dohk-**tehr**
Help!	Au secours!	o suh-**koor**
Stop!	Arrêtez!	a-reh-**tay**
Fire!	Au feu!	o fuh
Caution!/Look out!	Attention!	a-tahn-see-**ohn**

Dining Out

A bottle of . . .	une bouteille de . . .	ewn boo-**tay** duh
A cup of . . .	une tasse de . . .	ewn tass duh
A glass of . . .	un verre de . . .	uhn vair duh
Ashtray	un cendrier	uhn sahn-dree-**ay**
Bill/check	l'addition	la-dee-see-**ohn**
Bread	du pain	dew pan
Breakfast	le petit-déjeuner	luh puh-**tee** day-zhuh-**nay**
Butter	du beurre	dew burr

Cheers!	A votre santé!	ah vo-truh sahn-**tay**
Cocktail/aperitif	un apéritif	uhn ah-pay-ree-**teef**
Dinner	le dîner	luh dee-**nay**
Dish of the day	le plat du jour	luh plah dew zhoor
Enjoy!	Bon appétit!	bohn a-pay-**tee**
Fixed-price menu	le menu	luh may-**new**
Fork	une fourchette	ewn four-**shet**
I am diabetic	Je suis diabétique	zhuh swee dee-ah-bay-**teek**
I am on a diet	Je suis au régime	zhuh sweez oray-**jeem**
I am vegetarian	Je suis végé-tarien(ne)	zhuh swee vay-zhay-ta-ree-**en**
I cannot eat . . .	Je ne peux pas manger de . . .	zhuh nuh **puh** pah mahn-**jay** deh
I'd like to order	Je voudrais commander	zhuh voo-**dray** ko-mahn-**day**
I'm hungry/thirsty	J'ai faim/soif	zhay fahm/swahf
Is service/the tip included?	Est-ce que le service est compris?	ess kuh luh sair-**veess** ay comb-**pree**
It's good/bad	C'est bon/mauvais	say bohn/mo-**vay**
It's hot/cold	C'est chaud/froid	say sho/frwah
Knife	un couteau	uhn koo-**toe**
Lunch	le déjeuner	luh day-zhuh-**nay**
Menu	la carte	la cart
Napkin	une serviette	ewn sair-vee-**et**
Pepper	du poivre	dew **pwah**-vruh
Plate	une assiette	ewn a-see-**et**
Please give me . . .	Donnez-moi . . .	doe-nay-**mwah**
Salt	du sel	dew sell
Spoon	une cuillère	ewn kwee-**air**
Sugar	du sucre	dew **sook**-ruh
Waiter!/Waitress!	Monsieur!/Mademoiselle!	muh-**syuh**/mad-mwa-**zel**
Wine list	la carte des vins	la cart day **van**

MENU GUIDE

French	English
Garniture au choix	Choice of vegetable side
Menu à prix fixe	Set menu
Plat du jour	Dish of the day
Selon arrivage	When available
Supplément/En sus	Extra charge
Sur commande	Made to order

Breakfast

Confiture	Jam
Miel	Honey
Oeuf à la coque	Boiled egg
Oeufs au bacon	Bacon and eggs
Oeufs au jambon	Ham and eggs
Oeufs sur le plat	Fried eggs
Oeufs brouillés	Scrambled eggs
Omelette (nature)	Omelet (plain)
Petits pains	Rolls

Starters

Anchois	Anchovies
Andouille(tte)	Chitterling sausage
Assiette de charcuterie	Assorted pork products
Crudités	Mixed raw vegetable salad
Escargots	Snails
Hors-d'oeuvres variés	Assorted appetizers
Jambon	Ham
Jambon de Campagne	Smoked ham
Jambonneau	Cured pig's knuckle
Mortadelle	Bologna sausage
Pâté	Liver purée blended with meat
Quenelles	Light dumplings (fish, fowl, or meat)
Saucisson	Dried sausage
Terrine	Pâté sliced and served from an earthenware pot

Salads

Salade de thon	Tuna salad
Salade mixte	Mixed salad
Salade niçoise	Tuna and potatoes on mixed greens
Salade russe	Diced vegetable salad
Salade verte	Green salad

Soups

Bisque	Seafood stew
Bouillabaisse	Fish and seafood stew
Crême de . . .	Cream of . . .
Potage	Light soup
julienne	Shredded vegetables
parmentier	Potato
Pot-au-feu	Stew of meat and vegetables

Soupe	Hearty soup
du jour	Of the day
à l'oignon gratinée	French onion soup
au pistou	Provençal vegetable soup
Velouté de . . .	Cream of . . .
Vichyssoise	Cold leek and potato cream soup

Fish and Seafood

Anguille	Eel
Bar	Bass
Bigorneaux	Winkles
Bourride	Fish stew from Marseilles
Brandade de morue	Creamed salt cod
Brochet	Pike
Cabillaud	Fresh cod
Calmar	Squid
Carpe	Carp
Coquille St-Jacques	Scallops in creamy sauce
Crabe	Crab
Crevettes	Shrimp
Cuisses de grenouilles	Frogs' legs
Daurade	Sea bream
Ecrevisses	Prawns
Ecrevisses	Crayfish
Eperlans	Smelt
Harengs	Herring
Homard	Lobster
Huîtres	Oysters
Langouste	Spiny lobster
Langoustines	Dublin bay prawns (scampi)
Lotte	Burbot
Lotte de mer	Angler
Loup	Catfish
Maquereau	Mackerel
Matelote	Fish stew in wine
Merlan	Whiting
Morue	Cod
Moules	Mussels
Palourdes	Clams
Perche	Perch
Poulpes	Octopus
Raie	Skate
Rascasse	Fish used in bouillabaisse
Rouget	Red mullet
Saumon	Salmon
Sole	Sole
Thon	Tuna
Truite	Trout

Meat

Agneau	Lamb
Boeuf	Beef
pavé	Thick slice of boned beef
Boulettes de viande	Meatballs

Brochette	Kabob
Cassoulet toulousain	Casserole of white beans and meat
Cervelle	Brains
Chateaubriand	Double fillet steak
Côtelettes	Chops
Choucroute garnie	Sausages and cured pork served with sauerkraut
Contre-filet	Loin strip steak
Côte de boeuf	T-bone steak
Côte	Rib
Entrecôte	Rib or rib-eye steak
Epaule	Shoulder
Escalope	Cutlet
Filet	Fillet steak
Foie	Liver
Gigot	Leg
Langue	Tongue
Médaillon	Tenderloin steak
Pieds de cochon	Pig's feet
Porc	Pork
Ragoût	Stew
Ris de veau	Veal sweetbreads
Rognons	Kidneys
Saucisses	Sausages
Selle	Saddle
Steak/steack	Steak (always beef)
Tournedos	Tenderloin of T-bone steak
Veau	Veal

Methods of Preparation

A point	Medium
A l'étouffée	Stewed
Au four	Baked
Bien cuit	Well-done
Bleu	Very rare
Bouilli	Boiled
Braisé	Braised
Frit	Fried
Grillé	Grilled
Rôti	Roast
Saignant	Rare
Sauté/poêlée	Sautéed

Game and Poultry

Blanc de volaille	Chicken breast
Caille	Quail
Canard/caneton	Duck/duckling
Cerf/chevreuil	Venison (red/roe)
Coq au vin	Chicken stewed in red wine
Dinde/dindonneau	Turkey/young turkey
Faisan	Pheasant
Grive	Thrush
Lapin	Rabbit

Lièvre	Wild hare
Oie	Goose
Perdrix/perdreau	Partridge/young partridge
Pigeon/pigeonneau	Pigeon/squab
Pintade/pintadeau	Guinea fowl/young guinea fowl
Poularde	Fattened pullet
Poule au pot	Chicken stewed with vegetables
Poulet	Chicken
Poussin	Spring chicken
Sanglier/marcassin	Wild boar/young wild boar
Volaille	Fowl

Vegetables

Artichaut	Artichoke
Asperge	Asparagus
Aubergine	Eggplant
Carottes	Carrots
Champignons	Mushrooms
Chicorée	Chicory (Endive)
Chou-fleur	Cauliflower
Chou (rouge)	Cabbage (red)
Choux de Bruxelles	Brussels sprouts
Courgette	Zucchini
Cresson	Watercress
Endive	Endive
Epinard	Spinach
Haricots blancs/verts	White kidney/French beans
Laitue	Lettuce
Lentilles	Lentils
Oignons	Onions
Petits pois	Peas
Poireaux	Leeks
Poivrons	Peppers
Radis	Radishes
Tomates	Tomatoes

Potatoes, Rice, and Noodles

Pâtes	Pasta
Pomme de terre	Potato
allumettes	matchsticks
dauphine	mashed and deep-fried
duchesse	mashed with butter and egg yolks
en robe des champs	in their skin
frites	french fries
mousseline	mashed
nature/vapeur	boiled/steamed
Riz	Rice
pilaf	boiled in bouillon with onions

Sauces and Preparations

Béarnaise	Vinegar, egg yolks, white wine, shallots, tarragon
Béchamel	White sauce
Bordelaise	Mushrooms, red wine, shallots, beef marrow

Bourguignon	Red wine, herbs
Chasseur	Wine, mushrooms, onions, shallots
Diable	Hot pepper
Forestière	Mushrooms
Hollandaise	Egg yolks, butter, vinegar
Indienne	Curry
Madère	With Madeira wine
Marinière	White wine, mussel broth, egg yolks
Meunière	Brown butter, parsley, lemon juice
Périgueux	With goose or duck liver purée and truffles
Poivrade	Pepper sauce
Provençale	Onions, tomatoes, garlic
Tartare	Mayonnaise flavored with mustard and herbs
Vinaigrette	Vinegar dressing

Fruits and Nuts

Abricot	Apricot
Amandes	Almonds
Ananas	Pineapple
Banane	Banana
Brugnon	Nectarine
Cacahouètes	Peanuts
Cassis	Blackcurrants
Cerises	Cherries
Citron	Lemon
Citron vert	Lime
Dattes	Dates
Figues	Figs
Fraises	Strawberries
Framboises	Raspberries
Fruits secs	Dried fruit
Groseilles	Red currants
Mandarine	Tangerine
Marrons	Chestnuts
Melon	Melon
Mûres	Blackberries
Myrtilles	Blueberries
Noisettes	Hazelnuts
Noix de coco	Coconut
Noix	Walnuts
Orange	Orange
Pamplemousse	Grapefruit
Pastèque	Watermelon
Pêche	Peach
Poire	Pear
Pomme	Apple
Pruneaux	Prunes
Prunes	Plums
Raisins secs	Raisins
Raisins blancs/noirs	Grapes green/blue

Desserts

Crêpe suzette	Thin pancake simmered in orange juice and flambéed with orange liqueur
Crème Chantilly	Whipped cream
Flan	Custard
Gâteau au chocolat	Chocolate cake
Glace	Ice cream
Mousse au chocolat	Chocolate pudding
Tarte aux pommes	Apple pie
Tourte	Layer cake

Alcoholic Drinks

A l'eau	With water
Avec des glaçons	On the rocks
Apéritifs	Cocktails
Kir/blanc-cassis	Chilled white wine mixed with black-currant syrup
Bière	Beer
Blonde/brune	Light/dark
Eau-de-vie	Brandy
Liqueur	Cordial
Porto	Port
Sec	Straight
Vin	Wine
sec	dry
brut	very dry
léger	light
doux	sweet
rouge	red
rosé	rosé
mousseux	sparkling
blanc	white

Nonalcoholic Drinks

Café	Coffee
noir	black
crème	milk/cream
au lait	with milk
décaféiné	caffeine-free
express	espresso
Chocolat chaud	Hot chocolate
Eau minérale	Mineral water
gazeuse	carbonated
non gazeuse	still
Jus de . . .	. . . juice (see fruit)
Lait	Milk
Limonade	Lemonade
Limonade gazeuse	Ginger ale
Schweppes	Tonic water
Thé	Tea
crème/citron	with milk/lemon
glacé	iced tea
Tisane	Herb tea

INDEX

WHEREVER YOU TRAVEL, *H*ELP IS NEVER FAR AWAY.

From planning your trip to providing travel assistance along the way, American Express® Travel Service Offices are always there to help.

Provence

L'Agence (R)
15 Cours Mirabeau
Aix-en-Provence
42/26 93 93

Canebière Voyages (R)
39 La Canebière
Marseilles
91/13 71 21

Riviera

American Express Travel Service
8 rue des Belges
Cannes
93/38 15 87

American Express Travel Service
11 Promenade des Anglais
Nice
93/16 53 51

Travel

http://www.americanexpress.com/travel

American Express Travel Service Offices are found in central locations throughout France.